BYRON'S *DON JUAN*

In this first full-length study of Byron's masterpiece in over thirty years, Richard Cronin boldly presents *Don Juan* as the epic poem of its age. Impressively illuminating the whole literary nineteenth century through a single work, he asks what kind of epic can be said to represent an era more readily defined by newspapers and magazines than by competitors such as Wordsworth's *Excursion* or Southey's *Joan of Arc*. Delving into questions of form and choice of hero, he also explores the controversies that informed the poem's reception, its contemporary interactions, and its influence on later nineteenth-century literature. *Don Juan*, he argues, is the epic poem demanded by an age of cant and dissembling, when people's feelings and the world they lived in had become disconnected. In it, he finds a powerful defence of liberal thinking at a time when that kind of thinking was under threat.

RICHARD CRONIN taught for more than forty years at the University of Glasgow. His first monograph was *Shelley's Poetic Thoughts* (1981), and his most recent are *Romantic Victorians: English Literature, 1824–1840* (2002), *Paper Pellets: British Literary Culture after Waterloo* (2010), *Reading Victorian Poetry* (2011), and *George Meredith: The Life and Writing of an Alteregoist* (2019). He co-edited *Emma* for the Cambridge Edition of the Works of Jane Austen (2005), *Robert Browning* for 21st-Century Oxford Authors (2014), and *A Companion to Victorian Poetry* (2002). This is his ninth monograph.

CAMBRIDGE STUDIES IN ROMANTICISM

Founding Editor
Marilyn Butler, University of Oxford

General Editor
James Chandler, University of Chicago

This series aims to foster the best new work in one of the most challenging fields within English literary studies. From the early 1780s to the early 1830s, a formidable array of talented men and women took to literary composition, not just in poetry, which some of them famously transformed, but in many modes of writing. The expansion of publishing created new opportunities for writers, and the political stakes of what they wrote were raised again by what Wordsworth called those 'great national events' that were 'almost daily taking place': the French Revolution, the Napoleonic and American wars, urbanization, industrialization, religious revival, an expanded empire abroad, and the reform movement at home. This was an enormous ambition, even when it pretended otherwise. The relations between science, philosophy, religion, and literature were reworked in texts such as *Frankenstein* and *Biographia Literaria*; gender relations in *A Vindication of the Rights of Woman* and *Don Juan*; journalism by Cobbett and Hazlitt; and poetic form, content, and style by the Lake School and the Cockney School. Outside Shakespeare studies, probably no body of writing has produced such a wealth of commentary or done so much to shape the responses of modern criticism. This indeed is the period that saw the emergence of those notions of literature and of literary history, especially national literary history, on which modern scholarship in English has been founded.

The categories produced by Romanticism have also been challenged by recent historicist arguments. The task of the series is to engage both with a challenging corpus of Romantic writings and with the changing field of criticism they have helped to shape. As with other literary series published by Cambridge University Press, this one will represent the work of both younger and more established scholars on either side of the Atlantic and elsewhere.

See the end of the book for a complete list of published titles.

BYRON'S *DON JUAN*

The Liberal Epic of the Nineteenth Century

RICHARD CRONIN

University of Glasgow

 CAMBRIDGE
UNIVERSITY PRESS

Shaftesbury Road, Cambridge CB2 8EA, United Kingdom

One Liberty Plaza, 20th Floor, New York, NY 10006, USA

477 Williamstown Road, Port Melbourne, VIC 3207, Australia

314–321, 3rd Floor, Plot 3, Splendor Forum, Jasola District Centre, New Delhi – 110025, India

103 Penang Road, #05–06/07, Visioncrest Commercial, Singapore 238467

Cambridge University Press is part of Cambridge University Press & Assessment, a department of the University of Cambridge.

We share the University's mission to contribute to society through the pursuit of education, learning and research at the highest international levels of excellence.

www.cambridge.org
Information on this title: www.cambridge.org/9781009366236

DOI: 10.1017/9781009366229

First published 2023

A catalogue record for this publication is available from the British Library.

A Cataloging-in-Publication data record for this book is available from the Library of Congress

ISBN 978-1-009-36623-6 Hardback

Cambridge University Press & Assessment has no responsibility for the persistence or accuracy of URLs for external or third-party internet websites referred to in this publication and does not guarantee that any content on such websites is, or will remain, accurate or appropriate.

For Matilda,
and, as always, for Dorothy

Contents

Acknowledgements

I began writing this book in lockdown. It helped, as writing *Don Juan* helped Byron, to ease my ennui, and it helped to distract me, as writing the poem helped distract Byron, from other things. But it is a book that I had been thinking about for fifty years. In that time I have incurred many debts. My most important is to Dorothy McMillan, who read about half of the book. Of one chapter in particular I would be unable to say where Dorothy's contribution ended and where my own began. Jane Stabler and John Gardner read drafts of the whole book, and made valuable suggestions, all of which I have shamelessly incorporated. I have known and admired Jane's work on Byron ever since she was a graduate student, and it has informed my reading of Byron ever since. Neither John Gardner nor David Stewart has yet written on Byron at any length, but my understanding of the period has been shaped by their work, and my understanding of Byron has been deepened by my conversations with them. Peter Graham is the author of one of the very best studies of *Don Juan*, and I am indebted to him, too, and to Rosa Florou for invitations to give the talks on Byron in Messlolonghi and in Athens, where many of the ideas that I develop in this book were first advanced. I am also grateful to the other scholars who have invited me to talk or to write on Byron and cognate subjects, amongst them Bernard Beatty, Clare Bucknell, Lilla Crisafulli, Nora Crook, Nick Halmi, Michael O'Neill, Nick Roe, Mark Sandy, Maria Schoina, Jane Stabler (my debts to whom are embarrassingly multiple: she also allowed me to read her own outstanding edition of *Don Juan* before publication), Matthew Ward, Timothy Webb, David Woodhouse, and Sarah Wootton. In the forty years that I taught at Glasgow I was blessed with many colleagues who shared my interest in Byron. I learned a great deal from all of them. I learned most of all, perhaps, from Drummond Bone, but I learned much too from Alex Benchimol, Bob Cummings, Philip Drew, Simon Kovesi, Nigel Leask, Seamus Perry, Jack Rillie, Jeffrey Robinson, Cliff Siskin, Jan Todd, Nicola Trott, and Duncan Wu (what starry colleagues

I have had at Glasgow over the years). I also learned much from the many hundreds of students who talked with me about Byron. I am grateful too for the comments of the two scholars invited to read the book by Cambridge University Press, to James Chandler, the general editor of the series in which this book appears, and to Bethany Thomas and George Laver for the help and encouragement I have been given.

Abbreviations

Introduction

Don Juan was an epic poem, Byron assured Thomas Medwin, a poem 'as much in the spirit of our day as the Iliad was in Homer's'.[1] Epics were the poems that gave a character to their age. They were the poems through which a people might come to recognise their identity, as Britons, as Europeans, as, in a still more ambitious possibility, members of the human race. But in the years in which Byron wrote and published *Don Juan*, it was far from clear what the character of Byron's nation might be, let alone the character of Byron's continent or Byron's world. When George Canning was returned for Liverpool in 1820, in the election triggered by the death of the old king, the local Tories gave a dinner to congratulate him. In his address Canning congratulated the government, of which he was a prominent member, on the difference between the nation as it had been a few months before and the nation as it was now, in the opening months of the reign of George IV. There were no more mass meetings calling for parliamentary reform of the kind that had brought violence to the streets of Manchester on 16 August 1819. The government had banned them. The prohibition, Canning insisted, safeguarded rather than curtailed the liberties of British citizens. The crowd of some 60,000 people who had gathered in St Peter's Field and been dispersed by the Manchester yeomanry in what became known as the Peterloo Massacre had been a concourse of strangers, a coming together of a multitude that had 'neither property, nor domicile, nor connexion' in the town in which they met. It had been no more than 'an aggregation of individuals', an assembly of those who had 'no permanent relation to one another, no common tie'.[2] They had come together to hear the radical reformer Henry Hunt, but Hunt himself had no connection with Manchester: he was a Wiltshire farmer, or, as Canning preferred to describe him, 'an itinerant hawker of grievances'. Canning counters Henry Hunt and all those who had come to hear him by celebrating 'neighbourhood'. He lauds local associations. It had been the business of the French revolutionaries to attack all those bonds between neighbours because their project required them 'to reduce the nation to a collection of individuals'. It was only by doing so that they could go on 'to congregate them into mobs'. The thousands who met at Manchester to petition for reform had been just such a mob. The Six Acts passed by the Tory government in the wake of Peterloo had proved their worth. They had put a stop to the reform movement. Those measures, Canning told his constituents, put him in mind of a poem. One might say of them what has been said of 'some of the most consummate productions of literary art': no one could have predicted them, and yet all of us felt as soon as they were proposed that the measures recommended were exactly what we had been thinking of ourselves.[3]

The first two cantos of *Don Juan* had been published the year before, but *Don Juan* is not at all the kind of poem that Canning had in mind. It is not a poem that succeeds by finding ways of saying what all of us had thought but could not have put so well. No more is it a poem that offers the nation a mirror in which it might contemplate a flattering reflection of itself. *Don Juan* is a very different kind of poem. My aim throughout this book is to describe what kind of poem that might be, but I can begin by pointing out that it is the poem of a man who does not share Canning's vision of a nation as a large neighbourhood that accommodates the smaller neighbourhoods of which it is composed while somehow retaining their character. For Canning the nation was the locus in which all those little neighbourhoods could recognise their common identity. But a nation for Byron is much what it was, according to Canning, for the French revolutionaries: it was simply 'an aggregation of individuals'. It was not a thought that filled him with dismay. All through *Don Juan* Byron delights in aggregations of the kind that appalled George Canning. The poem begins with just such an aggregation. In its first four stanzas Byron canvasses the claims of more than thirty candidates to be the hero of his poem, from the butcher Cumberland to the Marquis de Condorcet. In the third canto he takes two stanzas, 17 and 18, to list all the miscellaneous items that Lambro selects from his plunder to take home as gifts for his daughter. The sultan's seraglio is another aggregation, a collection of women selected for their variousness. There is Lolah, 'dusk as India', Katinka, the Georgian, 'white and red', and Dudu, who is so 'large and languishing and lazy' (VI, 41). In two stanzas in the seventh canto (3 and 4), Byron lists twelve famous authors who have very little in common, except that all of them, according to Byron, dismiss life as 'not worth a potato'. In the same canto Byron refers to fifteen Russian heroes whose names would be immortal if only they could be pronounced, even though of all those heroes with names '[e]nding in "ischskin," "ousckin," "iffskchy," "ouski,"' he 'can insert but Rousamouski' (VII, 16). There are several aggregations of poets, amongst them the eleven who in the eleventh canto rival Byron for the title of 'greatest living poet' (XI, 57–60). The 'catalogue' of potential brides that Adeline offers Juan, a catalogue from which Aurora Raby is unaccountably omitted, is another aggregation (XV, 41–3), and the list of the dishes that Lady Adeline offers her guests is much more of an aggregation than a menu (XV, 62–74), which is appropriate because the guests themselves are not so much a company as yet another aggregation. Lord Henry has invited some 'thirty-three / Of highest caste' (XIII, 82); he has invited a bevy of young women, all of whom, like 'the six Miss Rawbolds', are in pursuit of a coronet (XIII, 85); and he has invited, too, a job lot of guests chosen for their entertainment value: 'the young bard Rackrhyme', 'Sir John Pottledeep, the mighty drinker', 'the preux Chevalier de la Ruse', a gambler of doubtful reputation, 'Dick Dubious the metaphysician', 'Sir Henry Silvercup, the great race-winner', and 'Jack Jargon the gigantic guardsman' amongst them. Lord Henry's guests may seem 'an heterogeneous mass', but heterogeneity is, Byron suggests, the only antidote to the dullness of 'a humdrum *tête-à-tête*' (XIII, 84–94). It is certainly the antidote that Byron offers his readers, because *Don Juan* itself is an aggregation, a collection of cantos devised like Lord Henry's guest list and the sultan's harem to be various enough to appeal to every taste.[4] *Don Juan* is the epic poem of a poet not eager to invite his readers to bask as they read his poem in a warm sense of their shared identity. He had rather that the poem left them with the sense that they were no more united than, in Canning's account, were all those people who gathered to listen to Henry Hunt in Manchester, and that is one reason that I choose to describe *Don Juan* as a liberal epic.

For George Canning Byron's penchant for aggregations would have revealed him as suspect, as a man whose sympathies still lay with the French revolutionaries despite the disastrous outcome of all their experiments. Great Britain, Canning believed, was the product of a quite different vision. It was a nation made up of organic communities, neighbourhoods, the character of which was reflected in the great nation to which they belonged. But Canning was speaking in 1820 in Liverpool, and he was speaking of events in Manchester. Liverpool, its economy boosted by the transatlantic slave trade, was by 1820 a port rivalled in importance only by London and Bristol. In 1780, Manchester was still just a small market town, but by 1801 its population had grown to more than 70,000, not much less than the population of Liverpool. It was already well on its way to becoming what it was for Disraeli, 'the great METROPOLIS OF LABOUR'.[5] Liverpool and Manchester were not neighbourhoods but large mercantile and industrial towns, their populations still more evidently heterogeneous than Lord Henry's guest list, and by 1821 it was Liverpool and Manchester as they were in reality, not as Canning chose to imagine them, that lent their character to the nation.

Byron understood as much, not because he had a better knowledge than Canning of the nation, let alone of the great towns of the north, but because he knew the people that he was writing for. As their sales figures show, no writers had a better understanding of what William St Clair has called 'the reading nation' of the Romantic period than Walter Scott and Byron,[6] and that nation, they understood very well, was not made up of a community of readers bound to each other by common ties. The reading nation was much better thought of as a heterogeneous mass. The whole of Canning's speech was re-printed in *Blackwood's Edinburgh Magazine* because the magazine shared Canning's nostalgia for the nation as a community, for a nation that retained as well as protected the character of all those little neighbourhoods of which it was composed. But the *Blackwood's* writers understood very well that the Tory parochialism that they championed did not comfortably accord with the magazine's commercial interests. They recognised that the success of their magazine depended on their skill in addressing the reading nation as it was, not as they dreamed it might be. They may have remembered fondly the closed, familiar readership that Addison and Steele had addressed a hundred years before, but their own readership, they knew, was very different. It was a heterogeneous readership, and *Blackwood's* succeeded by offering that readership the heterogeneous content that it demanded.[7] That was one reason why *Blackwood's*, despite its disapproval of Byron's politics, read *Don Juan* so much more astutely, and recognised its genius so much more wholeheartedly than any other Regency periodical. Even Canning understood, even if he did not admit it, that his vision of Britain as a nation of neighbourhoods was fanciful. He brought his speech to an end in a conclusion that abruptly contradicted his own argument. He issued a warning of the dangers of 'confusion'. A line had been drawn, he claimed, and the only question that remained was on which side of that line to take one's stand, whether to seek to overthrow the existing institutions of the nation or to unite in their defence. Canning offered those who had gathered to hear him a vision of the nation as an organic community, but he offered that vision to an audience that understood just as well as Canning that the nation was divided, and that at present it could be defined only by its divisions. *Don Juan* is the age's epic because Byron knew that very well. The poem's 'notorious lack of form', Jerome McGann contends, should be understood as a necessary outcome of Byron's 'attempt to draw distinctions'. His is a poem interested in 'separations', a poem interested in bringing out 'differences',[8] which is why it may properly be claimed as the epic poem of the nation that was still coming into existence as Byron wrote it. When I describe this kind of poem as a 'liberal' epic, I am aware that the epithet carries political resonances, but for me it describes the poem's formal still more than its ideological characteristics, which is why it does not surprise me that amongst the first critics to recognise its special qualities should have been the rabid Tories who wrote for *Blackwood's*.

Chapter 1 asks what kind of poem *Don Juan* is, whether Byron's claim, 'my poem's epic', is valid or whether, as he told John Murray, it was a poem written with no intention other than to 'giggle and make giggle'.[9] It arrives at the conclusion that Byron wrote *Don Juan* at a time when the epic poem, the poem that truly expressed the spirit of its age, could succeed only if it agreed also to be trivial. The epic poem of the 1820s could only achieve epic status by being, to echo a phrase of Angela Esterhammer's, profoundly trivial.[10] Chapter 2 presents *Don Juan* as an anti-heroic epic. The poem begins 'I want a hero', and it ends still in the same predicament, because Don Juan, the figure from the pantomime that Byron selects for his hero, so signally fails to fulfil that role. Byron has difficulty finding a hero because there were just too many heroes to choose from. He examines the claims of thirty-two candidates in the poem's first four stanzas. He had always looked at heroism sceptically. The heroes of the early poems that made him famous are, as Jerome McGann points out, heroes condemned to operate in a world that offers them no scope for their heroism.[11] In the plays that he wrote while he was working on *Don Juan*, Byron subjected the idea of heroism to a still more sceptical examination. But the early poems and the plays, however much they may question the content of heroism, retain its form. They are fictions organised around their central characters. In *Don Juan* Byron chooses a hero who fails to dominate his own poem, a hero who is always finding himself pushed to the sidelines of his own story. Byron is unusual amongst epic poets in thinking of his poem not as the 'single wonder of a thousand years' (*English Bards and Scotch Reviewers*, 194), but as taking its place in the contemporary publishing industry. His cool awareness that *Don Juan* is a poem offered for sale in the literary marketplace disqualified for many readers its title to be a work of literature at all, let alone to be the epic poem of the age, but, as I suggest in Chapter 3, one reason that Byron's poem has a better claim to embody the age's spirit than *The Prelude* or *The Excursion* or, for that matter, Southey's *Joan of Arc* or *The Curse of Kehama* is because it can accommodate so many of the kinds of writing produced in Britain in the 1820s, from advertisements in newspapers to novels to epic poems. Byron is happy to be counted amongst all the other 'authors luminous, voluminous' publishing in the period, content, if only playfully, to be just one of the 'twice ten thousand daily scribes', and for his poem, *Don Juan*, to take its place amongst all the 'pamphlets, volumes, newspapers', that they produce (IX, 35). His is after all a poem that celebrates differences, the difference between newspapers and epic poems amongst them.

In Chapter 4, I turn to the difference that concerns him most often in the poem, the difference between men and women, and to another difference that makes the relationship between men and women so fraught, the difference between what people say they think and what they really think. 'Philo-genitiveness' is, Byron remarks, 'a word quite after [his] own heart', but there is another word, 'a shorter a good deal than this', though coupled with it by alliteration, a word that Byron and his readers are entirely familiar with, although it is a word that cannot be allowed into the poem (XII, 22). A still more scabrous pair of words, 'cant' and a word that differs from it only in a single vowel, is still more central to the poem. It is again an unpublishable word, a word that must be excluded from the poem as Byron excludes its Latin cognate when he quotes a passage from Horace in Canto IX. There are words that can be spoken in public and words that can only be spoken in private. Byron is interested in swearing, in 'Billingsgate' language, and in 'Continental oaths' still more 'incontinent' 'which no Aristocratic / Spirit would name' (XI, 42–3). Language of that kind is often heard but much more rarely read. It is language that cannot be printed, and the difference between what should and what should not be published is the subject too of Chapter 5. *Don Juan* is thickly seeded with references to Byron's own domestic circumstances. Many of his readers, his friendliest, most sympathetic readers amongst them, believed that those private allusions ought to have rendered his poem unpublishable. Canning imagined England as a community, a nation that shared the characteristics of all the little communities that it sheltered. But Byron knew that was no longer the case, if it ever had been. The population of England in the 1820s was heterogeneous. In a community the private and the public melt into each other, the transition from one to the other is seamless, but in an England that was simply 'an aggregation of individuals', the public life and the private life were separate. There was a jarring whenever they came together.

necessarily?

The distinction between them had to be insisted on and stringently policed. *Don Juan* drew attention to that difference by so flagrantly ignoring it, which was what persuaded so many of Byron's friends that it was a poem that should never have been publicly circulated. It was an 'Epic Satire', a poem in which Byron addressed the state of Europe and the state of Britain, and it was also, as I point out in this chapter, a poem written by a man who had been abandoned by his wife, and responded to the hurt done him by writing a poem that all through its sixteen cantos holds that wife up to public ridicule.

In Chapter 6, I focus on the swift transitions that so distressed many of the poem's first readers. In the *London Magazine*, for example, John Scott deplored 'the quick alternation' in *Don Juan* 'of pathos and profaneness, – of serious and moving sentiment and indecent ribaldry'. Scott added, 'This is not an English fault.'[12] The chapter will trace how soon the habits that struck Scott as foreign came to be thought of as supremely English, as Shakespearean, and what that means not just for the reception of *Don Juan* but for how people's understanding not just of the history of literature but of the world around them had changed. In Chapter 7, I focus on the difference that functions in *Don Juan* as the type of all the other differences that the poem explores, the difference between what Byron has to say, and the form, ottava rima, in which he has to say it. The chapter asks what it might mean for a poem so frankly to confess how the poet is at the mercy of the demands of rhyme ('This should be *entre nous* for Julia thought / In French, but then the rhyme would go for nought' (I, 84)) and of metre, as when he admits that he had added a word to a quotation from Horace simply because 'prosody' demanded it (VI, 18). Byron was a cricketer, and in *Don Juan* he is willing to admit that from time to time he is a poor fielder, a butterfingers: the stanza, like the story of *Beppo*, slips forever through his fingers. But Byron's offences against rhyme and metre keep his readers always aware of the difference between what he means to say and what the verse form he has chosen allows him to say.[13] In Chapter 8, I bring the book to a conclusion by asking what Byron means by insisting that his is a liberal age even though he was writing at a time when liberalism seemed to be, if not defeated, then at least everywhere in retreat.

In this chapter, I return to the speech by George Canning with which I began. Canning feared a population that was no more than an aggregation of individuals, and his fear required him to distract himself from England as it now was. He did so by inventing in his address to his Liverpool constituents a fictional country, a nation best thought of as a large neighbourhood made up of little neighbourhoods. *Don Juan* is, by contrast, a poem that delights in aggregations: of generals, of poets, of items in a shop window, of guests at a country house, of dishes on a menu. Byron differs in this from Canning, and he differs too from the greatest of his fellow poets. *Don Juan* is, amongst other things, Byron's riposte to that 'drowsy, frowzy poem call'd the "Excursion"' (III, 94). Wordsworth is a poet interested in how things coalesce, in how one thing and another may be interfused, the more deeply interfused the better. Byron in *Don Juan* is by contrast the poet of confusion, a poet happy to take his place, as Juan takes his at Lord Henry's dinner, '[c]onfused, in the confusion' (XVI, 87). In *The Prelude* London leaves Wordsworth sick and dizzy because it resists his unifying imagination, which is exactly what Juan (and Byron too) finds so exciting about it. As he enters the city for the first time, Juan makes his way through 'coaches, drays, choked turnpikes, and a whirl / Of wheels, and roar of voices and confusion' (XI, 22). For Wordsworth London is an anomaly, for Byron it is the true capital of a world that offers 'no spot where man can rest eye on, / Without confusion of the sorts and sexes, / Of beings, stars, and this unriddled wonder, / The World' (XI, 3). Byron complains that the confusion 'vexes' his spirit, but he does not really mean it. The world that he describes, the world that offers no spot to rest the eye on, 'at the worst's a glorious blunder'. His is a poem that values rather than regrets difference, which is why, as I conclude in Chapter 8, it is a liberal poem, and why it is the first poem adequately to represent the nation that was coming into existence as Byron wrote it. It is why *Don Juan* deserves to be recognised as the liberal epic of Byron's century, the only Romantic poem that looks forward to the epic achievement of the Victorian novels that are its true successors. I will end by arguing that the novelists, however much they may be Byron's true heirs, fail quite to match his achievement. Disraeli was right to predict shortly before Victoria came to the throne that the epics of the nineteenth century would be written in prose.[14] The novelists who produced the epics of the Victorian age are Byron's true heirs, but they followed without superseding him. There are ways in which *Don Juan* remains the one true epic of the nineteenth century.

CHAPTER I

My Poem's Epic

It should not much concern us, Jerome McGann believes, whether or not *Don Juan* should be thought of as an epic poem. It is only a 'pseudo-problem': 'The work is epic because Byron wanted it to be thought of as such, and because the consensus of history has agreed.'[1] Which would seem to be the end of the matter, except that it is not at all clear that Byron did want his poem to be thought of as an epic, and, even if he did, it is still less clear that most readers of the poem have agreed with him. 'So you and Mr. Foscolo &c.', he wrote to John Murray, 'want me to undertake what you call a "great work" an Epic poem I suppose or some such pyramid – I'll try no such thing'.[2] Instead he sent Murray the poem he had just finished, the second canto of *Don Juan*. Byron very often registered the pride he took in his poem: 'As to "Don Juan" – confess – confess – you dog – and be candid – that it is the sublime of that there sort of writing – it may be bawdy – but is it not good English? – it may be profligate – but is it not life, is it not the thing?'[3] But Douglas Kinnaird, the dog that Byron is address-ing, is not invited to recognise *Don Juan* as an epic, only as 'the sublime of that there sort of writing'. *Paradise Lost*, as Byron puts in his Dedication to *Don Juan*, had made 'the word Miltonic mean sublime', and, ever since Milton, poets had insisted on the strenuous course of education that those amongst them who harboured epic ambitions needed to undertake. Coleridge 'would not think of devoting less than 20 years to an Epic Poem'. Ten of these would be devoted to composition, but he would not begin writing until he had spent a decade warming his mind with 'universal science': 'I would be a tolerable Mathematician, I would thoroughly know Mechanics, Hydrostatics, Optics, and Astronomy, Botany, Metallurgy, Fossilism, Chemistry, Geology, Anatomy, Medicine – then the mind of man – then the minds of men – in all Travels, Voyages, and Histories.'[4] When Murray suggested that Byron dedicate himself to the composition of a great poem, he got short shrift, even though Byron did not expect it to take half so long: 'I hate tasks – and then "seven or eight years!" God send

9

us all well this day three months – let alone years – if one's years can't be
better employed than in sweating poesy – a man had better be a ditcher.'[5]
The education that had fitted Byron to write *Don Juan* may have been just
as strenuous as the education Coleridge envisioned, but it was, as Byron
reports it to Kinnaird, very different in character: 'Could any man have
written it – who has not lived in the world? – and tooled in a post-chaise? in
a hackney coach? in a Gondola? against a wall? in a court carriage? in a vis-
a-vis? – on a table? – and under it?'

Only once, outside the poem itself, is Byron recorded as making
a straightforward claim for the epic status of *Don Juan*. Thomas
Medwin, Shelley's cousin, who got to know Byron in Pisa, recalls him
saying:

> If you must have an epic, there's 'Don Juan' for you. I call that an epic: it is
> an epic as much in the spirit of our day as the Iliad was in Homer's.[6]

Medwin claims that this conversation was 'committed to paper half an hour
after it had occurred'. He is not a particularly reliable witness – at one point
he has Byron telling him, 'I believe you know more of me than any one
else'[7] – but there is no reason on this occasion to disbelieve him even though
Byron seems not to have repeated the claim to his other acquaintances. None
of his friends admired the poem more than Shelley, who was fully converted
only when the second instalment of the poem, Cantos III–V, was published
in 1821. 'This sort of writing', he told Byron, 'is what I wished you to do
when I made my vows for an epic'. *Don Juan* was not the epic he had hoped
for, but in spite of that it left Shelley 'content'. Byron's poem seemed to
Shelley sui generis – 'Nothing has ever been written like it in English – nor if
I may venture to prophesy, will there be; without carrying upon it the mark
of a secondary and borrowed light.'[8] Even Medwin, who recorded Byron's
claim, was unpersuaded by it. He had often heard it discussed which was the
finest of all Byron's works. He had heard *Childe Harold*, *Manfred*, *Cain*, and
The Corsair nominated, 'even', he adds, 'Don Juan'.[9]

The poem's reviewers were just as unconvinced. Leigh Hunt's nephew,
Henry Leigh Hunt, reviewed *Don Juan* enthusiastically in the *Literary
Examiner*, and dismissed as irrelevant objections to the poem's irregularity:
'after all, Don Juan is not an epic'.[10] The reviewer for the *Monthly
Magazine* stands alone amongst contemporary reviewers in demurring.
Even though 'their moral qualities were very low', the poem's first two
cantos gave promise that, if he were to continue the poem, Byron would
produce 'one of the finest epics in a gay spirit that has enriched any
language'.[11] The *British Critic* took the more common view. It saw in the

same two cantos only 'a narrative of degrading debauchery in doggrel
rhyme'.[12] The poem's 'moral qualities' were reflected in its style: Byron
had 'fallen into a sort of slip-shod manner of versifying, in which his genius
delights to lounge in the laxity and slovenliness of indecent and unprin-
cipled disorder'.[13] This was in response to the third, fourth, and fifth cantos
of the poem. In the later cantos, things only got worse. The fourth
instalment (Cantos IX–XI), it seemed to the *Literary Gazette*, only served
to show the inevitable consequence when a 'nobleman adopts the style of
a porter in which to utter the sentiments of a bagnio'.[14] It seemed obvious
to these early reviewers that the poem's low subject matter coupled with its
low style made nonsense of any notion that it was the work of a poet who
harboured epic ambitions. But in 1819, when Byron began to publish *Don
Juan*, the judgements of reviewers in the weeklies and the monthlies were
inconsequential in comparison with the verdicts of the two great quarterly
reviews, and the *Edinburgh* and the *Quarterly*, rivals though they were, and
divided by literary taste no less than by politics, were united at least in this:
they neither of them reviewed any of the six instalments of *Don Juan*.
Byron smilingly forgave Francis Jeffrey, the editor of the *Edinburgh*, in his
eleventh canto: 'Old enemies who have become new friends / Should so
continue – 'tis a point of honour' (X, 12). Even though it was the Tory
review, the behaviour of the *Quarterly* may have rankled more. The
Quarterly was edited by William Gifford – 'I always thought of Gifford
as my *literary* father', Byron wrote, 'and myself as his "*prodigal* son"'[15] – and
its proprietor was his own publisher, John Murray. Reginald Heber
explained the *Quarterly*'s policy in a composite review of Byron's dramas:
'We knew not any severity of criticism which could reach the faults or
purify the taste of Don Juan, and we trusted that its author would himself,
ere long, discover, that if he continued to write such works as these, he
would lose the power of producing any thing better.'[16] Byron was well
aware that, as he puts it in the poem, 'the Edinburgh Review and
Quarterly / Treat a dissenting author very martyrly' (I, 211), but it was
not disagreement with Byron's opinions that persuaded both reviews to
ignore *Don Juan*. It was the conviction that the poem was beneath their
notice. The policy was maintained after Byron's death even by his most
enthusiastic followers. In the decade after his death Byron had no more
fervent admirer than Edward Bulwer (he later became Edward Bulwer-
Lytton), unless it were Benjamin Disraeli. In a survey of the literary state of
the nation in his *England and the English* Bulwer finds that Byron had
expressed 'a yet more deep and enduring sentiment of the time' than could

be found even in the work of Walter Scott. The early work, the first two cantos of *Childe Harold* and the eastern tales, were overrated for precisely that reason: 'a far higher order of genius' was displayed in the later productions.[17] Modern critics would agree, except that the later work Bulwer has in mind are the tragedies, works that had been reviewed seriously and at length both in the *Edinburgh* and in the *Quarterly*. Byron's masterpieces, according to Bulwer, are *Marino Faliero, The Two Foscari, Cain,* and *Sardanapalus.* As for *Don Juan*, it remains a poem that Byron might just as well not have written. Bulwer makes not a single reference to it.

Bulwer was writing in 1833, consciously resisting a growing tendency to question Byron's reputation. It would soon become the fashion, according to John Nichol, to dismiss Byron as 'a sentimentalist, a romancer, a shallow wit, a nine days' wonder, a poet for "green, unknowing youth"'.[18] The salvaging of Byron's reputation did not begin until 1866, when Swinburne published a selection from his works, and it was Swinburne, unlike early admirers such as Bulwer, who confidently identified *Don Juan* as the greatest of Byron's poems:

> Between 'Childe Harold' and 'Don Juan' the same difference exists which a swimmer feels between lake-water and sea-water; the one is fluent, yielding, invariable; the other has in it a life and pulse, a sting and a swell, which touch and excite the nerves like fire or like music. Across the stanzas of 'Don Juan' we swim forward as over 'the broad backs of the sea'; they break and glitter, hiss and laugh, murmur and move, like waves that sound or that subside. There is in them a delicious resistance, an elastic motion, which salt water has and fresh water has not. There is about them a wide wholesome air, full of vivid light and constant wind, which is only felt at sea. Life undulates and death palpitates in the splendid verse which resumes the evidence of a brave and clear-sighted man concerning life and death. Here, as at sea, there is enough and too much of fluctuation and intermission; the ripple flags and falls in loose and lazy lines: the foam flies wide of any mark, and the breakers collapse here and there in sudden ruin and violent failure. But the violence and weakness of the sea are preferable to the smooth sound and equable security of a lake: its buoyant and progressive impulse sustains and propels those who would sink through weariness in the flat and placid shallows. There are others whom it sickens, and others whom it chills; these will do well to steer inshore.[19]

Swinburne begins his fine tribute by echoing the contrast that Byron draws between himself and the Lake poets. Wordsworth, Coleridge, and Southey think themselves the only poets worthy of notice, Byron complains: 'There is a narrowness in such a notion, / Which makes me wish you'd change your lakes for ocean' (*Don Juan*, Dedication, 5). But Swinburne's claim is grander than the claim Byron makes for himself. Although he never uses the word, when he compares reading *Don Juan* to plunging into the sea, Swinburne is presenting it as an epic poem. Andrew Lang recognised as much when he borrowed the phrase 'the broad backs of the sea' in his prose translation of *The Odyssey*.[20] Twentieth-century critics, some of them at least, were happy to agree. For MacNeile Dixon, in 1912 *Don Juan* is the one true epic of the nineteenth century. It is 'an epic in the modern manner, probably the only manner in which the taste of latter days would willingly accept it'. This is not too far from Herbert Tucker's view when in his enthralling account of the epic aspirations of nineteenth-century poets he describes *Don Juan* as 'the epic for an age of bullshit'.[21] But it is not the case, as Tucker's robust description of the poem suggests, that, after the misgivings of Byron's contemporaries and after the Victorian attack on Byron's reputation, the epic status of *Don Juan* came to be generally accepted. Some of its twentieth-century admirers thought of *Don Juan* as a poem of a very different kind. In 1978, Kingsley Amis's *New Oxford Book of English Light Verse* replaced W. H. Auden's *Oxford Book of Light Verse* that had come out forty years before. When Amis wanted to insist on the difference between the two volumes he pointed out that there was not a single stanza of *Don Juan* that appeared in both.[22] Amis is making the point that he and Auden had very different notions of what constituted light verse. One thing they were agreed on, though, was that *Don Juan* was the supreme example of the kind in English. Amis includes more of it than of any other poem, and so too had Auden, or would have done had he not found space for the whole of *The Miller's Tale*. Auden's Byron is not the author of 'an epic in the modern manner'. He is 'the first writer of Light Verse in the modern sense'. He succeeds as a poet only 'as long as he takes nothing very seriously; the moment he tries to be pro- found, and "poetic" he fails'.[23] Auden scarcely makes it seem an epic achievement.

In the poem itself, of course, Byron insists repeatedly that *Don Juan* is an epic poem: 'My poem's epic and is meant to be', 'my name of Epic's no misnomer' (I, 200). The reading public are invited to recognise his 'epical pretensions to the laurel' (I, 209). If he has a failing it is in 'being too epic' (III, 111). The poem is divided into cantos because such divisions are required by 'the ancient epic laws' (V, 159). When Byron commands 'Thou shalt believe in Milton, Dryden, Pope' (I, 205), we are to remember that Dryden and Pope are not only satirists, they are also the great English translators of Virgil and Homer. When he wants to paint a battle Byron prepares by invoking 'eternal Homer' even though he is quite aware that '[t]o vie with thee would be about as vain / As for a brook to cope with ocean's flood' (VII, 80). He defends himself for calling his hero, Juan, an ass by pointing out that 'great Homer thought / This simile enough for Ajax' (VIII, 29). If his language is sometimes 'rather rough', it is no rougher than the language often found 'in Dante's / Verse' (VII, 3). He is like Dante too in that his poem is the product of his middle age. Dante wrote *The Divine Comedy*, '[n]el mezzo del cammin di nostra vita', when he found himself, as Byron puts it, at 'Life's half-way house' (VI, 75), and *Don Juan* likewise is written during

> That horrid equinox, that hateful section
> Of human years, that half-way house, that rude
>   Hut, whence wise travellers drive with circumspection
> Life's sad post-horses o'er the dreary frontier
>   Of age.   (X, 27)

Milton is 'the prince of poets – so we say; / A little heavy, but no less divine' (III, 91). *Don Juan* is, Byron admits, a different kind of poem. For one thing it is a lot less heavy. Milton's name may be synonymous with the sublime, but the sublime 'when long', when sustained all through a lengthy poem, is 'a little apt to weary us' (XIII, 1). Byron seems confident that *Don Juan* is less tedious than *Paradise Lost*, but he claims Milton and Dante as his confrères all the same, if only because all three poets have been 'hapless in their nuptials' (III, 10). And yet these claims to epic status, however often repeated, always leave the reader uncertain how far Byron expects them to be taken seriously and how far he offers them facetiously. We are never sure whether Byron is claiming a place in the great tradition of epic poets, or whether he is presenting *Don Juan* as an anti-epic, a poem best defined by its difference from its epic predecessors.[24] When he dedicates his poem to Bob Southey, Byron points the difference between Southey, who produces an epic poem 'every spring' (III, 97), and the true epic poet, Milton. Far from being an 'epic renegade' like Southey (Dedication, 1), Milton 'closed the tyrant-hater he begun', and the consequence has been that 'Time, the avenger, execrates his wrongs / And makes the word "Miltonic" mean "sublime"' (Dedication, 10). But if Byron were serious in his epic pretensions, he would surely have claimed a share in that sublimity. In *The Lament of Tasso* and *The Prophecy of Dante*, he does just this. He allows his voice to merge with the voices of the great heroic poets of Italy. But that is not what happens in *Don Juan*. The 'knights and dames' he sings are '[s]uch as the times may furnish', and they are times in which the muse cannot 'fly' and must be content to 'flutter' (XV, 25 and 27). In *Don Juan*, he tells us, he has no ambition to mount Pegasus, 'the wingéd steed', and enter into competition with the great poets of the past. He is happy instead to be off 'wandering with pedestrian muses' (Dedication, 8), one reason for which is that epic poems like Milton's are so apt to be 'a little heavy'. It would not be hard to prove that the 'grand ingredient' of the epic or 'épopée' is 'ennui' (III, 97), which is why Byron is content to take his stand upon 'an humbler promontory':

> never straining hard to versify,
> I rattle on exactly as I'd talk
> With anybody in a ride or walk.   (XV, 19)

Byron seems to have thought of epic poems as a little like those enormous rooms 'without a soul / To break the lifeless splendour of the whole' that he is reminded of when Juan enters the sultan's palace. When we enter a room like that '[a] kind of death comes o'er us all alone'. Byron much prefers '[a] neat snug study on a winter's night', comfortably furnished with '[a] book, friend, single lady, or a glass / Of claret, sandwich, and an appetite' (V, 56–8). It is as if epic ambitions are vainglorious, like the projects of those who design great houses for themselves, forgetting that in the end their only residence will be the grave, which is for them as for all of us the only 'place of rest' (V, 63).

   Epic poets had always made a practice of authenticating their claim to epic stature by repudiating their predecessors. Virgil's Aeneas, so civic-minded, so willing to sacrifice his own wishes to the best interests of the community, is clearly offered as a corrective to Homer's hero Achilles, who recognises no law except the dictate of his own desires. Milton, in the famous proem to Book IX of *Paradise Lost*, insists that his theme is '[n]ot less but more heroic than the wrath / Of stern Achilles'. His own poem supersedes rather than replicates the classical epic and the Italian epics of Tasso and Ariosto by locating the heroic ideal in 'the better fortitude / Of patience and heroic martyrdom' rather than in '[w]ars, hitherto the only argument / Heroic deemed'. Milton reproduces the hero of classical epic, he offers his own version of Achilles and Aeneas, but in his poem the classical hero is revealed as diabolic. Milton names him Satan. Byron's older contemporary, William Blake, fully shared Milton's disdain for 'the silly Greek & Latin slaves of the sword', but he rests his claim to be an epic poet on his exposure of the inadequacy of even Milton's heroic ideal. Milton had accepted a feeble compromise, reconciling the law and the spirit, God the father and God the son, and in

Blake's *Milton* he must be brought back to earth to recognise and to repent his mistake. Milton had claimed for *Paradise Lost* a 'higher argument' than those chosen by Homer, Virgil, and their Italian renaissance successors. Wordsworth in the prospectus to his own unwritten epic, *The Recluse*, doubts whether even Milton's muse, Urania, will be adequate to the task he has set himself. He may need a 'greater muse' because he plans to explore 'the Mind of Man', which contains depths more profound than Milton's Hell, places deeper far than the 'darkest pit of lowest Erebus', and heights in comparison with which 'the heaven of heavens is but a veil'. Epic poets carve out a place for themselves by repudiating the values of their predecessors. There are odd occasions when Byron seems to think of *Don Juan* as a poem of this kind. The American poet Joel Barlow had chosen Columbus as the hero of his epic poem, but Byron offers himself as the 'Columbus of the moral seas', and the man who explores those seas will encounter things stranger than ever Columbus came across (XIV, 102–2). In the cantos on the siege of Ismail, Byron joins with Milton and with Blake by offering his own fierce denunciation '[o]f conquest and its consequences, which / Make epic poesy so rare and rich' (VIII, 90). But even in these cantos there is a mordancy that sharply distinguishes Byron from the Milton of *Paradise Lost* or the Blake of *Jerusalem*. If Byron's poem reaches after epic seriousness, it is as what Byron calls later in the poem 'Epic Satire' (XIV, 99).[25] But even the claim to be an epic satirist is intermittent. Byron is just as likely to deny that he has any serious purpose at all. His only goal, he told John Murray, was 'to giggle and make giggle',[26] and in the poem itself he insists that the only end he had in view was 'to be a moment merry' (IV, 5). It seems a decidedly unepic ambition.

In the poem Byron most often thinks of epic poetry as formally defined. Epics are poems whose poets are given to invoking their muses: 'Hail, Muse et cetera' (III, 1). His poem must be an epic because it is

> Divided in twelve books; each book containing,
> With love, and war, a heavy gale at sea,
> A list of ships, and captains, and kings reigning,
> New characters; the episodes are three:
> A panoramic view of hell 's in training,
> After the style of Virgil and of Homer,
> So that my name of Epic 's no misnomer.   (I, 200)

He is uncertain when he sets out how many books his epic should be divided into, unsure whether to follow Virgil and make it twelve or match

Homer and allow himself twenty-four (II, 216), but by the time he reached the twelfth canto, his ambitions had grown:

> I thought, at setting off, about two dozen
>   Cantos would do; but at Apollo's pleading,
> If that my Pegasus should not be founder'd,
>   I think to canter gently through a hundred.   (XII, 55)

In the event, by the time the composition of the poem was interrupted, Byron had embarked on the seventeenth canto. He does not find room for a catalogue of ships, but there are other kinds of list: lists of generals, lists of poets, lists of dandies, even lists of courses consumed by those who attend one of Lord Henry's dinners. If he offers no descent to the underworld or panoramic view of hell, he has the siege of Ismail:

> All that defies the worst which pen expresses;
>   All by which Hell is peopled, or as sad
> As Hell – mere mortals who their power abuse, –
>   Was here (as heretofore and since) let loose.   (VIII, 123)

His poem includes, he tells us, all the proper epic ingredients:

> I 've got new mythological machinery,
> And very handsome supernatural scenery.   (I, 201)

> Reader! I have kept my word, – at least so far
>   As the first Canto promised. You have now
> Had sketches of love, tempest, travel, war –
>   All very accurate, you must allow,
> And Epic.   (VIII, 138)

> Remember, reader! you have had before
>   The worst of tempests and the best of battles
> That e'er were brew'd from elements or gore.   (XII, 88)

Byron is apt, in passages such as these, to write as if epic were best defined by how many different kinds of thing it could accommodate. He believes, perhaps, like Joseph Trapp and others, that the special characteristic of the epic poem is that it 'comprehends within its Sphere all the other Kinds of Poetry whatever'.[27] Commentators on *Don Juan* often emphasise how many kinds of writing it finds room for. Frederick Beaty, for example, detects the presence of 'classical epic, Roman satire, Italian epic romance, mock-heroic poetry, the picaresque novel, the novel of manners, the pantomime, Gothic romance, the ballad, the lyric, and neo-classical satire'.[28] But Byron's own idea of epic seems a little less untrammelled.

When he fails to follow epic conventions he points it out, as when he decides 'to begin with the beginning' rather than 'in "medias res"', which, on Horace's authority, has become 'the heroic turnpike road' (I, 6). His major difference from his epic predecessors is a difference he rather plumes himself on. Unlike them, he makes his appeal 'to facts'. Facts are 'the grand desideratum!' (VII, 81), 'tis the part / Of a true poet to escape from fiction' (VIII, 86), and in this respect at least he is himself a true poet, more or less:

> Besides, my Muse by no means deals in fiction:
>   She gathers a repertory of facts.
> Of course with some reserve and slight restriction.   (XIV, 13)

It is not so much a verbal tic as a quiet reminder of his respect for unadorned circumstance that leads Byron to use the phrase 'in fact' more than thirty times in the sixteen cantos of his poem. Byron's epic predecessors are all of them prehistoric in the sense that all of them, even Milton, wrote before history had fully established itself as an intellectual discipline. It is because Byron, unlike his epic predecessors, is a modern man that in his account of the siege of Ismail he follows Castelnau's *Essai sur l'histoire ancienne et moderne de la nouvelle Russie* so closely, however much he may deplore the celebratory tenor of Castlenau's account of Suwarrow's victory. It is because of the high value he places on fact that, in his account of a shipwreck, he, unlike Virgil, has recourse to books. He draws his details from volumes such as Sir John Graham Dalyell's *Shipwrecks and Disasters at Sea*. His respect for history, for facts, is one of the things that made Byron a man of his time,[29] and, as Medwin remembered it, his claim that *Don Juan* should be recognised as an epic poem had exactly the same basis. It was an epic because it was the poem of its time, 'as much in the spirit of our day as the Iliad was in Homer's'.

Byron may pretend within the poem that an epic is a poem that is divided into twelve books, a poem that has war in it, and a shipwreck, and a descent to the underworld and supernatural machinery, but he is quite aware that by 1819 that was not how epic poetry was most commonly understood. The epic poem, as Byron's readers would have thought of it, was the poem that most completely expressed 'the spirit' of the society out of which it was produced. Macpherson's Ossianic poems, according to Hugh Blair, fulfilled all the formal requirements for epic poetry, but they did so as an inevitable consequence of the perfection with which they expressed the spirit that animated Ossian's world, the spirit of 'the first ages of society'.[30] The problem was that, unlike Ossian, Byron lived, or believed that he lived, in an unheroic age. The 'knights and dames' that he was given to sing were '[s]uch as the times may furnish' (XV, 25). What would Ossian be without Fingal? What would an epic poem look like that fully expressed the spirit of an age that had no heroes? If Tucker is right, and *Don Juan* is 'the epic for an age of bullshit', what kind of epic will it be that can perfectly express the spirit of such an age?

One answer might be that it will be a mock-epic rather than an epic.[31] 'Thou shalt believe in Milton, Dryden, Pope', Byron writes, and he is not just thinking of Dryden's Virgil and Pope's Homer. He also has in mind *Mac Flecknoe* and *The Dunciad*. Dryden and Pope could be epic poets only in translation, because they too, like Byron, thought that they lived in unheroic times, and for the poet who wishes to express the spirit of such times the epic impulse can survive only if it learns to mock itself. There are traces of the mock-epic, as eighteenth-century poets would have understood it, in *Don Juan*, but there are rather few of them, and when they do appear they seem peripheral to the main business of the poem.[32] In Canto XV Lord Henry's guests prepare for the public dinner that he offers them like Homeric heroes arming for battle:

> Great things were now to be achieved at table
>   With massy plate for armour, knives and forks
> For weapons.   (XV, 62)

In *The Rape of the Lock* a game at cards becomes an epic combat, but Byron wisely chooses not to enter into competition with Pope on Pope's own ground. All he does is to register, briefly, the possibility. *The Rape of the Lock* portrays a world that at once entrances and outrages because it refuses to distinguish between the grave and the trivial. It is a world that finds its just expression in a particular figure of speech, zeugma. It is a world where 'Thou, great Anna! whom three Realms obey / Dost sometimes Counsel take – and sometimes tea' (III, 7–8), a world where it is just as important to a young woman whether she 'stain her Honour or her new Brocade' (II, 107). Zeugma is a figure that Byron finds a place for in *Don Juan*. It is, after all, a post-Waterloo poem, a poem written in a world and for a world where the shock of Napoleon's defeat is registered by a drop in the price of corn: 'What strange thoughts / Arise, when we see Emperors fall with oats!' (IX, 32). When Lambro cocks his pistol, Byron warns that 'one instant more / Had stopp'd this Canto and Don Juan's breath' (IV, 42). In Canto II, when the wind gets up, the porthole of Juan's cabin springs a leak which makes '[h]is berth a little damp, and him afraid' (II, 25). Women are almost always disappointed in marriage, and what follows?

> Some take a lover, some take drams or prayers,
>   Some mind their household, others dissipation.   (II, 201)

Sailors fear autumn as the season of storms: it is the season when 'loud tempests raise / The waters, and repentance for past sinning' (V, 6).[33] But Byron uses the figure less elegantly than Pope. Byron's verbs tend not to be equally congruent with both their complements. We 'take' drams but do we really take prayers, and a wife might well 'mind' her household, but would she really mind dissipation? Storms do 'raise' the waves at sea, but repentance is not like a ghost: it is not usually said to have been raised. Pope's world is absurd, at once delightful and outrageous in its absurdity: Byron's world is comic, and, like most comedy, fails quite to conceal the melancholy that it disguises. Byron's first use of zeugma in *Don Juan* is also the neatest. Waters seeping into a cabin would make the bunk damp and the person lying on the bunk afraid, but the figure does not detach the reader from the fiction as it does in Pope's poem. We would be frightened too if we felt our blankets getting wet. Pope sometimes contrives the zeugmatic effect not by making one verb take two objects but simply by making a list. On Belinda's dressing table there are combs and pins, 'Puffs, Powders, Patches, Bibles, Billet-doux' (I, 138). Some of Byron's lists work a little like this. Nothing compares with a glass of hock and soda water to a man who wakes up parched with a hangover. Not even 'Burgundy in all its sunset glow',

> After long travel, ennui, love, or slaughter,
> Vie with that draught of hock and soda water.   (II, 180)

But Pope is sharply aware of the difference between Bibles and billets-doux, whereas Byron, for an octave or two, is finding a very different pleasure in seeing the world as it must appear to a languid aristocrat who scarcely cares to distinguish between uncomfortably long journeys, fits of boredom, love affairs, and carnage. Caesar, Pompey, Mahomet, and Belisarius have one thing in common: 'They all were heroes, conquerors, and cuckolds' (II, 206). The grouping is incongruous, no doubt, like the assortment of items on Belinda's dressing table, but in Pope's poem the incongruity defines a particular social group, Pope's coquettes, a section of society as tiny as it is fragile. In Byron's line it is the kind of incongruity that does more than describe a few warlords: it defines our general humanity. We may not all be conquerors and cuckolds, but we are all of us compounded of odd, discordant qualities. The line in *Don Juan* most like Pope's is perhaps the line describing the suite that attends Juan and Haidée at their island feast. The pair have assembled for their entertainment '[d]warfs, dancing girls, black eunuchs, and a poet' (III, 78). But the poet at the feast is only at first glance as incongruous as the Bible on Belinda's dressing table. In *Don Juan*, Byron is entirely willing to entertain the thought that poets, even though their representative was once 'great Homer', must now be content to rank alongside dwarfs and dancing girls. Writers have become so fashionable, he remarks, that they 'balance even the scale' with prizefighters (XIV, 20). Mock-epic is right for Dryden and Pope because it is the mode that best registers confusions that they do not share. It will not do for Byron because he does not claim a vantage that allows him to gaze down on absurdities in which he remains unimplicated.

If *Don Juan* is not a mock-epic, it is perhaps a comic epic, a genre which, for Byron, Homer's *Margites* being lost, had its origin in the early seventeenth century, when Cervantes published *Don Quixote*. Cervantes was important to Byron.[34] In *Don Juan* he makes his first appearance in one of Byron's fabulously unlikely lists:

> I say no more than hath been said in Dante's
> Verse, and by Solomon and by Cervantes;
>
> By Swift, by Machiavel, by Rochefoucault,
>   By Fenelon, by Luther, and by Plato;
> By Tillotson, and Wesley, and Rousseau,
>   Who knew this life was not worth a potato.   (VII, 3–4)

If all these, writers who seem to have so little in common, agree that life is not worth a potato, it becomes a proposition that it would be foolhardy to challenge. It is on his second appearance in the poem that Cervantes is particularised:

> I should be very willing to redress
>   Men's wrongs, and rather check than punish crimes,
> Had not Cervantes, in that too true tale
> Of Quixote, shown how all such efforts fail.
>
> Of all tales 'tis the saddest – and more sad,
>   Because it makes us smile: his hero 's right,
> And still pursues the right; – to curb the bad,
>   His only object, and 'gainst odds to fight
> His guerdon: 't is his virtue makes him mad!
>   But his adventures form a sorry sight; –
> A sorrier still is the great moral taught
> By that real Epic unto all who have thought.

> Redressing injury, revenging wrong,
>   To aid the damsel and destroy the caitiff;
> Opposing singly the united strong,
>   From foreign yoke to free the helpless native; –
> Alas! Must noblest views, like an old song,
>   Be for mere fancy's sport a theme creative?
> A jest, a riddle, Fame through thin and thick sought!
> And Socrates himself but Wisdom's Quixote?
>
> Cervantes smiled Spain's Chivalry away;
>   A single laugh demolished the right arm
> Of his own country; – seldom since that day
>   Has Spain had heroes. While Romance could charm,
> The world gave ground before her bright array;
>   And therefore have his volumes done such harm,
> That all their glory, as a composition,
> Was dearly purchased by his land's perdition.   (XIII, 8–11)

Don Quixote 'pursues the right', which is why he is a true hero, but he is a hero in a world in which such a pursuit serves only to mark a man out as insane. It is a world where redressing injury, aiding damsels, opposing wrong even when a society is united in its wrongdoing, and liberating one's country from foreign rule are the projects of a madman, a world where all such virtues survive, like the romances that once celebrated them, only as 'an old song'. *Don Quixote* is an exercise in nostalgia, comic because it celebrates epic virtues that can only be properly exercised in a world that is past. The dream that such a world might be retrieved can be entertained only by a lunatic.

Cervantes offered a model that was followed by many English novelists of the eighteenth century. In Fielding's *Joseph Andrews*, his 'comic epic-poem in prose', the Quixote is Joseph's friend, Abraham Adams, whose pursuit of the right becomes as ridiculous as Quixote's because Adams lives his life in the insane belief that England, his country, is a Christian nation. He is mad because he lacks his wife's common sense. Mrs Adams, as Byron recalls, recognises that we should be Christians only when we go to church: 'Scriptures out of church are blasphemies' (XIII, 96). In *Tom Jones*, Squire Allworthy lives in Paradise Hall, blithely unaware that both he and his country seat have their places in a fallen world, and the result is that Squire Allworthy is less able to see the world around him and the people in it as they really are than his neighbour, Squire Western, whose energies seem almost entirely corporeal. Byron recognised his kinship with Fielding and the other quixotic novelists of the eighteenth century. He is happy to leave

all those who will not allow his poem into their homes to the 'purer page /
Of Smollett, Prior, Ariosto, Fielding' (IV, 98). He reminded John Murray
that if his poem is 'voluptuous', Smollett was 'ten times worse' and
Fielding 'no better'. He advised Douglas Kinnaird that, if he thought
Don Juan 'indecent', he should read, amongst other things, 'Fielding's
night Scene of Slipslop and Adams – and Mrs. Waters and Molly Seagrim
in the thicket – and Square in the garret',[35] and when Lord Henry gathers
his house guests at Norman Abbey, Byron regrets that there are none of
them so distinctive, so characterful, as the 'Squire Westerns' of old and
their daughters, the 'Sophias' (XIII, 110). And yet *Don Juan* is not really, or
at least not often, a quixotic poem. Byron may acknowledge Cervantes, but
he does not choose to follow in his footsteps. He is not like Juan's tutor,
Pedrillo, happy to follow in Juan's 'wake, like Sancho Panca' (II, 37). *Don
Juan* makes room on occasion for nostalgia. Aurora Raby's Catholicism is
quickened by it: she 'deem'd that fallen worship far more dear / Perhaps
because 'twas fallen' (XV, 46). Still more plangently there is Haidée. When
she dies of a broken heart after she is separated from Juan, she and the
father responsible for her death survive in song and in story as types of what
once was and never more may be: 'many a Greek maid in a loving song /
Sighs o'er her name; and many an islander / With her sire's story makes the
night less long' (IV, 73). But Byron's is not a poem given over to nostalgia
even if it occasionally makes space for it. It is a poem that far more often
turns its face to the future:

> But let me change this theme which grows too sad,
>   And lay this sheet of sorrows on the shelf;
> I don't much like describing people mad,
>   For fear of seeming rather touch'd myself –
> Besides, I've no more on this head to add;
>   And as my Muse is a capricious elf,
> We 'll put about, and try another tack
> With Juan, left half-kill'd some stanzas back.   (IV, 74)

There is another crucial difference. Cervantes and Fielding write their
comic epics in prose. In his preface to *Joseph Andrews*, Fielding makes
light of it, dismissing the notion that a fiction cannot properly be classified
as epic unless it is written in metre, but all the same it is an important
difference. It marks a decisive break with the long tradition of verse epics.
In *Tom Jones*, Molly is attacked as she leaves church by the other young
women of the parish who are outraged by her finery, and jealous of it too
no doubt. Molly defends herself stoutly, but it is Tom Jones who secures

victory by scouring 'the whole coast of the enemy, as well as any of Homer's heroes ever did'. The battle is 'sung by the muse in Homerican style'. Sustained epic parody of the kind that Fielding goes in for has no place in *Don Juan*. Fielding feels free to parody Homer, because he writes in prose: his medium in itself separates him from the verse epics of the past. Byron's poem remains haunted by them. His ottava rima may be very different from Homer's and Virgil's hexameters and from Milton's blank verse, but, as he knows very well, it is Tasso's stanza and Ariosto's. *Don Juan* has a more anxious relationship with its epic predecessors than the comic epics of Cervantes and Fielding, which is why Byron's demands that *Don Juan* be recognised as an epic poem are so hard to place, why they leave the reader so uncertain whether they are to be taken seriously or dismissed as facetious.

From 1819 until the last cantos were published in 1824, the poem was ignored by the two quarterlies, and either ignored or disparaged by most, if not all, of the other periodicals. George Darley exaggerated when he claimed in a piece for the *London Magazine* that *Don Juan* had 'almost totally escaped the promiscuous hands of reviewers', but it was reviewed much more rarely than any other of Byron's major poems, and much more rarely than might have been predicted, given that it was the longest poem by the most celebrated poet of the age. But, as Darley recognised, 'the reason of this neglect on the part of the periodical press is evident, – the immorality of the work alluded to'. Darley claims that his paper will serve a useful function: it will make the beauties of the poem available to readers without their having to read the poem through.[36] Byron was already dead, but *Don Juan* remained a poem that, as Byron himself reported, could not be admitted 'into families' (IV, 97). In Byron's lifetime, the *London* had not noticed *Don Juan*, except in John Scott's essay in his series 'Living Authors', in which Scott remarks of the appearance of *Don Juan* after *Childe Harold* that it was 'as if the statue of Apollo, in the Vatican, had left its pedestal, to appear as that of Pasquin, the squib publisher, in the common Roman market place'.[37] The *New Monthly* regretted the publication of the first two cantos in a brief review,[38] and was thereafter silent. But one magazine bucked the trend.

Blackwood's Edinburgh Magazine paid more attention to *Don Juan* than to any other poem published in the five years from 1819 until 1824. It was a *Blackwood's* trademark to accommodate wildly divergent assessments of the same writer, even of the same work, but in its notices of *Don Juan* the magazine outdid itself. In July 1823, 'Timothy Tickler', in a notice jointly written by William Maginn and J. G. Lockhart, characterised the first

cantos of the poem published by John Hunt (Cantos VI, VII, and VII) as
'heartless, heavy, dull, anti-British garbage'. These latest cantos demonstrated that Byron was now 'wallowing in a sty of mere filth'. Two months
later Lockhart began his review of Cantos IX, X, and XI by dismissing this
'absurd critique', and giving it as his firm opinion that '*Don Juan* is,
without exception, the first of Lord Byron's works'.[39] One reason that
the *Blackwood's* writers returned to *Don Juan* again and again is that they
recognised the poem as a mirror in which they could contemplate the
features of their own magazine. When Lockhart wonders at Jeffrey's refusal
to notice the poem in the *Edinburgh*, and explains it as betraying Jeffrey's
fear of the reprisal that he might provoke if he were to review it disobli-
gingly, he surely does so conscious that Jeffrey had also established it as
a policy that he would allow no reference in the *Edinburgh* to *Blackwood's
Magazine*. Jeffrey's motive, the *Blackwood's* writers must have recognised,
was in both cases the same. Both poem and magazine were ignored as
scurrilous, and hence beneath notice. Even in its wildly contradictory
judgements, nowhere more flamboyantly displayed than in its notices of
Don Juan, *Blackwood's* was Byronic. It was after all Byron who had
wondered, 'if a writer should be quite consistent / How could he possibly
show things existent?' (XV, 87). In 1820, the magazine published a letter
purporting to be from Byron, acknowledging that in 'The Mad Banker of
Amsterdam', a poem in ottava rima serialised in the magazine,
J. G. Lockhart had 'out-Byron'd Byron'.[40] The claim was less a measure
of the brilliance of Lockhart's poem than of the effrontery of the magazine,
but Lockhart did contribute to the magazine a version of Byron's defence
of *Cain* done into couplets that comes close to justifying the claim. In
a letter to John Murray, Byron had protested that if *Cain* was blasphemous,
so was *Paradise Lost*: 'the very words . . . "Evil be thou my good," are from
that very poem, from the mouth of Satan'. Lockhart translates the sentence
into a couplet that is wittier than Byron's prose, and also somehow more
Byronic:

> But my poor shoulders why throw all the guilt on?
> There's as much blasphemy, or more, in Milton.[41]

The most striking expression of the belief shared by many of its contributors that the magazine had a special affinity with the Byron of *Don Juan* is
the fourth instalment of the magazine's most famous occasional series, the
Noctes Ambrosianae. The series records the conversations when the magazine's contributors meet to eat heartily and drink still more freely in
Ambrose's tavern in Edinburgh's Gabriel's Road under the benign auspices

of the magazine's fictitious editor, Christopher North. But in the fourth
episode, which was supplied by William Maginn, the scene is 'transferred
(by poetic licence) to Pisa'.[42] There, the magazine's resident Irishman
Ensign Morgan Odoherty, a character loosely based on William Maginn,
engages in a conversation with Byron, fuelled by liberal potations of
Montefiascone and brandy. The principal topic is the brilliance of
Blackwood's Magazine, but Maginn also gives his opinion of Byron's latest
poem: 'Consider, my Lord – consider, I say, what a very immoral work
Don Juan is – how you therein sport with the holiest ties – the most sacred
feelings – the purest sentiments.' He pauses to remind Byron 'the bottle is
with you', and then goes on to admit that, however much he disapproves of
the poem, 'I had rather have written a page of Juan than a ton of Childe
Harold.' *Blackwood's* was a belligerently Tory magazine, and Maginn was
its most belligerently Tory contributor. He admired *Don Juan* because,
however much he disagreed with Byron's politics, he recognised that
Blackwood's and *Don Juan* shared an aesthetic. Indeed Maginn's ability
to hold together wildly contradictory judgements of Byron's poem was one
aspect of the aesthetic that the magazine and the poet held in common.

In the very first of the notices of *Don Juan* in *Blackwood's*, *Don Juan* is
praised as 'by far the most admirable specimen of the mixture of ease,
strength, gayety, and seriousness extant in the whole body of English
poetry'. The crucial term here is 'mixture', which is as much a quality of
the poem's moral character as of its manner. Evident in the poem is 'a
more thorough and intense infusion of genius and vice – power and
profligacy – than in any poem which has ever before been written in the
English, or indeed in any other modern language'.[43] Three years later we
are told that *Don Juan* offers 'the finest specimens of serious poetry
[Byron] has ever written; and it contains the finest specimens of ludicrous
poetry that our age has witnessed'.[44] But what is most remarkable about
the poem is the swiftness of Byron's transitions between the two, and it is
in this that it most resembles *Blackwood's Magazine*. *Blackwood's*, as
Ensign Odoherty describes it to Byron, is 'a real Magazine of mirth,
misanthropy, wit, wisdom, folly, fiction, fun, festivity, theology, bruising, and thingumbob'.[45] It achieved its special character because this
miscellaneous content was not organised into sections: the fun, the
theology, and the thingumbob were allowed to jostle against one another.
In the magazine at large, and in the conversations that make up the *Noctes
Ambrosianae* in particular, the shifts from verse to prose, from high
seriousness to comic absurdity, from German idealism to whisky punch
and cured herrings, are bewilderingly rapid. The magazine called

attention to its methods by noticing the objection of a doubtlessly fictitious home counties clergyman:

> A Berkshire Rector has been pleased to wonder
> Why we've dismissed the primitive arrangement.
> He hates, he says, from verse to prose to blunder,
> Our quick transitions seem to him derangement.
>
> Begging our good friend's pardon, we prefer
> To mix the dulce with the utile,
> And think it has in fact a charming air
> Such different things in the same page to see.
>
> A sonnet there, a good grave essay here,
> Chalmers, Rob Roy, Divorce-law, the New Play,
> Next (our divan, amid their toils to cheer)
> Some squib upon our neighbours o'er the way.[46]

A principal reason for the *Blackwood's* preoccupation with *Don Juan* is
clearly that the poem and the magazine were put together in obedience to
the same principles.

One sign of this was the rapid appearance in *Blackwood's* of ottava rima
poems evidently written in imitation of *Don Juan*. Such poems appeared in
other magazines, too, even those that, unlike *Blackwood's*, found nothing
to admire in Byron's poem, which suggests that even Byron's most furious
detractors recognised that there was some sort of family resemblance
between *Don Juan* and magazines.[47] The very first of these imitations
even contrived to pre-date *Don Juan*. The first instalment of *The Mad
Banker of Amsterdam* by William Wastle (a *Blackwood's* pseudonym
assumed on this occasion by Lockhart) appeared in *Blackwood's* in
July 1818, exactly a year before the first two cantos of Byron's poem were
published. Lockhart, like Byron, acknowledged that he was inspired by
John Hookham Frere's Whistlecraft, the 'specimen' of a national epic on
King Arthur supposedly written by two Suffolk harness and collar-makers:
William and Robert Whistlecraft. Lockhart writes, he tells us, 'in this new
style of Frere's'. He mounts on a Pegasus borrowed from Frere, and boasts,
'tis a fine hack'. But Lockhart's real model was *Beppo*, Byron's first exercise
in Frere's new style. It may have been Frere's example that persuaded
Byron of the comic possibilities of ottava rima for an English poet, but
Lockhart thought it 'mere humbug' to accuse Byron of copying Frere.[48]
Beppo had been published earlier in 1818, in March, and Lockhart, even, it
may be, before Byron himself, at once saw the possibilities of the new
manner that Byron had adopted. *The Mad Banker of Amsterdam* goes

nowhere. It appeared in *Blackwood's* in four instalments.[49] After the first, Lockhart moves from Amsterdam to Edinburgh and seems unsure what to do when he gets there. There is some mockery of Jeffrey and phrenologists, and a brief history of Scottish monarchs that includes a sentimental eulogy of Mary Queen of Scots, but in the end the poem simply peters out. Early in 1820 a letter in *Blackwood's* supposedly written by James Hogg but in fact almost certainly contributed by Lockhart himself reported that 'Don Juan has put [Wastle] quite out of countenance with the Mad Banker, I now fear, he will never conclude.'[50] But in the poem's first two cantos Lockhart reveals himself as much the most perceptive of *Beppo*'s early readers. Lockhart's crucial tactic was to shift Byron's scene from Italy to Holland. Lockhart recognised Byron as the 'grand Napoleon of the realms of rhyme' (XI, 55) long before Byron claimed the title. He makes for himself a more modest claim. He claims only the rank of the great Napoleon's younger brother, Louis Bonaparte, who was installed as King of Holland by his brother in 1806, and quickly acquired, once he had mounted his throne, 'a taste for smoking and gin toddy'. The story Lockhart begins to tell concerns the love of a Prussian banker, long resident in Amsterdam, for a buxom Dutch widow, but Lockhart's point lies in the contrast between his poem and Byron's, between the two canal cities, Byron's Venice and Amsterdam, the 'capital of snugness and the Dutch', between the Venetian gondolas that travel the Venetian canals so lightly, 'their dusk livery of woe' (*Beppo*, 157) in such piquant contrast to the opportunities they offered their passengers, and the treckschuyts that move so much more heavily along the canals of Amsterdam, and, still more importantly, on the contrast between the women of the two nations. Venetian women for Byron bring back to life those faces which we 'once have seen, but ne'er will see again', those sweet 'forms, which flit by us, when we / Are young', forms that fix our eyes as they pass us '[i]n momentary gliding', and that we remember afterwards as beings '[w]hose course and home we knew not, nor shall know, / Like the lost Pleiad seen no more below' (*Beppo*, 104–12). In Amsterdam by contrast the most admired woman is a 'bouncer', a 'plump, jolly, juicy lady', like the widow with whom the mad banker is enamoured:

> Once on a washing-green I spied her slips,
> And found them full three yards about the hips.

It is the kind of coarse, broad humour that *Blackwood's* favoured, but it opens the way for a contrast between Italian and Dutch art, between Byron's women, 'like so many Venuses of Titian's', women who are 'like a picture of Giorgione' (*Beppo*, 85–8), and the women of Amsterdam, '[s]uch dames as sat to Rubens and Jan Stein'. And it opens the way too for a contrast between the two languages, between the language that has given us the 'gondola' and the language that has given us the 'treckschuyt', between Byron's Italian, 'that soft bastard Latin / Which melts like kisses from a female mouth, / And sounds as if it should be writ on satin' (*Beppo*, 345–7), and the harsh, guttural language of the Dutch. It is a point that Byron made too, but not until he wrote Canto X of *Don Juan*, when Juan travels through Germany and comes across words, 'Hundsfot' and 'Verflucter', that clog the mouth as effectively as the slow German coaches clog the roads (X, 71).

The modern magazine was invented in October 1817, when William Blackwood re-branded the magazine he had launched six months earlier. The *Edinburgh Monthly Magazine* became *Blackwood's Edinburgh Magazine*, edited by Blackwood himself with the help of two young Scots, both of them graduates of Oxford, John Wilson and John Gibson Lockhart. From its very first issue the new magazine aimed at notoriety. The issue opened with a sixteen-page review by John Wilson of Coleridge's *Biographia Literaria* magnificent in its sustained and intemperate injustice. It instigated the magazine's long campaign against Leigh Hunt with the first of Lockhart's papers on the Cockney School of Poetry; it included a Biblical parody, 'the Chaldee manuscript', well calculated to outrage the pious burghers of Edinburgh; it launched a virulent attack on William Wilberforce for his tentative suggestion that the insurgents in a recent slave rebellion in Barbados might have had grievances; and it included some blank verse lines by John Wilson telling how the Queen of Fairies is so rapt as she listens to the Ettrick Shepherd's song that she 'half forgets her own green paradise'. Wilson's lines introduced a tender lyric by James Hogg, an elegy for a girl, born outside wedlock, who had died just as she stood on 'tiptoe' between 'childhood and unstable youth'. It was not just the inflammatory nature of some of its contents, but the abrupt transitions between them that ensured for this first issue of the new magazine its sensational success, and that made it the model for later magazines such as the *London*, the *New Monthly*, and *Fraser's*. It was also the characteristic of the magazine that equipped Lockhart to recognise at once the importance of the new direction Byron had taken with *Beppo*.

From 1817, for the next twenty-five years, all through the years that Byron was writing *Don Juan* and beyond, the literary market in Britain was dominated by the magazines.[51] For one thing, the magazines paid better than any other kind of writing. But that was not cause for unmixed satisfaction even to those who profited by it. Edward Bulwer became editor of the *New Monthly* in 1831, but in *England and the English* he remembers a German acquaintance who readily acknowledged that it was 'a great literary epoch' in Britain, an age of 'magnificent writers', and at once adds, but 'where, to ask a simple question, are their writings?' It is, Bulwer acknowledges, a great period for 'imaginative literature', for poets and novelists, but he agrees with his German friend that in all other fields there are 'very few great books', and his explanation is that all the people who should be writing those books are spending their time writing for magazines instead. Because they have chosen 'a temporary form of publication', even 'the profoundest writers' have been content to produce writing that, brilliant though it might be, remains 'superficial'.[52] It was a charge to which even the most admired of the periodical writers were sensitive. 'If we are superficial, let us be brilliant', Hazlitt writes: 'If we cannot be profound, let us at least be popular.' Such remarks seem defensive, and Hazlitt is quick to remind his readers that unsigned magazine papers were sometimes gathered together and published between hard covers: 'many of these fugitive, unowned productions [amongst them, many of Hazlitt's own], have been collected, and met with no unfavourable reception, in solid octavo or compact duodecimo'.[53] Charles Lamb agreed that magazine writing occupied a shadowy middle ground, in between the fleeting and the permanent. He would not, he tells us, bind 'a set of Magazines ... in full suit': 'The dishabille, or half-binding (with Russia backs ever), is our costume.'[54] Only the half-binding is appropriate to the in-between status of magazine writing. The magazine writers were so quick to recognise *Don Juan* as their own poem, because it seemed to them to have a similar status, somewhere between the permanent and the throwaway.

J. G. Lockhart was much the most perceptive contemporary critic of *Don Juan*, and he sometimes claimed epic stature for the poem. The shipwreck in the second canto, 'as a piece of terrible painting', outdid anything in the *Aeneid*.[55] Nothing can be done, according to Lockhart, 'in literature, or in any of the sister arts, except by taking things as they are, or representing things as they are', and it is in this that Byron excels, and it is because of this that his true kinship is with Homer. But much more often Lockhart claims for *Don Juan* a different kind of epic value, a value that derives from its being the most complete and most truthful expression of the England of its era: 'There is nobody but yourself who has any chance of conveying to posterity a true idea of the spirit of England in the days of his

Majesty George IV.'[56] Later, in *Blackwood's*, he insisted that *Don Juan* was 'a great work – a work that must last', because any work must last that speaks the 'prevailing sentiment of a large proportion of the people of any given age of the world'.[57] By then that was the quality that most commonly identified the epic work: the epic offered the most complete expression of the spirit of an age. But what does it mean to write an epic that conveys the spirit of the nation 'in the days of his Majesty George IV', that is, the epic of a period that even Lockhart, a Tory and a staunch supporter of the king, cannot mention without lapsing into a prose that seems slyly mock-heroic? What kind of work will the epic poet of a trivial age, of an age of bullshit as Herbert Tucker describes it, produce? It will be, it may be, an epic poem as likely to prompt comparison with *Hudibras* as with Homer, a poem in which epic dignity is repeatedly violated by doggerel rhyme, a poem produced by a poet who has not, like Milton, equipped himself for his task by undergoing a strenuous and long-extended education embracing not just poetry but all of human knowledge, but by a man who had fitted himself for his task by undergoing a very different kind of education, by a man who had 'tooled in a post-chaise, in a hackney coach, in a gondola, against a wall, in a court carriage, in a vis-a-vis, on a table, and under it'. All through the 200 years since it was first composed, *Don Juan* has prompted disagreement, even amongst its greatest admirers, as to whether it ought to be thought of as an epic poem or as the supreme English example of light verse. It is worth considering whether it might more properly be thought of as a poem that fulfilled the epic requirement to express the spirit of the nation at a time when that spirit could only be expressed by a poet who was a master of light verse.

After Byron died in 1824 poetry became a drug on the market. By 1830 Edward Moxon was the only London publisher willing to bring out volumes of poetry written by a single author, and he almost always did so only on condition that the poet bore the costs. Byron's most successful female follower, Letitia Landon or L. E. L., resisted the new distaste for poetry better than most, but in 1830, in *Romance and Reality*, she finally acknowledged that 'the novel is now the very highest effort – the popular vehicle for thought, feeling, and observation – the one used by our first-rate writers'.[58] *Romance and Reality* was a novel, and a novel of a particular kind. One of the earliest examples of the kind was Thomas Lister's *Granby*. Walter Scott read Lister's novel in 1826 as soon as it was published and described it as belonging to 'that very difficult class which aspires to describe the actual current of society'.[59] Scott's one attempt in that kind three years earlier must have been what persuaded him of its difficulty. *St*

Ronan's Well had not been a success. It was not just the concern for the present moment that distinguished *Granby*. Lister's interest was confined to a particular section of society. The women in the novel study only one column in the *Morning Post*, the 'Fashionable Changes', the column in which the doings of their own class are recorded: 'We never look at anything else – we abstain upon principle.'[60] *Granby* was almost the first of the fashionable novels, novels exclusively concerned with that tiny, privileged group whose sense of its own identity is confirmed when it finds its doings printed in the society pages of the morning newspaper. The characters in these novels are chosen from amongst 'the two thousand Brahmins who constitute the world',[61] but they appealed to a wide readership. They particularly appealed, as Bulwer, the most successful of them, recognised, to the middling classes, to those who 'sought for representations of the manners which they aspired to imitate'.[62]

On 1 April 1826, Colburn placed a puff in the *New Monthly Magazine* for a new novel of this kind. He describes Disraeli's *Vivian Grey* as 'a sort of Don Juan in prose, detailing the adventures of an ambitious, dashing and talented young man of high life'. Disraeli would have approved of the comparison. He and Edward Bulwer were both fervent Byronists. Disraeli persuaded his father to employ Byron's old servant, Tita Falcieri. Bulwer leased Byron's old rooms in Albemarle Street and took his discipleship to the unusual lengths of conducting an affair with Lady Caroline Lamb. The fashionable novel, in its male incarnation as the dandy novel at any rate, is an offspring of *Don Juan*.[63] Catherine Gore intimates as much in *Cecil* in which the hero, Cecil Danby, is a close friend of Byron's. The two men had known each other in London, but it is in Italy, when Byron was at work on *Don Juan*, that they become intimate. It was Byron who first defined the world that these novels describe, the fashionable world that consists, as Byron puts it in *Beppo*, only of '[y]ourself and friends, and half a hundred more' (466), a world populated by 'twenty score / Of well-bred persons' (470–1). In the English cantos of *Don Juan*, the 'great world' is only a little more populous. It is made up of 'about twice two thousand people' (XI, 45), the 'twice two thousand, for whom earth was made' (XIII, 39).

Disraeli was one of the first to be persuaded that the epic of the future would take the form of a novel. Vivian Grey announces that he plans to write an epic, 'but it shall be in prose': 'The reign of Poesy is over, at least for half a century.'[64] One reason that any new epic must be in prose is that the verse epic of the 1820s, as Disraeli knew very well, had already been written.[65] Byron had already done it. But however much they may recognise that the epics of the future would take the form of a novel the fashionable novelists never suggest that they harbour epic ambitions for the kind of novel that they write themselves. They often speak of their own efforts as slightingly as their most contemptuous reviewers, as if they accept that their own productions are unlikely to survive the fashions in clothing, the verbal tics, and the shopping habits that they so faithfully record. Vivian Grey asks, 'Amid the myriad of volumes which issued monthly from the press, what one was not written for the mere hour?',[66] and fashionable novelists seem to accept that theirs are works of precisely this kind. Disraeli, as he confesses in *The Young Duke*, scribbles 'pages lighter than the wind' that will issue in 'volumes which will be forgotten ere [he] can hear that they are even published'.[67] The novels are like the young women who people them: they 'come into season with the green peas, and go out with the strawberries'.[68] In 1836, Bulwer speaks of 'the three years' run of the fashionable novels' even though it was a vogue that had already lasted for a decade and would last for ten years more.[69] It is as if he is anxious to represent his own achievement as a fashionable novelist as even more ephemeral than it was. But fashionable novels, however self-deprecating the novelists might be, sometimes suggest that it is precisely their focus on the fleeting and the trivial that gives them their value. As Catherine Gore puts it, they are 'the amber which serves to preserve the ephemeral modes and caprices of the day'.[70] In *Cecil,* she lends the thought to her hero:

> The truth is that, like a straw thrown up to determine the course of the wind, the triflers of any epoch are an invaluable evidence of the bent of the public mind. They are always floating on the surface – always ostensible! – they are a mark for general observation. Statesmen and Beaux are the only really public men. Posterity will see, in Brumel and Castlereagh, the leading characters of the Regency.[71]

It may be that she borrowed her simile from Bulwer, who applies it to the fashionable novels themselves rather than their characters. The novels were 'a shrewd sign of the times: straws they were but they showed the upgathering of the storm'.[72] But it may equally well be the case that Gore and Bulwer were both of them indebted to *Don Juan*. 'Fling up a straw', Byron writes, ''twill show the way the wind blows'. And poesy itself, he adds, is just 'such a straw' (XIV, 8). If *Don Juan* is an epic, it is an epic of an entirely new kind, an epic written on the assumption that literature might achieve its historical significance through rather than in spite of its flimsiness. It may be precisely because it is as light as a straw that it can accurately chart the currents of the stream or the direction of the wind. It may be precisely because it is so light a poem, not in spite of it, that *Don Juan* has a better claim to convey to posterity 'a true idea of the spirit of England in the days of his Majesty George IV' than the epics that Southey brought out every spring, or the epic on Hyperion that Keats began, or *The Recluse*, the epic that Wordsworth planned, or even than *The Prelude*, the poem in which Wordsworth traced how he became the kind of poet qualified to write an epic, and found when he had done he had not written a prelude to the great poem he had in mind but had already completed the only kind of epic poem that he could compass. All these poems were, as Byron puts it in *Don Juan*, '*too* epic' (III, 111), and a poem that was too epic could never be the true epic poem of the 1820s. 'The cultural moment of the mid-1820s', Angela Esterhammer writes, 'turns out to be profoundly ephemeral',[73] and the true epic of the 1820s would be, like its age, a paradoxical epic, 'profoundly ephemeral'.

    Don Juan is a generic hybrid, or, it might be better to say, it is, as far as genre goes, a contradiction in terms. Epic poems survive their age. Homer is the first of epic poets because he could 'charm / All ears', 'all ages'. He is 'eternal Homer' (VII, 80). But the epic poem of the 1820s is written by a poet who mocks poets (Wordsworth chief amongst them) who make their 'appeal to the unborn'. Byron succeeded in his own lifetime, when he could enjoy it. Better still he had triumphed when he could enjoy it most, in his youth, '[t]he only time when much success is needed'. As for posterity, 'Why I'm posterity – and so are you; / And who do we remember?' (XII, 17–19). *Don Juan* is the epic poem of a poet who has given up epic pretensions, an epic poet who seems as ready as a periodical writer like Hazlitt to settle for being popular even if that meant surrendering the ambition to be profound. When Byron looks for a hero he does not find him in classical mythology or military history. Instead he chooses Don Juan, a figure that he knows will be familiar to all his readers from the pantomime (I, 1). *Don Juan* is an epic pantomime,[74] and pantomime, unlike epic, does not live through the ages: it lives only in the two or three hours of its performance. In Italy, Byron admired Tommaso Sgricci, whose poems were improvised rather than written, and recognised a kinship between Sgricci's talent and his own. *Don Juan* is remarkable for its 'conversational facility': Byron finds a way of turning into rhyme whatever comes 'uppermost', '[j]ust as I feel the "Improvisatore"' (XV, 20). But improvisation is not just an Italian talent. In England, Byron had been friendly with the great pantomime performer of the Regency, Joseph Grimaldi. When they met at Berkeley Castle in October 1812, it was a meeting of one clown with another. The two improvised a comic performance for the delight of their fellow guests.[75] But Grimaldi's genius survives only in report. The gambols and the facial expressions that convulsed his audiences died with him. Byron's clowning in *Don Juan* has outlived him, preserved in print. And yet *Don Juan*, unlike any other epic poem, still has something in it that smacks of live performance. A poem like *Paradise Lost* stays in the memory, solid, grand, as stable as a monument. *Don Juan* is a poem that does not fix itself in the mind.[76] We remember snatches of it, but it is a poem that lives fully only as it is being read. It is a little like 'the world of eight years past':

> 'Twas there –
> I look for it – 'tis gone, a Globe of Glass!

> Cracked, shivered, vanished, scarcely gazed on, ere
> A silent change dissolves the glittering mass.   (XI, 76)

Don Juan is that strange paradox, an epic poem that still somehow manages to keep something of the character of a Grimaldi performance,[77] that is, of a performance that lasts only as long as Grimaldi holds the stage, and disappears with him into darkness the moment the theatre lights grow dim.

CHAPTER 2

I Want a Hero

On 14 May 1824, when news of Byron's death reached England, Hazlitt was writing his essay on Byron for *The Spirit of the Age*. The moment that the news reached him is marked in the published text by a row of seven asterisks. Hazlitt thinks it 'better, and more like himself' to let what he had already written stand, but what follows is very different from what had gone before. The essay had begun pugnaciously. Everything that Byron wrote was inflected by his sense of his rank. In the letter published in *The Liberal*, 'To the Editor of the *British Review*', he subjected William Roberts to 'the sort of *quizzing* he might use to a person who came to hire himself as a valet to him at *Long's*' (the New Bond Street hotel), and in his dispute with the Reverend William Lisle Bowles on the merits of Pope, he clapped his fellow poet on the back 'with a coarse facetious familiarity, as if he were his chaplain whom he had invited to dine with him, or was about to present to a benefice'. The lordly manner renders the liberalism that Byron affects in his politics 'preposterous'. But the assault is interrupted by the row of asterisks, and when Hazlitt takes up his pen once more, it is to remark how at the touch of death 'the drossy particles fall off, the irritable, the personal, the gross, and mingle with the dust'. Death 'strips a man of every thing but genius and virtue', and Byron had died 'a martyr', giving his life in 'the cause of freedom, for the last, best hopes of man'. It is of no consequence that the Dean has refused to sanction his interment in Westminster Abbey: 'The poet's cemetery is the human mind, in which he sows the seeds of never-ending thought – his monument is to be found in his works.'[1] In the first part of the essay, Byron is vividly, vulgarly alive, quizzing one fellow, clapping another on the back, but it all comes to an abrupt halt when news of Byron's death reaches Hazlitt, and in the final paragraph of the essay Byron is transfigured. He has become statuesque, as if he were cast in bronze or carved in marble.

In the decades that followed Byron's death, the monument of himself that Byron had left in his works was supplemented by monuments in stone.

In 1826, a committee, set up by Byron's friend Hobhouse, decided on a memorial statue. Sir Francis Chantrey refused the commission, and the committee turned to the Danish sculptor Bertel Thorwaldsen. Byron had sat to Thorwaldsen at Rome in 1817. It had not been an entirely happy experience. Byron had proved a difficult subject. He had resisted Hobhouse's suggestion that he be represented crowned with a laurel wreath – 'I won't have my head garnished like a Xmas pie with Holly – or a Cod's Head and Fennel – or whatever the damned weed is they strew round it' – but he had other affectations. Thorwaldsen had been unable to dissuade him from striking a pose. 'You need not assume that look', Thorwaldsen had told him, but Byron had persisted. He complained of the finished bust that it was nothing like him because he was in person 'more unhappy', but, Thorvaldsen insisted, 'it was universally admitted to be an excellent likeness'.[2] In 1834, ten years after Byron's death, the commemorative statue was completed and shipped to England, where it remained stored in a Customs House for another decade. Hobhouse was awaiting the death of John Ireland, Dean of Westminster Abbey, who had refused permission for the statue to be installed in his church, and Ireland lived on until he was eighty. Then, in 1842, when at long last he died, his successor proved just as intransigent, and Hobhouse at last accepted the request from Trinity, Byron's Cambridge college, that the statue be placed, where it still stands, in its library. Byron holds a book half open in his left hand, with his right hand he holds a pencil to his chin, and his left foot rests on a fallen Greek column in witness of the cause for which he died. There are other statues of Byron. There is the one in London, in Park Lane (Byron is pensive, and accompanied by Boatswain, his newfoundland dog), and in Rome a copy of the Trinity College sculpture stands in the Borghese Gardens. There are statues, as one would expect, in Greece. In Athens, just outside the National Gardens, Greece in the figure of a woman crowns Byron, who seems oddly diminutive in her presence. Most movingly of all, in Messolonghi, the sacred city of Greece, a statue of Byron looks over the Garden of Heroes, the garden that commemorates those of all nations who fell in the Greek struggle for independence.

Byron took the story for *Werner* from 'The German's Tale', one of Harriet Lee's contributions to *The Canterbury Tales* (Byron thought it was by Harriet's sister, Sophia[3]). Lee's hero, like Byron's Corsair, is named Conrad. His heroic status is confirmed when a turn of his head 'presented that bold outline sometimes formed in a moment of inspiration by the chisel of a master'. Conrad, that turn of his head reveals, had been 'cast in the mould of a hero, and had nothing to do with the common and every-day race of men'.[4] Harriet Lee thinks of heroes as being like statues, and Byron agreed. In *The Deformed Transformed*, the hunchback Arnold exchanges his misshapen body for the body of the first of all heroes, Achilles. If Achilles had not satisfied his 'nice taste', he would have swapped his body for the body of a statue, he would have chosen to be 'ideal marble' brought to life, but even as Achilles he is more like a statue than a man.[5] To become a hero is to transmute one's flesh and blood into marble or bronze. Marino Faliero in Byron's play dreams of making that exchange. When he imagines his ideal self, he does not think of his own ageing body but of a body cast in bronze. He thinks of Verrocchio's great equestrian statue of Bartolomeo Colleoni. The statue, in Faliero's account, was the reward that the state had conferred on Colleoni, one of his ancestors, in gratitude for his delivery of Venice from the enemy host that threatened it.[6] Faliero tries to emulate that feat, but the enemies from whom he seeks to rid Venice are enemies within. He plots to oust the ruling aristocracy, and instead of the marble or the bronze repose that had been his goal he suffers a shameful traitor's death. Byron had been prompted to write the play when he noticed how thoroughly all memory of Marino had been extirpated. Even his portrait had been removed from the great hall of the Doge's palace where it should have hung alongside all the other doges of Venice, the space that it would have occupied painted over in black. Byron reverses that decision. He paints his own portrait of the disgraced Doge, but it is a portrait, not the heroic statue of himself that Marino had craved.

The book that Thorwaldsen's Byron holds in his left hand half open is a copy of *Childe Harold*, which is fitting because the fourth canto of *Childe Harold* is Byron's most sculptural poem. It begins in Venice, a city where the doges are statues, even if '[s]tatues of glass' (IV, 127), a city that finds its proper emblem in the 'steeds of brass / Their gilded collars glittering in the sun' that stand in St Mark's basilica (IV, 109–10). In Florence there is the Uffizi '[w]here sculpture with her rainbow sister vies' (IV, 543). Poets in the canto are honoured by being commemorated in busts, like the bust for which Byron sat to Thorwaldsen in Rome. There is 'Ariosto's bust' (IV, 361) and, more tellingly, there are the busts shamefully absent from Santa Croce, the busts of Dante, Petrarch, and Boccaccio, the 'Bard of Prose'. Their absence is felt: it impresses itself on visitors still more deeply than any of the memorials on display (IV, 523–6). In Rome, there is the statue of Pompey at the base of which Caesar was assassinated (IV, 775–6), there is the bronze of the Capitoline Wolf suckling Romulus and Remus (IV, 784–8), and in the Vatican there is the Laocöon, in which the father's love for his sons gives him dignity even in his pain (IV, 1332–40). Most memorably, also in the

Capitoline, there is the Dying Gladiator (now known as the Dying Gaul), his head bowed, hearing but not heeding the baying crowd, remembering as he dies the home and the family that he would never see again: 'his eyes / Were with his heart, and that was far away' (IV, 1261–2).

Thorvaldsen was quite right to show Byron holding a copy of *Childe Harold* rather than *Don Juan*. In *Don Juan* for one thing sculpture is rather less admired. In *Childe Harold* Byron had regretted the absence of the poets' busts from Santa Croce, but by the time he came to write *Don Juan*, it had come to seem ridiculous that a poet's achievement should be marked by '[a] name, a wretched picture, and worse bust' (I, 218). Haidée, Byron remarks, is '[f]it for the model of a statuary', and at once rebukes himself for offering her so vapid a compliment. Sculptors are

> (A race of mere impostors, when all's done –
> I've seen much finer women, ripe and real,
> Than all the nonsense of their stone ideal.) (II, 118)

He instances 'an Irish lady, to whose bust / I ne'er saw justice done, and yet she was / A frequent model' (II, 119). He may have been thinking of Lady Adelaide Forbes, the granddaughter of Thomas Moore's patron, the Earl of Moira. Byron had once entertained thoughts of becoming 'seriously enamoured' with her, and when he was in Rome he was struck by how much the Apollo Belvedere resembled her: 'I think I never saw such a likeness.'[7] Haidée does become statuesque, but only once. When Lambro intrudes on Juan and Haidée as they lie 'pillow'd cheek to cheek, in loving sleep' (III, 29), Juan starts up and snatches a sabre. Lambro cocks his pistol – 'It has a strange quick jar upon the ear, / That cocking of a pistol' (IV, 41) – and Haidée throws herself between the two men she loves:

> 'On me', she cried, 'let death
> Descend – the fault is mine; this fatal shore
> He found – but sought not. I have pledged my faith;
> I love him – I will die with him: I knew
> Your nature's firmness – know your daughter's too'. (IV, 42)

At this moment Haidée, who just a moment before had been 'all tears / And tenderness', reveals herself as a heroine, and as she does so her flesh becomes stone: she stands '[p]ale, statue-like, and stern' (IV, 43). The transformation is magnificent, but it is also an anticipation of the death that will overtake her just a few stanzas later. She sees Juan cut down and falls unconscious, never to revive. In death her face retains its expression, but it is 'such as marble shows / When exquisitely chisell'd', an expression 'fix'd as marble's unchanged aspect throws / O'er the fair Venus' (IV,61). She keeps her beauty but only by becoming a statue of herself. When her body stiffens into stone she brings to mind the statues that Byron had admired in Rome and celebrated in the fourth canto of *Childe Harold*, 'the Laocoon's all eternal throes, / And ever-dying Gladiator's air' (IV, 61). But what strikes him now is that although the statues are so striking by virtue of their 'energy', it is an energy that 'looks not life', the reason for which is simple: statues never change. They cannot be lifelike 'for they are still the same' (IV, 61). The beauty of a statue is unchanging, and that kind of beauty, Byron wants to say, is dead.

Trelawny remembered that when he took his leave of Byron on Cephalonia, Byron had remarked, mordantly enough, that no matter how things turned out in Greece, the experience would give him literary material: 'if things are farcical, they will do for Don Juan; if heroical, you shall have another canto of Childe Harold.'[8] *Don Juan*, Byron knew, was an unheroic poem. Heroes, as Harriet Lee puts it, have 'nothing to do with the common and every-day race of men', but in *Don Juan* Byron's attention is focused on the common and everyday. When Lambro threatens her lover, Haidée is frozen into a heroic posture, and looks as if she had been carved 'by the chisel of a master', but that is a rare moment in a poem that prefers the 'ripe and real' to the sculptor's ideal forms. The poem stretches out its hand to grasp the world much in the manner that Juan reaches out his hand on his second encounter with a ghost, not to find a sculpted figure made of cold marble, but to grasp the 'glowing bust, / Which beat as if there was a warm heart under' that belongs to 'her frolic Grace – Fitz-Fulke!' (XVI, 122–3). That encounter takes place in Norman Abbey where there are sculptures, most memorably, in the topmost 'niche' of the arch that survives as a 'glorious remnant' of the original Abbey, the 'Virgin Mother of the God-born child, / With her son in her blessed arms, look'd round' and 'made the earth below seem holy ground' (XIII, 61). But that sculpture is quite unlike the Abbey's current mistress, the Lady Adeline Amundeville. Byron recognises a kinship between the statue and one of the poem's characters, but the kinship is with one of Lady Adeline's guests. Aurora Raby has been raised a Catholic, in a faith that, like the Abbey, is 'fallen', and remains in her eyes 'far more dear / Perhaps because 'twas fallen' (XV, 46). Lady Adeline is so unlike the Virgin not because she is unchaste, but because she has not been cast in stone. She is changeable, so changeable that Juan, as he watches her work the room when her husband gives a public dinner, 'began to feel / Some doubt how much of Adeline was *real*':

> So well she acted, all and every part
>   By turns – with that vivacious versatility,
> Which many people take for want of heart.
>   They err – 'tis merely what is called mobility,
> A thing of temperament and not of art,
>   Though seeming so, from its supposed facility,
> And false – though true; for surely they 're sincerest
> Who are strongly acted on by what is nearest.   (XVI, 97)

Byron adds a note pointing out that 'mobility' is a translation of the French 'mobilité', which he defines as 'an excessive sensibility of immediate impressions'. Although it is a quality, he adds, 'sometimes apparently useful to the possessor', as it is to Lady Adeline when she performs so expertly the role of hostess at Lord Henry's public dinners, it is 'a most painful and unhappy attribute'. That remark, as no doubt Byron intended, has prompted all commentators on the passage, from Thomas Moore onwards, to point out that it is a quality that Lady Adeline shares with Byron himself. As Moore put it, 'That Lord Byron was fully aware not only of the abundance of this quality in his own nature, but of the danger in which it placed consistency and singleness of character, did not require this note to assure you.'[9] It is a quality commonly found, Byron goes on to remark, in 'orators', in 'actors, artists and romancers', in 'speakers, bards, diplomatists, and dancers', in '[h]eroes, sometimes though seldom – sages never' (XVI, 98). And that is why heroes and philosophers, Alexander and Aristotle, may properly be commemorated in statues and busts, whereas no sculptor can fashion a true likeness of people like Lady Adeline and Byron. Such people are not themselves when their features are fixed. The long list of professions to which those gifted or cursed with mobility are suited is enough to indicate that people of this kind are in a large majority, which is one reason why most people do not look like their busts – Byron did not think that he looked like Thorwaldsen's bust of him, however excellent others thought the likeness – and they do not look like their portraits either. Portraits even of the living look like portraits of the dead. When we look closely at the eyes, even though they may be brightened by a dab of white paint, we see at once that 'death is imaged in their shadowy beams', and that is because

> A picture is the past; even ere its frame
> Be gilt, who sate hath ceased to be the same.   (XVI, 19)

The thought comes to Juan, unable to sleep, as he walks through the picture gallery of Norman Abbey. Portraits are not like the people they represent because the people change and the portraits do not. But what is true of painting is still more true of sculpture, because statues have a chilly immobility that painting never quite matches. Statues are lifeless, like Lord Henry's house guests, who are 'as polished, smooth, and cold / As Phidian forms cut out of marble Attic' (XIII, 110).

In *Don Juan*, Byron is suspicious of sculpture because he is suspicious of the heroic. In some sense he always had been. Byron had, it is true, from the first been closely associated with 'his tall scornful heroes, all of one family, with hearts as black as their heads, and lips curling as regularly and duly as their whiskers'. In the early poems that had made him famous he 'struts and mouths under the tinsel and pasteboard trappings of the melodramatic hero'.[10] But by the time he came to write *Don Juan* he had come to the conclusion that such characters were as hackneyed as his more sophisticated readers had already begun to find them. 'I have met today the personification of my Corsair', he remarked after being introduced to Edward Trelawny in 1822, and he went on to suggest that Trelawny slept with Byron's poem under his pillow.[11] He was amused rather than impressed. In *Don Juan*, Byron had already assumed a very different character. He had exchanged the hero's costume for the jester's, as the reviewer in the *British Critic* remarked, and was now content to jingle 'the cap and bells of the motley jackpudding'.[12] But those early heroes of his, Harold and the Giaour and Selim and Conrad and Lara and Alp and Hugo, had in any case all shared an oddly ambivalent status. They are heroes, as Jerome McGann puts it, in a world that offers them no scope for their heroism, heroes of poems that take as their subject 'the debasement of the western ideal of heroism'.[13] Lambro in *Don Juan* is their last surviving representative. The years have rolled on, and Byron's heroes are no longer the young men they once were. Lambro, like Byron himself, has entered 'the most barbarous' of all the middle ages, 'the middle age / Of man' (XII, 1). His affections are centred on his daughter rather than his mistress: he is 'the best of fathers' (III, 17). He is, it is true, a 'piratical papa' (III, 13), but buccaneering for him is a trade. He is a professional man not a swashbuckler, 'a sea-attorney' (III, 14), a 'sea-solicitor' (III, 26), a businessman who has made the happy decision to operate in a deregulated market where there is 'no custom-house nor quarantine / To ask him awkward questions' (III, 20). Piracy was a capital offence, but, Byron playfully suggests, its criminal status is not established by principle. It is really just a matter of words:

> For into a prime minister but change
> His title, and 'tis nothing but taxation.   (III, 14)

Lambro has qualities that might have fitted him to govern a nation, not just the little island that he has made his home. 'You never could divine his real thought', a facility which, Byron suggests rather tartly, shows 'the true breeding of a gentleman' (III, 41). Be that as it may, it is certainly a useful aptitude for a statesman, as is Lambro's capacity not to signal when he is about to strike. When Lambro is 'in his real and serious mood', his every action is 'calm, concentrated, and still, and slow' (III, 48). But Lambro is a prime minister in waiting whose potential can never be fulfilled because he belongs to a country that has lost its nationhood. As the turncoat poet puts it in the patriotic song with which he entertains the guests at Haidée's feast, 'The heroic lay is tuneless now / The heroic bosom beats no more!' (III, 715–6). The 'spirit of old Greece' had '[f]lash'd o'er [Lambro's] soul a few heroic rays' (III, 55), but to little effect. All that those dying gleams have done for him is to make him into a pirate: 'His country's wrongs and his despair to save her / Had stung him from a slave to an enslaver' (III, 53).

Lambro is almost the last in the line of Byronic heroes. He is a diminished, middle-aged version of the heroes of the earlier tales, but he is their legitimate successor. It is a line of heroes, but heroes of the only kind extant in an unheroic age, heroes who have no arena available to them in which their heroism can be adequately displayed. In the sequence of plays that Byron wrote while he was at work on *Don Juan* – many of his serious-minded readers thought the plays the substantial achievement and *Don Juan* just the relaxation with which Byron entertained himself in the intervals between their composition, and sometimes Byron shared that view – the idea of the hero is subjected to a still more sceptical examination. For Marino Faliero the only heroic action possible is to engage in a conspiracy to oust the very class to which he belongs, but the conspiracy requires him to associate with men whose company feels to him like a degradation. Cain, like Marino, aspires to be a hero and finds that the only act of heroic self-assertion available to him is even more uncomfortable: he murders his own brother. But however sceptically these narratives explore the idea of heroism, they keep faith with its form. In the early tales and in the dramas that followed them, the hero exerts the gravitational force that gives the poems and the plays their shape. The heroes are the individuals that the stories are organised around. These are centripetal narratives. *Don Juan* by contrast is centrifugal. It is not just that the poem moves restlessly from story to story as Juan moves from place to place, repeatedly trying another tack: it is more that none of those stories is quite able to engross the story-teller's attention. None of them is able to cure the narrator of his besetting fault, digression, his habit of '[l]eaving [his] people to proceed alone' while he soliloquises 'beyond expression' (III, 96). *Don Juan* puts in question the idea of the heroic, and, still more radically, it also puts in question its shape.

Take Lambro, for example. Even on the island that he owns, the island of which he is the absolute ruler, Lambro finds himself pushed to the periphery. When he returns home after a successful voyage – although he had been 'detain'd / By winds and waves', he had made 'some important captures' (III, 15) – he is surprised to find the island's inhabitants feasting. He asks one 'vinous Greek' what the occasion is, but neither he nor his two neighbours deign to reply. They are 'new comers', and have no idea who is addressing them. Lambro continues on his way, reaching his house 'by a private way', unrecognised even by those he passes: 'the few who met him hardly heeded, / So little they expected him that day' (III, 49). They pass him by as if he had become invisible, just a ghost of himself. Lambro violently reasserts his centrality soon enough. He seizes his daughter when she throws herself between him and Juan, and she is helpless in his grasp. When Lambro's men attack him, Juan falls, bleeding from 'two smart sabre gashes', and is at once removed to one of Lambro's galliots and stowed under the hatches. Lambro makes himself master in his own house once more, but to what end? For twelve days he watches while his daughter pines away, and when she dies she takes away his only reason for living. She 'had been / The only thing which kept his heart unclosed' (III, 57). Haidée is remembered by 'many a Greek maid in a loving song', and 'many an islander / With her sire's story makes the night less long' (IV, 73). It is a legacy of sorts, but Lambro leaves no trace on the twelve cantos of the poem that remain. 'I've no more on this head to add', Byron remarks, and at once he puts about and tries another tack (IV, 74). Haidée retains a muted presence in the poem – even in the presence of Gulbeyaz Juan 'could not yet forget her' (V, 124) – but in all the rest of the poem Lambro is not once mentioned.

'I want a hero', *Don Juan* begins, and in that opening phrase Byron compresses into the one word, 'want', the lack and the longing, the dearth and the desire, that will propel the poem all through its sixteen cantos.[14] He wants a hero, and, unable to find a true one, he falls back on 'our ancient friend Don Juan', a character familiar to all his readers from the pantomime. The poem traces Juan's career as he develops from the sixteen-year-old adolescent living with his mother in Seville to the 'full-grown Cupid' of twenty-one, '[a] little spoilt, but by no means so quite' (XIV, 41), who accepts Lord Henry's invitation to Norman Abbey. His is on the face of it a career chock-a-block with event; an adulterous affair with an older woman, shipwreck, the love idyll on the Greek island, adventures in the slave market and the harem, the savagery of the war cantos, the enervating months in the Russian court as the favourite of Catherine the Great, and then the mission to England where Juan finds himself enmeshed in all the intricacies of English social life, swithering between the married Lady Adeline and the virginal Aurora Raby before he allows himself to be seduced in a moment of distraction by a third woman, the Duchess of Fitz-Fulke, a 'somewhat full-blown blonde' (XIV, 42). It is an eventful life, but, despite that, Juan, rather like Lambro, is repeatedly pushed to its margins, his role reduced to little more than a bystander in the poem of which he is supposed to be the hero. In the very first canto it is Donna Inez, his monstrous mother, and Donna Julia, his first love, who occupy the centre of the stage. Juan is present in all the canto's most important scenes, but he is a silent presence. Even Don Alfonso, Julia's fifty-year-old husband, and Antonia, her maid, are allowed speaking roles. Juan's silence is underlined by a love affair that unites him with so very voluble a mistress. Julia displays her capacity for sustained eloquence in the six stanzas of the letter of farewell she writes to Juan and still more remarkably in the thirteen stanzas in which she upbraids her husband when she is surprised by him and his retinue in her bedroom. All through those thirteen stanzas she brilliantly assumes the role of the wronged wife even though Juan lies all the while concealed beneath her bedclothes:

> Perhaps 'tis of Antonia you are jealous,
>   You saw that she was sleeping by my side
> When you broke in upon us with your fellows:
>   Look where you please – we 've nothing, sir, to hide;
> Only another time, I trust, you 'll tell us,
>   Or for the sake of decency abide
> A moment at the door, that we may be
> Drest to receive so much good company.   (I, 156)

The poem's hero, tucked underneath her blankets, says not a word.

In the English cantos Juan has become a worldly, self-confident, somewhat conceited young man, but even in these last cantos he remains, as Jane Stabler and Caroline Franklin understand, subordinate to the three women who vie for his affections.[15] At Norman Abbey Juan, we are told, 'shone in the best part of dialogue', but what that means is that he has learned the art of keeping quiet: 'there never was a better hearer' (XIV, 37). When Lord Henry gives a public dinner, Juan addresses 'gay nothings' to Aurora (XV, 78), but we never learn what they might be: they remain, quite literally, 'nothings'. It had been just the same in Ismail. Juan had told the two cossacks threatening little Leila exactly what he thought of their behaviour, but what he said remains a mystery: 'I shall not say exactly what he *said*, / Because it might not solace "ears polite"' (VIII, 93). When asked if he is well, on the morning after his encounter with the ghost, he is reduced to stammering incoherence, 'Yes – no – rather – yes', 'He was quite well. /Quite well; yes; no' (XVI, 32–3). Only once in all the sixteen cantos of the poem is Juan allowed a memorable remark. In Canto V he makes a joke, and not at all a bad one. When Baba the eunuch insists that Juan don the 'effeminate garb' that his soul loathes, he assures John Johnson that, despite his dress, he remains determined to preserve his honour: 'the Sultan's self shan't carry me, / Unless his highness promises to marry me' (V, 84). It is a sprightly couplet, but a single couplet is not much to boast for the hero of a poem of sixteen cantos. It is surely not just a coincidence that the canto in which Juan speaks most often and with most effect is the canto much of which he spends dressed as a woman. Byron's Juan is sexually passive, as Byron sometimes imagines that he was himself: 'I have been more ravished myself than anybody since the Trojan war', he claimed on one occasion.[16] Only once in the whole poem does Juan take the sexual initiative, when he is put to bed with Dudu in the harem. Sexual and linguistic confidence go together and Juan manages to display the two kinds of confidence only in a canto in which he wears women's clothes, answers to the name Juanna, and is referred to by female pronouns: undressing before getting into bed with Dudu, Juan declines Dudu's assistance, and 'rather suffered' for doing so by '[p]ricking her fingers with those cursed pins' (VI, 61). Throughout the other fifteen cantos of the poem Juan seems always in the predicament to which he is reduced on the ghost's second appearance. His mouth opens '[a]s wide as if a long speech were to come', but for all that his mouth is open he remains quite silent (XVI, 115). Byron had learned from Scott the usefulness of a hero, who, because he has no very marked characteristics, is the better able to reflect the character of the societies through which he moves, but Juan is even more anodyne than Edward Waverley or Frank Osbaldistone. He is more like a twentieth-century character, more like Robert Musil's hero, *The Man Without Qualities*.

'I want a hero', the poem begins, and Juan supplies that want. At least he promises to, but it is a promise that he never quite fulfils. Instead, Juan is repeatedly sidelined in the poem of which he is supposedly the hero, and not only by the women who find him so attractive. Take, for example, his journey from Dover to London. As he walks up Shooter's Hill he is assailed by four footpads, fires his pocket pistol into the 'pudding' of one of them, and puts the other three to flight. It is one of several occasions in the poem when he seems to accomplish a properly heroic exploit, except that the man he has shot at once takes centre stage, and gives a dying speech of such colourful bravado that Juan is reduced to the status of his mute audience:

> as the fuel
> Of life shrunk in his heart, and thick and sooty
>   The drops fell from his death-wound, and he drew ill
> His breath, – he from his swelling throat untied
> A kerchief, crying 'Give Sal that!' – and died. (XI, 16)

'Tom, the highwayman', according to Jerome Christensen, 'is Byron's last hero'.[17] He is, as Christensen surely recognises, only a pantomime hero. His death is a performance, like Sergeant Troy's when he plays Dick Turpin in the travelling circus in *Far from the Madding Crowd*. But, then, one of the reasons that Byron chooses Juan as the hero of his poem is because '[w]e all have seen him in the pantomime'. The dying Tom elbows Juan aside, and in this he rehearses the slights to which Juan is subjected throughout a poem in which the narrator, the character that for ease, and because the poem repeatedly insists on the identification, I call Byron, so often and so thoroughly subordinates his hero to himself. Juan becomes Byron's feed, stooge to the principal comedian, the straight man whose chief role it is to prompt the dazzling turns in which Byron establishes himself at the top of the bill, unchallenged star of his own poem.

Byron begins *Don Juan* in want of a hero not because there are too few heroes to choose from but because there are too many. In the first four stanzas of his poem Byron considers the claims of thirty-two of them before finally settling on Don Juan. His technique is to catalogue his heroes in lists. Six heroic French Revolutionary generals, for example, are disposed of in a single line: 'Joubert, Hoche, Marceau, Lannes, Dessaix, Moreau'. François Marceau occupies just two syllables of the poem. In the third canto of *Childe Harold* he had been allowed two full stanzas. When the traveller passes the small pyramid that marks the place of his burial, he is invited to pause and honour a soldier who even in the midst of battle 'kept / The whiteness of his soul'. He was a hero even to his enemies. When his French comrades marked his death by firing a volley of musket shots over his grave, it was echoed by a volley fired by the Austrian troops who had fought against him (III, 56–7).[18] Marceau is transported from *Childe Harold* to *Don Juan*, and in the course of that journey he is stripped of all his individuality. He becomes just one name amongst many. The lists of heroes are at times so arbitrary as to seem almost random: 'Petion, Clootz, Danton, Marat, La Fayette.' The reference to Clootz may be pointed. In 1821, Byron suggested to Murray that one of his plans for Juan was to have him 'finish as Anacharsis Cloots in the French Revolution'.[19] Clootz was guillotined in March 1794 in front of the largest crowd ever assembled to witness an execution. But what can one make of a line of heroes that places side by side the aristocratic Marquis de Lafayette, Jérôme Pétion, who had defeated Lafayette when he stood for election as Mayor of Paris, and Jean-Paul Marat, 'l'ami du peuple' and Lafayette's sworn enemy. All of them, as Byron remarks, '[w]ere French, and famous people, as we know', and all of them were active in the French Revolution, but they do not seem to have very much else in common in life or even in death. Cloots was guillotined when he was thirty-eight. Lafayette survived the Revolution and lived on until 1834, when he was an old man of seventy-six, still the hero on two continents so dryly celebrated by Thomas Carlyle. Marat was fifty when Charlotte Corday stabbed him in his bath, and after the fall of Robespierre Pétion escaped execution by committing suicide. His body was found half-eaten by dogs. Like Clootz, he was thirty-eight. The heroes in these opening stanzas are named but named in lists, and names, however famous they may be, become all but anonymous when presented in that way. They are hidden in plain view. The lists work rather like the proper names in the war cantos. Amongst the Englishmen serving with the Russian forces, hoping to make their name no doubt, were '[s]ixteen call'd Thomson, and nineteen named Smith' (VII, 18). But how can a man become famous, the poem asks, when his very name renders him anonymous? The Russian troops encounter a similar problem, at least when they appear in an English poem. Their deeds were heroic enough to make their names immortal: all that stands between them and everlasting fame is 'pronunciation', for how can a man become a household name when his name is unpronounceable (VII, 14). Ever since Homer, heroes have relied on poets to confer on them their immortality ('Troy owes to Homer what whist owes to Hoyle' (III, 90)). But all those brave soldiers with names '[e]nding in "ischkin", "ousckin", "iffskchy", "ouski"', for all that they may be 'names at Moscow', defy any attempt to turn them 'into rhyme' (VII, 16). 'Heroes', Byron tells us, 'are but made for bards to sing' (8, 14), and those Russian names, bravely though Byron attempts the feat, resist accommodation in English iambics. They remain cacophonous, bearing witness only, in Anthony Howe's phrase, to 'modernity's heroic unfitness'.[20] Some names are too common for their bearers to become heroes, and some are too exotic. It is hard to make heroes of men whose names have 'twelve consonants a-piece' (VII, 15), and it is just as hard to make a hero of a man called Smith. But that is not the only difficulty with which the modern hero has to grapple. Homer's heroes won their fame in single combat. They fought in battles very different from the mass warfare that Byron knew. 'More men were slain / With deadlier engines' when Suwarrow took Ismail than all the casualties in the ten-year siege of Troy (VII, 80), and that is the reason that they will be, almost all of them, unremembered. The men who fought in the battle for Ismail fought

> As gallantly as ever heroes fought,
> But buried in the heap of such transactions
>   Their names are rarely found, nor often sought.
> Thus even good fame may suffer sad contractions,
>   And is extinguish'd sooner than she ought:
> Of all our modern battles, I will bet
> You can't repeat nine names from each Gazette.   (VII, 34)

The bodies of these modern heroes are lost in the heaps of the dead, and their names disappear in lists of the dead and wounded, lists so long that even the most assiduous reader of Gazettes will struggle to get through them. At Ismail 'fifty thousand heroes' fought (VIII, 17), but what becomes of heroism when a hero is just one of fifty thousand? All those names make up 'a bulky volume' of heroism until the battle reduces their number to 'an elegant extract (much less massy)' (VIII, 34), but even in extract there are still far too many of them. Their names may be printed in the Gazette, but they will never be imprinted on the public memory.

The hero in epic tradition is first and foremost a warrior, which is why most of the thirty-two potential heroes listed in the poem's first four stanzas are fighting men, some serving on land and some at sea. All through his career Byron had looked askance at the military virtues. Childe Harold, "[b]orn beneath some remote inglorious star', is 'unmoved' when he cruises past the sites of epic naval engagements, 'Actium, Lepanto, fatal Trafalgar'. He 'loathed the bravo's trade, and laughed at martial wight' (II, 40). But Byron added to the poem's first canto a warm tribute to his schoolfriend John Wingfield, an officer in the Guards who had died at Coimbra while serving in the Peninsular war. Wingfield died of fever, not in action, and Byron regrets that he had been denied the soldier's grave that he deserved. He wanted for Wingfield the death that, in one of his last poems, he sought for himself. 'Seek out', he urged himself, 'less often sought than found – / A soldier's grave, for thee the best;|[21] It was a wish that he, like Wingfield, was to be denied. The ambivalence with which Byron regarded the warrior hero is best revealed in his various and conflicted responses to Napoleon, the greatest general of the age, who inspired in Byron hero-worship but a hero-worship that was always edged with disdain.[22] In *Don Juan*, Byron's contempt for the military virtues is concentrated in the cantos that treat the Siege of Ismail. Napoleon, Byron's tainted hero, undergoes metempsychosis and is reborn as the Russian general Suwarrow. Suwarrow shares Napoleon's special talent. He too has 'the spirit of a single mind' that can make the minds of 'multitudes take one direction' (VII, 48). Still more emphatically than Napoleon Suwarrow plays the part of 'le petit caporal'.[23] He supervises the bayonet practice, and even 'deigned to drill / The awkward squad', behaving as if he 'could afford to squander / His time a corporal's duty to fulfil' (VII, 52). But in him Napoleon's carelessness of human life becomes outright callousness. Suwarrow is a hero, and a hero is a man whose 'trade / Is butchery', a man who has learned to contemplate with indifference the fates of 'whole millions'. Suwarrow is momentarily moved when Juan's and John Johnson's women weep, clinging to their men at the moment of parting, but Byron notes how incongruous that is. It is evidence of the curious truth that 'sometimes a single sorrow / Will touch even Heroes, and such was Suwarrow' (VII, 69).

Even in *Don Juan* Byron recognises military men whose heroism he can regard unironically. Such men display their worth in the defence of their country against foreign aggressors, not in wars of conquest. Their Greek types are Militiades who won at Marathon the victory that inspired Byron's dream that 'Greece might still be free', and Leonidas, who gave his life in battle against Xerxes at Thermopylae. Their representative in the modern world is George Washington. For such men 'every battle-field is holy ground, / Which breathes of nations saved, not worlds undone' (VIII, 5). After the Congress of Vienna, Byron, like Shelley in *Hellas*, took the view that freedom had fled to the west. Both poets nurtured the dream that another Athens might arise in America. Byron called the boat he had built for him at Leghorn the Bolivar, and dallied for a while with the notion of emigrating to South America,[24] but in *Don Juan* it is North America that gives him his types of the modern hero. The pastoral hero of the modern age is Daniel Boone, the 'back-woodsman of Kentucky', who preferred to make his home in 'the rarely-trodden wild', and raised his 'sylvan tribe' of children in the 'free-born forest' (VIII, 61–7), and its civic hero is George Washington, whose reward for winning his country's freedom was 'thanks and nought beside, / Except the all-cloudless glory' that it earned him (IX, 8). Wellington, whose name, happily for Byron, chimes with

Washington's, is his 'grand antithesis' (XV, 2), his 'soul's antipodes' (XIV, 101). Unlike Washington, Wellington, 'or Vilainton' as he becomes in French pronunciation (IX, 1), made a good thing out of being a hero. 'Half a million for your Sabine farm / Is rather dear', Byron remarks (IX, 7). He exaggerates. A grateful nation paid £263,000 to purchase a country estate for Wellington at Stratfield Saye near Basingstoke, and he paid for his London home, Apsley House, himself, buying it from his older brother. He had been born into an Anglo-Irish family of limited means but by the time he died in 1852, the Wellesleys were well on their way to becoming the richest family in all England – a fitting outcome, Byron suggests, for a man '[c]alled "Saviour of the Nations" – not yet saved; / And Europe's Liberator – still enslaved' (IX, 5).

Heroes in *Don Juan* are first and foremost warriors, but Byron also recognises a second order of heroes, the poets. The two kinds of hero are closely associated. The first hero of all, 'the bravest of the brave, Achilles' (IV, 76), owes his eminence to a poet – he is 'Homer's Achilles' (II, 123) – and modern poets have been happy to offer modern heroes the same service:

> Europe has slaves, allies, kings, armies still,
> And Southey lives to sing them very ill.   (Dedication, 16)

Modern heroes may even return the compliment. Of the sixteen Thomsons who fought with the Russian army, fourteen '[h]ad been call'd "*Jemmy*" after the great bard' (VII, 19). Byron himself had once been hailed the 'grand Napoleon of the realm of rhymes' until *Don Juan* did for him what Moscow did for Napoleon. Both men have been ousted and replaced by a holy alliance of dunces (XI, 55–6). There are even generals who try their hands at poetry themselves, Suwarrow for one: 'this Russ so witty / Could rhyme, like Nero, o'er a burning city' (VIII, 134). As Byron reports in a note, Suwarrow had reported the taking of Ismail to Catherine in a 'kind of couplet; for he was a poet'.[25] He compressed into one 'Russian couplet rather dull / The whole gazette of thousands whom he slew', and when Catherine read his rhyme, it 'brought a smile to her lips' (IX, 60). Byron was not one of Hazlitt's greatest admirers, taking the view that he '*talks pimples* – a red and white corruption rising up (in little imitation of mountains upon maps), but containing nothing, and discharging nothing, except their own humours', which may give us cause to doubt the assurance that Leigh Hunt offered Hazlitt when he told him how glad Byron would be if Hazlitt were to become a contributor to *The Liberal*.[26] But Byron would have been happy to

agree with Hazlitt's claim that the 'language of poetry naturally falls in
with the language of power'.[27] He may mark Suwarrow as inhuman in his
willingness to make rhymes over a burning city, but he can scarcely be
unaware that he is doing the same himself, and on a far greater scale. But
for Byron, as for Leigh Hunt and Shelley and Hazlitt himself,
Wordsworth's 'Thanksgiving Ode' offered the most egregious evidence
in support of Hazlitt's contention: '"Carnage" (so Wordsworth tells you)
"is God's daughter,"' which, Byron goes on to remark, makes her 'Christ's
sister' (VIII, 9). It is not one of his happier jests, but it at least expresses his
outrage that poets such as Wordsworth and Southey should make common cause with the generals.[28] The poet's role, Byron grants even in *Don
Juan*, might and perhaps ought to be heroic. He claims such a role himself
in one of the rare moments in the poem when he allows himself a grand
gesture:

> And I will war, at least in words (and – should
>   My chance so happen – deeds), with all who war
>   With Thought.   (IX, 24)

It was the chance that the London Greek committee offered him when
they invited him to travel as the committee's representative to Greece.
He seized the opportunity, and became, as Hazlitt recognised, a hero at
the last. But it was an unlikely achievement. At least Byron makes it
seem so in *Don Juan*, a poem in which poets are not often presented as
heroes.

It is not just that Byron casts unflattering glances at the work of so many
of his contemporaries, he seems almost as disenchanted with his own. He
hates, he remarks, when introducing Haidée and her maid Zoe, 'that air / Of
clap-trap, which your recent poets prize' (II, 124), dryly aware as he says so
that he is himself the most illustrious example of those recent poets. The
society Blues, amongst them Lady Fitz-Frisky and Miss Maevia Mannish,
a name, I am sorry to say, that should be understood as a play on the
name of Felicia Hemans,[29] admired Juan but 'still regretted that he did
not rhyme' (XI, 53). Byron does not share the regret. He will not have
a poet for his hero for the same reason that he will not have a soldier,
because there are far too many of them to choose from: 'they're too
numerous' (XI, 61). As he walks home after he disembarks, Lambro passes
a Greek girl with 'long floating auburn curls' so beautiful they would set
'ten poets raving' (III, 30), a thought that makes the beauty of the hair
less striking than the number of the poets. The Lake poets thought
differently. Byron accused Robert Southey of thinking himself 'the only

Blackbird', and forgetting that he was only one of the 'four and twenty' 'baked in the pie' (Dedication, 1 and 3). It is a charge that he could have levelled more plausibly at Wordsworth, and not by coincidence it was Wordsworth who of all Byron's contemporaries insisted most energetically on the heroic status of the poet. But Byron knows that even the four and twenty singing birds imagined in the nursery rhyme are a gross underestimate of the number of poets active in the Regency. Amongst the 'ten thousand living authors' present at the London assemblies that Juan attends, '[t]hat being about their average numeral', Juan is introduced to 'the eighty "greatest living poets"' (XI, 54).[30]

Unable to choose a warrior as his hero and unable to choose a poet, flummoxed in both cases by a superfluity of choice, Byron settles on 'our ancient friend Don Juan':

> We all have seen him in the pantomime
> Sent to the devil, somewhat ere his time.   (I, 1)

As Byron indicates, Don Juan was best known to his English readership from pantomimes. Byron had chosen his hero, one reviewer remarked, because of his 'uncommon celebrity':

> Of all the heroes who have administered to public gratification, Don Juan may be ranked as the most successful. With so much éclat has he been personified by Sig. Ambrogetti, at the Opera, Charles Kemble, at Covent Garden, and Short, at the Surrey, that his name has reached the *ne plus ultra* of gallantry.[31]

Pantomime was popular entertainment. It appealed to people like Leigh Hunt who were happy to admit to sharing popular tastes rather than to poets in search of epic heroes: 'There is something *real* in pantomime: there is animal spirit in it.' Hunt was happy to own 'a great predilection for this kind of drama', 'at whatever hazard of our critical reputation'.[32] It was a hazard that Byron too was ready to risk. He recognised an affinity between pantomime and the kind of poem he was attempting in *Don Juan*. Pantomime was an elastic form. It allowed abrupt shifts between the comic and tragic, and between the magical and the mundane, the narrative could be interrupted at will to accommodate topical material, and it allowed its actors, especially the Harlequin and the Clown, to keep up a conversation with the audience. Don Juan was the proper hero of a poem that, as I pointed out in Chapter 1, Byron seems to have thought of from the first as an epic pantomime. But Jerome McGann believes that Byron had a more immediate provocation.

McGann argues that Byron chose his hero in response to the twenty-third and penultimate chapter of the *Biographia Literaria*, in which Coleridge presents Don Juan as the representative hero of the age.[33] Don Juan holds 'the doctrine of godless nature, as the sole ground and efficient cause not only of all things, events, and appearances, but likewise of all our thoughts, sensations, impulses, and actions'. His life is founded on the belief that '[o]bedience to nature is the only virtue: the gratification of the passions and appetites her only dictate: each individual's self-will the sole organ through which nature utters her commands', for all of which reasons Don Juan is the character who most completely embodies 'the spirit of modern jacobinism'. Coleridge, like Byron, knows Don Juan from the pantomime, but he traces an impressive literary ancestry for the pantomime character. He is the descendant of Molina's *El Burlador de Sevilla* and of his English incarnation in Shadwell's *The Libertine*, and less directly he is the progeny of Shakespeare's Richard III, Edmund, and Iago, and of Milton's Satan. His debased modern counterparts are to be found in 'the modern jacobinical drama' where he is reincarnated as Karl von Moor in Schiller's *Die Räuber* and as Bertram, the title character of Maturin's play. It is *Bertram* on which Coleridge focuses his attention. The chapter certainly irritated Byron. He thought it an attack on himself and the rest of the Drury Lane committee for having staged *Bertram* and an attack on Maturin for the offence of having his play successfully staged when the play offered by Coleridge had been rejected because 'it did not appear at all practicable'. The attack was the more galling because 'the worthy auto-biographer' was under an obligation to Byron. 'He is a shabby fellow', Byron concluded, but he would leave Coleridge and Maturin, he told Murray, 'to battle it out between them'.[34] McGann may well be right that Byron owed to Coleridge the suggestion that Don Juan was the proper hero for a modern epic, but Coleridge's and Byron's Don Juan remain very different. Coleridge's belief that the biggest threat to the post-Waterloo world came from 'the spirit of modern jacobinism' can only have struck Byron as manifestly absurd when, all over Europe, the old monarchies had been restored and liberal constitutions rescinded. Wellington had 'repaired Legitimacy's crutch': 'The Spanish, and the French, as well as Dutch, / Have seen and felt how strongly you *restore*' (IX, 3). Coleridge's Juan is a jacobinical atheist. Byron's never thinks of questioning the constituted authorities in any of the very different societies he visits, and he remains to the last faithful to the religion in which he was raised. When Lady Adeline wonders what he sees in Aurora Raby, he replies,

'She was a Catholic', and it would be 'fittest' if he were to choose a bride that she should be someone 'of his persuasion' (XV, 50). Byron, it may be consciously, fashions his hero as the antithesis of the Don Juan that Coleridge describes. The 'accustomed state' of Bertram, Maturin's debased version of the Juan character, is characterised by 'raving, blasphemy, and nonsense'. Byron's Juan is so little given to rant that he scarcely speaks at all. Coleridge is impressed by 'the cool intrepidity' that Don Juan displays in the presence of the supernatural. Shadwell's Don John dismisses a spectre with cool nonchalance: 'Farewell, thou art a foolish ghost.' Even in this Byron's Juan maintains his difference. When he meets a ghost he is 'petrified' (XVI, 22), and when he encounters it again he 'shook', and has to pull himself together before confronting it (XVI, 118). He is by this point the epic hero adapted to the British society that Byron has introduced him to, a society which applies '[a] sort of varnish over every fault', a society of people who are 'common-place, even in their crimes', and who display 'a smooth monotony / Of character' if they have any character at all (XIV, 16). The only kind of epic hero appropriate to such a world is a hero like Juan, a hero who has hardly any qualities. That lack of any fixed character is what makes him able to fit in so well no matter where he finds himself: 'he had, like Alcibiades, / The art of living in all climes with ease' (XV, 11). His chief talent is that he is capable of being whatever he is expected to be. He is 'all things unto people of all sorts' (XIV, 31).

Juan, it is true, has most of the heroic attributes, although they are the attributes of the hero of the novel rather than the epic poem. Despite being Spanish, he demonstrates his abilities as a foxhunting man: 'He clear'd hedge, ditch, and double post, and rail, / And never *craned*' (XIV, 33). A character in a novel would immediately forfeit heroic status if he were to crane, that is, pull up at a fence and check the landing on the other side before attempting it, although he might easily survive what might seem graver sins. As Byron once remarked, 'You may tell a man that he is thought libertine – profligate – a villain – but not that his nose want's blowing – or that his neckcloth is ill tied.'[35] Juan takes every opportunity allowed him to show his physical courage. When Alfonso draws his sword on the sixteen-year-old youth, 'Juan knock'd him down', and in the ensuing scuffle Alfonso is 'pommell'd to his heart's desire' (I, 183–4). When the *Trinidada* loses its masts, the crew, desperate for grog, try to break into the spirit-room, but are thwarted by Juan, who guards the door armed with a pair of pistols (II, 35). Attacked by a 'file' of Lambro's pirates, Juan cuts the shoulder of one half through and lays

another's cheek open before he is bested (IV, 48–9). In the assault on
Ismail he shows himself 'a broth of a boy' (VII, 24), and he is undaunted
on Shooter's Hill when waylaid by four footpads (XI, 8–13). Not even his
fear of ghosts prevents him from confronting the spectre that enters his
room and discovering, underneath 'the sable frock and dreary cowl', the
body '[i]n full, voluptuous, but *not o'er*grown bulk' of 'her frolic Grace –
Fitz-Fulke!' (XVI, 123). He is a sentimental as well as a stalwart hero. As
the *Trinidada* carries him away from Spain, his native land, and Julia, his
mistress, 'Juan wept, and much he sigh'd and thought, / While his salt
tears dropp'd into the salt sea' (II, 17). 'I loved a maid', he tells John
Johnson, and as he speaks '[a] single tear upon his eyelash staid /
A moment and then dropp'd' (V, 18). He remembers Haidée again
when Gulbeyaz asks him if he can love and as he thinks of her, he
becomes still more demonstrative: he 'burst into tears' (V, 117). Juan is
'heroically' determined to resist Gulbeyaz's advances to the death, but
then she bursts into tears herself and Juan finds that 'all his great
preparatives for dying / Dissolved like snow before a woman crying' (V,
141). When Juan scales the ramparts of Ismail, one of the first to do so, he
has the opportunity to reconcile his two characters as muscular and
sentimental hero. He comes upon '[t]wo villainous Cossaques' threatening with their sabres a ten-year-old child. 'One's hip he slashed, and split
the other's shoulder', and then, although his blood is up, he refuses to
take any further part in the battle until he is assured of the safety of little
Leila, the girl he has rescued (VIII, 92–4).

Juan lives an eventful life, a life full of incident, but all his adventures
leave him curiously unmarked. His attributes are generic rather than
individual. He shares them with Tom Jones, with Roderick Random,
with Edward Waverley and Guy Mannering, and with countless others.
They are the attributes that almost all novel heroes have in common. In
the chapter of *Biographia Literaria* from which in Byron's view he
emerged so shabbily, Coleridge argues that the most interesting literary
characters, Don Juan amongst them, are 'ideal', by which he means they
are at once generic and individual. It is why, he suggests, we might
properly object of a character meant to be ideal that the depiction is
'too much of a *portrait*'. No one could level that charge against Byron's
Juan. Despite all the attention paid to his appearance – 'And then he had
good looks; – that point was carried / *Nem. con.* amongst the women'
(XV, 84) – Juan remains too little of a portrait, which, Coleridge argues,
ought to ensure that as a character he lacks '*living* interest; for nothing
lives or is *real*, but as definite and individual'. Coleridge is fascinated by

the erotic power of Don Juan, the mysterious power that makes even the
most unlikely women succumb to his charms. For Byron there is no
mystery about it. Juan owes his sexual success to his capacity to be
whatever women are 'pleased to make or take him for'. His blankness is
his secret weapon. It is what allows women to 'fill the canvas up' in
whatever way they please, and, given Juan's good looks – given that he is
'tolerably fair' – their 'Imagination's quite enough for that' (XV, 16).
Juan's lack of character ought to be a defect, even a fatal defect, in the
poem. In fact, it is the condition of its extraordinary success. It is what
ensures that Juan never engrosses either Byron's interest or the reader's.

'Return we to Don Juan', Byron announces (II, 167) when he has been
distracted by thoughts of his Greek lessons at Athens, and the women he
knew in London in his years of fame, and all those other things that now
seem 'dreams of what has been, no more to be'. Juan may be the hero, but
all through the poem we are allowed from time to time to forget all about
him. Byron calls himself to order again when he digresses into an anecdote about Nero, asking what on earth Nero '[o]r any suchlike sovereign
buffoons' have to do with 'the transactions of [his] hero' (III, 110). He has
to interrupt himself again when he is remembering a youthful heartbreak
and remind himself that in the previous canto he had 'left our hero and
third heroine in / A kind of state more awkward than uncommon': Juan
and Gulbeyaz have been surprised in their tête-a-tête by the Sultan
himself (VI, 7). Byron interrupts himself once more in his overview of
the assault on Ismail, '[t]o track our hero in his path of fame' (VIII, 17).
But one often feels on such occasions that he interrupts himself reluc-
tantly. He is forever leaving his hero as well as his other characters to
'proceed alone' while he soliloquises 'beyond expression' (III, 96). Even
when Juan is 'severely wounded' (IV, 54) twenty octaves pass before the
reader is recalled to 'Juan, left half-kill'd some stanzas back' (IV, 74).
Later in the poem Juan is 'left upon his way to the chief City / Of the
immortal Peter's polished boors' (IX, 23), while Byron discourses on
Wellington, on why death is so often said to laugh, on indigestion, on
Pyrrhonism, on the doctrine of the fall, and on his own reputation for
misanthropy. Canto XIV opens with a meditative digression just as
various, from the urge to 'plunge' felt by all of us when we gaze from
a mountain top into the abyss to the horrors of shaving, before at last in
stanza 29 he recalls that at the end of Canto XIII, '[w]e left our heroes and
our heroines' enjoying Lord Henry's hospitality at Norman Abbey. Even
the final truncated canto is in its twelfth stanza before Byron remembers
the 'tender moonlight situation' in which '[o]ur Hero' had been left 'in

Canto the Sixteenth'. Juan is Byron's ingenious solution to the most pressing problem that he confronts in *Don Juan*. Who will best serve as the hero of a determinedly unheroic poem,[36] a poem that not only distrusts the heroic virtues but calls into question the idea that a poem is best shaped when it is organised around the single, dominant presence of its central character? Byron begins the poem, in its very first line, in want of a hero. When the poem is broken off, he is in exactly the same predicament, and that, odd as it may seem, is one of the poem's most striking triumphs.

CHAPTER 3

Especially upon a Printed Page

'It is the most readable poem of its length ever written' was Virginia Woolf's verdict. She meant, I suppose, that no one would say of *Don Juan* what Byron says of *Paradise Lost*, that, though 'no less divine', it was '[a] little heavy' (III, 91). Nearing the end, looking forward to the sixteenth canto, Woolf reflected that she had enjoyed 'almost every stanza'. 'None ever wished it longer than it is', Samuel Johnson wrote of *Paradise Lost*, but that was not how Woolf felt about *Don Juan*. Reading the poem had been a pleasure rather than a duty, despite which, or perhaps because of which, she did not think of *Don Juan* as one of 'the proper books'. She counted it rather amongst the 'illicit kinds of books' she found more interesting.[1] A Kingsley Amis hero points out how astonishing it would be if he were to pick up 'the *Íliad* or some other gruelling cultural monument' and it 'turned out to be a good read as well as a masterpiece'.[2] Woolf and Amis are both keenly alert to a feeling deep and widespread in western culture that great literature should not be too readable. Reading masterpieces should be effortful rather than fun. *Don Juan* is a scandalous poem, one reason for which is that it is scandalously readable, but it is readable, too, in a more literal sense. It is a poem designed to be encountered on the page in print, a poem meant to be read just as much, perhaps even more, than a poem designed to be listened to.

For Byron, Milton is 'the blind old man' (Dedication, 11). His blindness is the affliction proper to an epic poet – it gives him kinship with Homer – and it also works to underwrite his claim that his poem was 'unpremeditated', inspired by his muse, Urania, who comes to him at night, and 'dictates' to him as he slumbers (*Paradise Lost*, Book IX, 21–5). After Milton, similar claims were made by poets who could see perfectly well. Blake denied that he had written *Milton*, the poem in which he re-writes *Paradise Lost*: 'he affirms', reports one witness, that the poem 'was recited to him by the spirit of Milton'.[3] Blake was eccentric, but his contemporaries Wordsworth and Coleridge seem almost as anxious to deny that their poems were composed on paper. Coleridge famously claimed that he had dreamt 'Kubla Khan' during 'a profound sleep' of some three hours. When he awoke he had 'a distinct recollection' of a poem 200 to 300 lines in length. He had transcribed only fifty-four before he was interrupted, and found, when he went back to it, that all the rest of the poem 'had passed away like the images on the surface of a stream into which a stone has been cast'.[4] Wordsworth was less extravagant, but still insisted that it was not his habit to compose his poems at a desk. He made his poems in the open air, as he paced the gravel walk in his garden, or as he roamed still further afield. He began 'Tintern Abbey' as soon as he left the Wye valley, and did not write any of the poem down until he had arrived back in Bristol, by which time it was complete. Byron's compositional habits were quite different. He did not compose the stanzas of *Don Juan* as he took his daily ride; he wrote the poem at his desk, and the spirits that inspired him were not at all supernatural. Leigh Hunt reports that he 'used to sit up all night, writing Don Juan (which he did under the influence of gin and water)'.[5] Byron admits as much in a stanza that did not, in the end, find a place in the published poem, a stanza written, Byron reports, while he was 'reeling': '(Having got drunk exceedingly today / So that I seem to stand upon the ceiling.)'[6] Drunk or not, Byron composed *Don Juan* at his desk, on paper.

Coleridge and Wordsworth were both of them suspicious of print. After bringing out *Poems on Various Subjects* in 1796, Coleridge did not publish a substantial volume of verse until *Sybilline Leaves* in 1817. Wordsworth published more regularly, but after the failure of *Poems in Two Volumes* in 1807, he did not publish a volume of poetry for seven years. Both men refrained from printing some of their most important poems. Wordsworth recited *Peter Bell* to Hazlitt in 1798, but did not offer the poem to the public for twenty-one years. *The Prelude*, his greatest poem, was known in his lifetime only to those who heard him recite it, although a favoured few were given access to the manuscript. Coleridge's 'Kubla Khan' and 'Christabel' had circulated like this, in manuscript and through recitation, for eighteen years before Murray, with Byron's encouragement, eventually published them in a pamphlet of 1816. 'We had frequently heard of Mr. Coleridge's manuscript of Christabel', a reviewer remarked.[7] Coleridge and Wordsworth were the first poets Hazlitt met, which may explain why he thought it grounds for contempt that Thomas Campbell was always 'thinking how his poetry will look when it comes to be hot-pressed on superfine wove paper'.[8] Byron had more in common with Campbell than with Wordsworth and Coleridge. For one thing he was reluctant to read his poems even to his closest friends. He claims never to have read a poem aloud to anyone except Francis Hodgson: 'It is a horrible thing to do too frequently; – better print, and they who like may read, and if they don't like, you have the satisfaction of knowing that they have, at least, *purchased* the right of saying so.'⁹ He was emphatically not one of those poets he mentions in *Don Juan*, who, if they tell you they have written '*fifty* rhymes', 'make you dread that they'll recite them too' (I, 108).

''Tis pleasant, sure, to see one's name in print', Byron remarks in *English Bards and Scotch Reviewers* (51), and he acted on that belief throughout his career. When R. C. Dallas advised him not to publish *The Bride of Abydos*, Byron wondered that 'experience' had not 'taught him that not to print is physically impossible'.¹⁰ In *Don Juan* he asks himself why, given the lack of encouragement, he goes on publishing, and answers that writing has become a habit with him, and that he does not feel that the process of writing is complete until it is 'cast upon the stream, / To sink or swim' (XIV, 11). Byron was unusually reluctant to keep his poems in manuscript. The best example is *The Giaour*, published by Murray on 5 June 1813, as a poem of 684 lines. Thereafter, as Byron pointed out to Murray, his 'snake of a poem' kept 'lengthening its rattles every month',¹¹ until in its seventh edition of December 1813 it reached its final form as a poem of 1,334 lines. It was as if, not content to publish each poem as he finished it, he chose to publish his every draft. As disapproving reviewers pointed out, it was a habit that worked to his and his publisher's financial advantage.

Byron began his career with the view that a gentleman should not profit from his writings. He presented the copyright of *Childe Harold* and *The Corsair*, two of his most popular poems, to R. C. Dallas, a family connection who acted in a general way as Byron's factotum. In *English Bards and Scotch Reviewers*, he presents the extravagant terms that Walter Scott secured for *Marmion*, before he had written a single line of the poem, as evidence of literary prostitution. The episode revealed Scott's willingness to sell a poem for 'half-a-crown a line', and 'when the sons of song descend to trade' they lose any title they may have had to 'the poet's sacred name' (174–7). It was a posture for which J. G. Lockhart twitted him:

> Now, Sir Walter has made a fortune by his books, and you will do so in good season too; and nothing can be more proper, because, if you did not, your booksellers would sell your books just as dear as they do, and pocket double as much as they do; whereas, all the world knows that they have pocketed, and are pocketing, by both of you, quite as much as is at all good for them.¹²

But that was in 1821, by which time Byron had long been converted to Lockhart's point of view. When he refers in *Don Juan* to his '"buon camerado" Scott' (XII, 16), he claims a fellowship that has its source not just in the cordial meeting between the two men on 7 April 1815 in Murray's first-floor drawing room at 50, Albemarle Street, but in Byron's awareness that he and Scott were allied as the most handsomely rewarded writers of the age. In the years in which 'Christabel' was known only in manuscript or by those who had heard the poem recited (Byron first encountered the poem when it was recited to him by Walter Scott), it had a narrow circulation, but it circulated freely. Byron's commitment to print went along with his mature conviction that a poet's writings were a commodity from which he had a right to make money.

One difference between poems and novels is that novelists, unlike poets, pay attention to economics. Defoe is much more interested in money than Milton. *Don Juan* is one of the first poems in English written by a poet ready to confess himself a novel reader. The love shared by Juan and Haidée is not 'factitious', one reason for which is that they have neither of them read any novels (IV, 19), but they differ in this from the man who tells their story. 'A great impression in my youth / Was made by Mrs Adams', the narrator tells us, and he regrets that in the England he has to describe the characters are so much less strongly marked than Fielding's (XIII, 96). *Don Juan* is a poem that opens itself up to the novel. Byron may be teasing when he promises that his 'best canto, save one on astronomy, / Will turn upon "political economy"' (XII, 88), but one of the ways he registers his kinship with the novelists is by taking a keen interest in the economic circumstances of his characters, an interest that only grows stronger as the poem proceeds. When Donna Inez sends Juan off on his travels, she gives him a letter of good advice that he never reads, 'and two or three of credit' (II, 9). 'Near two hundred souls' are lost when the *Trinidada* goes down, and the drowned will face a longer stint in purgatory than is strictly necessary:

> till people know what's come to pass,
> They won't lay out their money on the dead –
> It costs three francs for every mass that's said.   (II, 55)

The shipwreck reduces Juan to a state of nature in which money counts for nothing. He is released from this condition when he is washed up on Haidée's isle. 'Haidée was Nature's bride' (II, 202), but the nature to which she is wedded is pastoral rather than Hobbesian, and it is characteristic of pastoral (it may be the characteristic that defines the genre) that the freedom from economic constraints that it celebrates is secured by the very economic activity that it pretends to repudiate. For Haidée, who never leaves the island, money only has a decorative value. Juan faints when he is cast up on the island, and opens his eyes to find Haidée bending over him: 'Her brow was overhung with coins of gold, / That sparkled o'er the auburn of her hair' (II, 116). For her, coins serve only as hair ornaments, but they were given to her by Lambro, her father, and Lambro is the Corsair re-imagined as an entrepreneur. Byron never lets his reader forget that his most colourful activities, however 'strange' they may seem, are just his way of 'raising cash' (III, 14). 'A little smuggling and some piracy' figure amongst Lambro's 'speculations', and a major source of his income comes from supplying the Constantinople slave market (II, 125–6). It is the fate to which he consigns Juan when he returns unexpectedly to the island after being reported dead and finds that his daughter and Juan have set up house together. Juan is bought by the sultan's eunuch Baba, a bargain completed when the jumble of coins with which Baba pays for his purchase is 'accurately scanned' and receipts are signed (V, 29). The slave market is offered as a brutal demonstration that everybody is bought and sold in one way or another, '[t]he most by ready cash' (V, 27). 'Love rules the court, the camp, the grove', Walter Scott had suggested in *The Lay of the Last Minstrel*. Byron quotes the line (not quite accurately), and offers his own rejoinder, 'But if love don't, cash does, and cash alone' (XII, 13–14). It is certainly cash that rules the Russian camp when Juan enlists with the Russian forces besieging Ismail. The mad bravery that the Russian troops display in their assault on the city is prompted, as Juan's companion John Johnson knows, by the knowledge that 'there is plunder in a city' (VIII, 101). Even rape is a less urgent enticement to the troops than pillage. When Juan is installed in his position as Catherine the Great's lover, his mother is delighted that he no longer needs her financial support: his position at the Russian court frees him from any need of 'drawing on his banker' (X, 31). From Russia Juan journeys to England, where his surprise at the 'long, long bills' presented at his Dover hotel (X, 69) is a portent that he has at last arrived in a country in which all activities, even adultery ('those damned damages' (XII, 65)), are subordinated to economics. It is a point forcibly brought home to him when he gets out of his carriage on Shooter's Hill to admire the view of London, and is at once held at knifepoint by a footpad who demands his money or his life (XI, 10).

In *Don Juan* it is money that makes the world go round, which does not at all persuade Byron to look at the world askance. He offers it rather as a truth that he has of late come to accept. As he enters middle age and begins to recognise that his 'days of love are over', he learns to settle for 'a good old gentlemanly vice'. He has made a decision to 'take up with

avarice' (I, 216). He flamboyantly assumes the role of stage miser, gloating
like Volpone over his accumulated hoards:

> How beauteous are rouleaus! how charming chests
>   Containing ingots, bags of dollars, coins
> (Not of old victors, all whose heads and crests
>   Weigh not the thin ore where their visage shines,
> But) of fine unclipt gold, where dully rests
>   Some likeness, which the glittering cirque confines,
> Of modern, reigning, sterling, stupid stamp: –
> Yes! ready money is Aladdin's lamp.   (XII, 12)

He expects his readers to be amused by the self-characterisation, of course
(although Leigh Hunt in *Lord Byron and Some of His Contemporaries*
insists that it is a more accurate self-portrait than Byron would have us
believe), but it still serves to make a point. However much Byron may
deprecate a world ruled by money, he refuses to make any claim that it is
a world that either the poet or his poem rises above. He had once thought
differently. In *English Bards and Scotch Reviewers*, Homer and Virgil
transcend time:

> The work of each immortal bard appears
> The single wonder of a thousand years.   (193–4)

And one reason why the *Iliad* and the *Aeneid* can float free from time is that
they embody an aesthetic value that has nothing to do with economic
value. They may be poems that we encounter on the page, but they exist
independent of their material circumstances. Their value has no relation
either to the price for which the poems might be bought or to the number
of copies sold. As far as Byron is concerned, the opulent morocco in which
Lord Carlisle binds his own works serves only to underline how feeble
those works are (*English Bards*, 739–40). By 1816, when Byron re-read
English Bards in Switzerland, it was a judgement that he was inclined to
pass on himself. He added a note in the copy he was reading: 'The binding
of this volume is considerably too valuable for its Contents.'[13] But by 1819,
when the first two cantos of *Don Juan* were published, Byron had come to
accept that a poem could not, any more than any other commodity, exist
independently of the material means of its production. Readers did not just
respond to a poem, they responded to the book they read it in, and what
was true of all poems was especially true of *Don Juan*. It is a poem, after all,
that Byron invites his readers to think of as a book. Those who object to
Juan and Haidée's unmarried relationship, for example, are invited to
'shut / The book which treats of this erroneous pair' (III, 12).

The first two cantos were published by John Murray on 15 July 1819 in a fine quarto volume that sold for a guinea and a half unbound, an extravagant price for a volume that ran to 227 pages only by dint of accommodating 'only 16 lines in a page, and a magnificent circumference of margin'.[14] The book was expensively produced, and sold at a price that made it available only to wealthy readers. But it was a volume that sent a mixed message to its purchaser. The name of the printer, Thomas Davison of Whitefriars, appeared on the title page, but the names of the author and publisher were missing, as if they were ashamed to acknowledge the volume. Despite that, it was not in any ordinary sense an anonymous publication. The identities of the author and publisher may have been withheld but they were never in question. Byron made no attempt at all to disguise his authorship. He made repeated and transparent references in the poem to his own domestic circumstances, and he drew attention yet again to a feat of which he was particularly proud. Juan, we are told, was a good enough swimmer to have swum across the Hellespont:

> As once (a feat on which ourselves we prided)
> Leander, Mr. Ekenhead, and I did. (II, 105)[15]

The identity of the publisher was almost as transparent. It was perfectly evident to the poem's first readers that the publisher of the book was John Murray, who chose not to give his name because he was also, as one commentator pointed out, 'the Publisher of the Board of Longitude, and of the Quarterly Review – the Bookseller to the Admiralty, and a strenuous supporter of orthodoxy and the Bible Society'.[16]

In 1796, Joseph Cottle had published *Joan of Arc*, the first of the epics that 'Bob Southey' brought out 'every spring' (III, 97). It was, according to Southey, 'the handsomest book that Bristol had ever yet sent forth'.[17] The two volumes of the poem sold for 16 shillings, a reasonable price, but Cottle registered his sense of the poem's importance by printing only twenty lines on each quarto page. It was an extravagance that prompted Coleridge to insist when Cottle published *Lyrical Ballads* that the lines should be 'closely printed, certainly, *more closely* than those of the Joan', and Wordsworth agreed, 'Oh by all means closer!'[18] But in 1814 Longman chose to publish Wordsworth's new poem, as Cottle had printed Southey's *Joan*, in the large format. It was, according to Byron, 'a rather long Excursion / (I think the quarto holds five hundred pages)'. Byron exaggerates. There were only 447 pages, and the volume was a little more closely printed than 'the Joan', 23 rather than 20 lines to a page. To compensate for that, it sold for an eye-watering 2 guineas. In the Romantic period literature was a generic category rather like pastoral, its life resembling the life Haidée lives on her island. Literature was writing that possessed an aesthetic value independent of its commercial value, but publishers had a tendency to signify the high aesthetic value of a poem by publishing it in quarto, with wide margins, and charging a steep price for it.

When the first two cantos of *Don Juan* were published in an expensive quarto volume with just sixteen lines on a page and wide margins, a claim was implied for the high aesthetic value of the poem, but the claim fitted oddly with the failure of either the publisher or the poet to own the poem, and fitted oddly too with the comic, scandalous character of the poem's content. There was soon another, still more perplexing oddity to grapple with. Almost as soon as Murray had published his quarto the first two cantos of Byron's poem were on sale in a duodecimo volume priced at 4s. It was a pirate publication, but Murray had no legal recourse.[19] In 1817, radical publishers had embarrassed Robert Southey, the poet laureate, by printing *Wat Tyler*, a play that Southey had written when he was a nineteen-year-old ultra-radical. Southey sued, but Lord Eldon ruled against him. Copyright could not be enforced if a work was deemed seditious or obscene. Murray's less scrupulous rivals realised at once that Murray was unlikely to go to court to defend his intellectual property in *Don Juan* when he had been unwilling to identify himself as the poem's publisher. The result was that, despite Murray's decision to publish the poem in an opulent quarto, it was almost at once 'in every one's hands'.[20] A pirated edition of the first five cantos included a preface purportedly written by a clergyman who remarks, 'This work entitled DON JUAN seems, I know not why, a sort of common property amongst the booksellers: for we have had editions of all sorts and sizes; from the original superb quarto, to the shabby "two-penny-trash," or weekly instalment of about twenty-four duodecimo, badly printed, pages.'[21] The odd history of its publication gave *Don Juan* from the outset a double character. It was a very different poem in an edition that cost four shillings than it had been when Murray first published it in an edition on sale at a guinea and a half. As a contributor to the *Quarterly Review* remarked in 1824, '"Don Juan" in quarto and on hot-pressed paper would have been almost innocent – in a whity-brown duodecimo, it was one of the worst of the mischievous publications that have made the press a snare'.[22] The cheap production 'brought it within the reach of purchasers on whom its poison would operate without mitigation'.

In 1822, Byron parted company with John Murray. Murray had published the first five cantos of the poem, but Byron gave all the later cantos to

John Hunt, who brought out Cantos VI, VII, and VIII on 15 July 1823. Byron had become increasingly irritated by Murray's timidity, and he was already closely associated with John Hunt and his brother Leigh through his involvement with *The Liberal,* which was edited by Leigh Hunt and published by John. The Hunt brothers conducted the radical weekly newspaper *The Examiner,* and Leigh Hunt had been the target of a campaign of ridicule waged by *Blackwood's Edinburgh Magazine* ever since 1817. He was the King of Cockaigne who presided over the Cockney School of poetry. Given all this, it was inevitable that the change of publisher should have sharpened responses to the poem.[23] Murray may have published *Don Juan,* but he had at least refused to acknowledge his role on the poem's title page, and Murray was a friend of government. Even if his social pretensions sometimes irked (William Hone was particularly struck by Murray's habit of referring to himself when he advertised his forthcoming publications as 'Mr. Murray' rather than John Murray), he was a gentleman.[24] In *Blackwood's* 'Timothy Tickler', when he read the new cantos could only lament, 'Alas! that one so gifted . . . should descend to the composition of heartless, heavy, dull, anti-British garbage, to be printed by the Cockneys, and puffed in the Examiner'. Byron had been so determined in his efforts to 'write himself down to the level of the capacities and the swinish tastes' of his new associates that, Tickler suspects, he had even agreed to incorporate in the new cantos a few stanzas written by Leigh Hunt.[25] John Hunt secured *Don Juan* against the activities of the pirates by selling each batch of three cantos for a shilling.[26] Reviewers offered the low price, and the cheap production that made it possible, as evidence of the decline in the quality of the poem. Murray had offered its first two cantos for sale in a quarto priced at a guinea and a half, but, as Timothy Tickler pointed out in his notice of Cantos VI, VII, and VIII, 'This continuation of Don Juan is obliged to be sold for a shilling.' William Jerdan in the *Literary Gazette* had a similar objection to 'this shilling's worth of dirty brown paper'. The price and the low quality of the paper were a lively reminder of the consequences when 'a nobleman adopts the style of a porter in which to utter the sentiments of a bagnio'.[27]

Instalments of *Don Juan* might be published by John Murray, or by William Benbow, publisher of radical pamphlets and pornography, or by John Hunt, and they might be purchased for as much as a guinea and a half or as little as a shilling. This was important because it established the double character that the poem had even for its earliest readers, who might insist, as J. G. Lockhart did in *Blackwood's,* that it was the poem of Byron's most 'decisively and triumphantly expressive of the greatness of his genius', or might choose to describe the poem, like the reviewer of the *British Critic*, as offering the reader only 'a narrative of degrading debauchery in doggerel rhyme'.[28] The circumstances of the poem's publication gained added importance because the reader is always being reminded that the poem has a material existence. In this *Don Juan* resembles the company at Lord Henry's public dinner: it is a poem 'engrossed / By matter', a poem 'so much materialised' (XVI, 90) that its reader is never allowed to forget that it is an article offered for sale by its publisher, an article from which both publisher and author hope to profit. Byron acknowledges as much in the poem itself. At the end of the first canto, to give just one example, Byron bids farewell to his 'gentle reader' and '[s]till gentler purchaser' (I, 221).

When he introduced *The Excursion* to his readers, Wordsworth referred to his poem as a 'Work' (he is careful to dignify the word with a capital letter), but for Byron *The Excursion* is a book, a 'quarto' that 'holds five hundred pages'. It has an interest for him as a material object. So, too, does the edition of Martial from which the young Juan is taught, an edition from which all the more obscene epigrams had been expurgated and relegated to 'an appendix', where 'we have them all at one fell swoop / Instead of being scattered through the pages' (I, 44–5). Byron thinks of his own poem too as a book. As I have noted, he recommends readers offended that Juan and Haidée are unmarried lovers to 'shut / The book which treats of this erroneous pair' (III, 12). He has, he reminds the reader, already given Lady Adeline's age 'in – I forget what page' (XIV, 54). He promises transcripts of the despatches that the messenger brings Lord Henry 'in a brief appendix / To come between mine epic and its index' (XIV, 68). It would never have occurred to Wordsworth to imagine *The Excursion* printed with an index. Byron is infatuated with print as a medium. Poems become poems when they are printed, when they appear on 'poetic pages' (XIV, 15). It is because they can be printed that words have the power to make 'thousands, perhaps millions, think'. Because it is printed on paper 'even a rag like this' has the power to outlive '[f]rail man', to survive 'himself, his tomb, and all that's his' (III, 88). Byron is so fascinated by the printed page that he even turns to it when on the look-out for metaphors. Middle age is a time of life 'something like a printed page'. It is an age at which a man's hair becomes grizzled, 'black letter upon foolscap' (XII, 1). The printed page even, and rather beautifully, offers a figure for desire. When Juan finds his soul stirred by thoughts of Julia, it is as if the page in the book that he is reading 'is rustled' by the wind (I, 95).

Byron's fellow poets are most of them disinclined to think of their books as material objects, printed on sheets and bound into volumes. Blake is the obvious exception, but Blake published his own books and developed his own method of printing them, 'in the infernal method by corrosives, which in Hell are salutary and medicinal, melting apparent surfaces away, and displaying the infinite which was hid'.[29] By printing his books as he did, Blake gained independence from the publishing industry. Byron had no such ambition, one indication of which is his fascination with all those printer's conventions that Blake repudiated. Byron gives his page variety by choosing Greek script when he uses the word 'nous' (I, 130) or when he refers to Aristotle's *Poetics* (III, 111). More extravagantly, he finds a way of translating a doctor's prescription into ottava rima:

> But here is one prescription out of many:
> 'Sodaesulphat.3vj. 3fs.Mannaeoptim.
> Aq. fervent.f. 3ifs. 3ij. tinct. Sennae
> Haustus' (And here the surgeon came and cupp'd him)
> 'Rx Pulv Com gr. iij.Ipecacuanhae'
> (With more beside if Juan had not stopp'd 'em).
> 'Bolus Potassae Sulphuret. sumendus,
> Et haustuster in die capiendus.'   (X, 41)

Byron even takes an interest in misprints. He imagines that the story told of Queen Semiramis, that she had 'an improper friendship for her horse', has its origin in a slip of the pen. The scribe wrote 'courser' when he meant 'courier'. Her disgrace, on Byron's emended reading, was no more bizarre than Queen Caroline's, an infatuation with a low-born lover (V, 61). More poignantly Byron recalls his acquaintance Captain Edward Grose of the 1st Foot Guards who was killed at Waterloo. Poor Captain Grose was denied even posthumous recognition because in the Waterloo Gazette the notice of his death '[w]as printed Grove, although his name was Grose' (VIII, 18).

In early editions of the poem the typography is still more lively, because Murray used asterisks to signal the absence of the passages that he and his advisers had chosen to censor. The fifteenth stanza of Canto I offended by referring jocularly to Sir Samuel Romilly's suicide and was replaced by eighteen asterisks in two rows of nine. The couplet of stanza 130 and the whole of stanza 131 were also left out (they offered some light-hearted observations on syphilis), and asterisks took their place. Some objected to the practice. In his sequel to the first two cantos William Hone remarks, 'I hate your printer's stars – and coward blanks.'[30] But those asterisks (whether Murray and his printer calculated on it or not) acted as a spur to the lubricious imagination of Byron's readers. Murray may have instituted the practice but Byron ratified it. When he decided to redact an unflattering reference to two clergyman poets, George Croly and Henry Hart Milman, in the eleventh canto, he advised John Hunt that half of stanza 57 and the whole of stanza 58 were to be omitted, 'and asterisks placed instead of the lines'.[31] J.G. Lockhart thought the device so effective that he borrowed it for his novel *Adam Blair*. Adam Blair is a minister of the Church of Scotland who is disgraced when he succumbs, just once and briefly, to the charms of Charlotte Campbell, a friend of his late wife. The fateful event is signified only by thirty asterisks, divided into five lines of six.[32] Lockhart published his novel in 1822, and the use of asterisks was still as provocative as it has been three years earlier. In *Knight's Quarterly Magazine*, 'the thirty ill-omened stars which frown at the commencement of the fourteenth chapter' are identified as the principal cause of the abuse to which the novel had been subjected.[33] In his fascination with the business of print, as in much else, Byron seems to follow the novelists rather than the poets – Laurence Sterne, for example, who refers the reader to his 'title page' to confirm how grievously his father was frustrated in his determination that no son of his should be called Tristram (Book I, chapter 19), who presents his reader with a 'marbled page' as a 'motly emblem' of his work (Book III, chapter 36), and who points out that chapter XXIV is missing not because the book-binder is 'a fool, or a knave, or a puppy', but because his book is the more complete without it (Book IV, chapter 25). Pierce Egan, whose novel *Life in London* is exactly contemporary with *Don Juan*, is even more typographically inventive (Egan had been trained as a compositor). It was one of the things that struck Thackeray when he read the novel as a boy. It left him thinking, 'How nobly those inverted commas, those italics, those capitals, bring out the writer's wit and relieve the eye.'[34]

Byron follows the novelists, too, in addressing himself so often to his reader, his 'still chaster reader' (I, 120), his 'prudish readers' (I, 209), his 'gentle reader' (I, 221), his 'kind reader' (IV, 6), his 'lively reader' (VI, 98), his 'common readers' (VII, 33), his 'atrocious reader' (XIV, 97), his '[g]rim reader' (XV, 95). He addresses his readers almost as often as Sterne and Fielding. His fellow poets addressed their readers too, but they did so in their prefaces, introductions, and advertisements. It is rare for Wordsworth, to give just one example, to invoke his reader within the poem (although he sometimes does, as in 'Simon Lee' and 'The Idiot Boy'), and that is because he prefers to present his poems as intimate communications, addressed like 'Tintern Abbey' to a 'dear, dear Sister', or like *The Prelude* to a 'dear friend'. Byron had once felt the same, as when he pauses at the end of the first canto of *Childe Harold* to pay private tribute to one 'known the earliest, and esteem'd the most! /

Dear to a heart where nought was left so dear!' (I, 92). The tactic works to remove the poem from the public arena, to offer it as a private communication that the reader of the printed text only overhears. But *Don Juan* is written on quite other principles. It is a poem that flaunts its status as a commodity, as an object offered for sale in the literary marketplace, a book that, like all the other books, is addressed not to a private individual but to the new mass readership of the early nineteenth century. By coincidence, I read, as I worked on this para- graph, a piece by Will Self in the *Times Literary Supplement*. Under the heading 'Grubby Business' Self discusses his earnings as a freelance journalist ('averaging at 30–50 pence a word') before coyly refusing to divulge to his 'dear and gentle reader' what rate of payment he has agreed with the *TLS*.[35]

Byron's fellow poets for the most part ignored the novel, anxious, it may be, not to call attention to so powerful a generic competitor. In *The Excursion*, it is true, the wanderer and his young friend find the Solitary's copy of *Candide*, but they contemplate it only as a fit relic of the sad life of its owner:

> The book which in my hand
>   Had opened of itself (for it was swoln
> With searching damp and seemingly had lain
> To the injurious elements exposed
> From week to week) I found to be a work
> In the French tongue, a novel of Voltaire,
> His famous Optimist.   (2, 438–44)

The volume is presented as clinching evidence that the Solitary had been an 'Unhappy Man'. It is, so far as I know, the only novel allowed to intrude into Wordsworth's verse unless one counts the famous appearance of *Don Quixote* in the fifth book of *The Prelude*. In his Preface to *Lyrical Ballads*, even when he is bemoaning his readers' preference for 'idle and extravagant stories' he is careful to stipulate that the stories he has in mind are 'in verse'. Byron was much more receptive to the novel. Novels were his favourite reading, the novels of Walter Scott in particular, unlike Wordsworth, who, according to De Quincey, had the unusual distinction of never having read 'one page of Sir Walter Scott's novels'.[36] Byron is happy to accommodate novels in *Don Juan*. Donna Inez, Juan's mother, is a didactic novel come to life, 'Miss Edgeworth's novels stepping from their covers' (I, 16). Juan and Haidée share a love that is not 'factitious' because '[n]o novels e'er had set their young hearts bleeding' (IV, 19), but their innocence of the novel ensures that however true their love may be it remains otherworldly. Caroline Lamb may lack their sincerity but she is far more representative of the world with which Byron is familiar, and she is not only a reader of novels but also the author of one, *Glenarvon*: 'Some play the devil, and then write a novel' (II, 201). Walter Scott had shocked Wordsworth by his easy confidence that literature might prove a more lucrative trade than the law, and that he might 'get more money than he would ever wish from the booksellers'.[37] But it was a confidence that Byron shared, which is one reason why he registers more fellow feeling with novelists, and with Walter Scott in particular, than with a poet like Wordsworth. He is at ease with the economics of literature, sympathetic even to booksellers when a cloud passes over their sunny countenances, as it passes over 'Longman and John Murray / When the sale of new books is not so fleet / As they who print them think is necessary' (VII, 26).

Byron shares with the novelists an understanding that books are articles for sale, but, despite that, he allows still more poets than novelists entry into his poem. The poem is dedicated to 'Bob Southey', although the dedicatory stanzas were not published until 1833, and Byron drafted a preface, not published until 1901, in which he introduces the poem with an elaborate parody of Wordsworth's note to 'The Thorn'. Instead of a retired sea captain we are to imagine *Don Juan* as narrated by 'a Spanish gentleman in a village in the Sierra Morena on the road between Monasterio and Seville, sitting at the door of a *posada* with the Curate of the hamlet on his right hand, a cigar in his mouth, a jug of Malaga or perhaps "right sherris" before him on a small table, containing the relics of an *olla-podrida*'. Byron was an admirer of *The Baviad*, the poem in which William Gifford was popularly supposed to have ended the careers of the Della Cruscan poets, whose reputation could not survive his withering scorn. *English Bards and Scotch Reviewers* is indebted to it. A main business of *Don Juan*, it might be thought, is to launch a similar attack on the Lake Poets. As Byron put it in the Biblical parody that early reviewers of the poem found so offensive:

> Thou shalt believe in Milton, Dryden, Pope;
> Thou shalt not set up Wordsworth, Coleridge, Southey.   (I, 205)

Southey makes thirteen appearances in the poem, Wordsworth twelve, and Coleridge five. The whole of *Don Juan* might be understood (it often has been) as impelled by the discovery that Byron announced in a letter to John Murray:

> I am convinced the more I think of it – that he [Thomas Moore] and *all* of us – Scott – Southey – Wordsworth – Moore – Campbell – I – are all in the

wrong – one as much as another – that we are upon a wrong revolutionary poetical system – or systems – not worth a damn in itself – from which none but Rogers and Crabbe are free – and that the present & next generations will finally be of this opinion.[38]

Byron had been confirmed in his view by re-reading Pope (mentioned seven times in *Don Juan*), and finding himself 'astonished' and 'mortified' by 'the ineffable distance' between 'the little Queen Anne's man' and himself and all his contemporaries. But *Don Juan* is not the kind of poem the chief business of which is to launch an attack on Byron's fellow poets.

When Byron set about modern poets in *English Bards and Scotch Reviewers*, taking up a task that, he says, more properly belonged to Gifford, he was aware that the model for all such attacks, his own and Gifford's included, had been established by Pope in *The Dunciad*, and he was aware, too, as Gifford seems not to have been, that it is a model that he was ill-equipped to emulate. Byron lacks Pope's confidence in his own judgements, and he lacks too Pope's confidence that in the couplets of his own poem he can embody the virtues that he finds wanting in the poets that he attacks. Byron's contention in the Dedication to *Don Juan* that the reputations of Southey, Wordsworth, and Coleridge will be outlasted by some of their contemporaries, that 'Scott, Rogers, Campbell, Moore, and Crabbe will try / 'Gainst you the question with posterity' (Dedication, 7), has been thought to show an embarrassing lack of prescience. *English Bards*, in which those chosen to 'bear witness' that England still nurtures fine poets are 'GIFFORD, SOTHEBY, MACNEIL' (818), offers an even more striking display of Byron's failure to predict the future of literary reputations. The Scottish poet Hector MacNeil, more commonly MacNeill, has been especially unsuccessful in claiming the attention of posterity. These are not casual errors on Byron's part, unlucky accidents to which we are all of us prone. He lacks the firm sense of how poetry ought to be written that secures Pope's judgements, and even Gifford's. His ethical judgements are just as unstable. In *English Bards* he reaches after a Juvenalian asperity, inveighing against foreign imports, the 'song from Italy, the step from France' (646), denouncing Moore for writing so unchastely,[39] and a dancer for making a lascivious display of 'her breast of snow' (628), before admitting that such postures ill beseem him: 'every Brother Rake will smile to see / That miracle, a Moralist in me!' (699–70). Nor, despite the change of opinion that he records in his letter to Murray, did *Don Juan* result from a dramatic conversion in which Byron rejected a Romantic for an Augustan aesthetic. If that had been the case, the poem would have been written in heroic couplets. *Don Juan* is a poem in ottava rima. It is not Pope but an Italian poet that Byron names as his predecessor ('Pulci was sire of the half-serious rhyme' (IV, 6)), and it is the defining feature of Pulci's ottava rima that it is 'half-serious'.[40] Rhymes, if they are half-serious, are freed to revel in the instability of the judgements they advance. Byron had found a verse form that allowed him to make a virtue of the uncertainties that bedevilled *English Bards*.

Don Juan is remarkable for the number of poets that it names. I have already mentioned twelve of them. There are in addition John Keats, Robert Burns, and George Croly, who appears in masquerade as 'the very Reverend Rowley Powley'; Barry Cornwall in whom Byron recognises 'a sort of moral me', 'that deep-mouth'd Boeotian "Savage Landor"' (XI, 58–9); and James Thompson, after whom sixteen of the Thompsons who served with Suwarrow were named (VII, 19). Of the Italians there are Ariosto and Dante as well as Pulci, and of those who did not always write in verse there are Molière, Congreve, Swift, and Voltaire. There is the expected troop of Greeks and Romans; Homer, Anacreon, Pindar, Sappho, Virgil, Horace, Ovid, Lucretius, and there is Shakespeare, who is quoted more than anyone. This would be unremarkable in one of those poems, loosely modelled on *The Dunciad*, the business of which was to offer a caustic survey of the current literary scene, poems such as Gifford's *Baviad* and *Maeviad*, *The Pursuits of Literature* by T. J. Mathias, or George Canning's *New Morality*. Byron had written *English Bards and Scotch Reviewers* in that tradition. The topic appealed even to poets anxious to reject Pope as a model. In his *A Feast of the Poets*, Leigh Hunt preferred to look back to seventeenth-century models, just as he had when he revived the masque in *The Descent of Liberty*. But *Don Juan* is not a poem like any of these. It is a narrative poem. It relates the adventures of the young Juan as he travels through Europe, and it is unprecedented for such a poem to busy itself with name-dropping so many poets, both contemporaries and poets of the past.

One reason Byron names so many is because one of the points that he wants to make about poets is that there are so many of them. There are even more poets than there are heroes, who are so plentiful that, as I pointed out in Chapter 2, Byron can list thirty-two of them in the first four stanzas of his poem. In the drawing rooms of London Juan is introduced to the 'eighty "greatest living poets"' (XI, 54), and the living poets are far outnumbered by the dead, which makes the case of poets who 'make their appeal to the unborn' to posterity, particularly hard:

> Why, I'm posterity – and so are you:
> And who do we remember? Not a hundred.   (XII, 19)

The thought might have been prompted by the collections of English poetry with which Byron would have been familiar. The prototype of these collections was John Bell's *The Poets of Great Britain*, published in 109 volumes from 1777 to 1783. Bell's collection claimed to be 'complete'. In fact, only fifty poets were collected, and some of those were not then, still less now, very widely known: Garth, Hughes, Fenton, Hammond, Broome. Alexander Chalmers' *Works of the English Poets* of 1810 reduced Bell's 109 volumes to 21, but Chalmers more than doubled the number of poets represented by finding room for poets such as Boyse, Cawthorne, Habington, Harte, Logan, Stepney, Walsh, and Yalden. The contents page of Chalmers' collection gives strong support to Byron's view that of all the poets of the past we remember 'not a hundred'. It amuses him to think of so many poets, all of them making their claim to be 'duly seated on the immortal hill' (Dedication, 6). But it is a genial not a caustic amusement.

Don Juan is dedicated to Southey, and 'shuffling Southey, that incarnate lie' (X, 13), is throughout the poem a principal object of Byron's contempt. Southey had made a personal attack on Byron in print,[41] and Byron was not quick to forgive such affronts. But in the Dedication he appears in company with Wordsworth and Coleridge, his fellow Lakers, and Byron's responses to them were more complex. Coleridge is a 'drunk' (I, 205), who coupled himself with Southey when the two men took as their wives two sisters, 'milliners of Bath', in preparation for establishing their 'Pantisocracy' in Pennsylvania, on the banks of the Susquehanna (III, 93). Like Wordsworth and Southey, Coleridge was a political renegade who had taken to writing for the *Morning Post*. But he was also a poet Byron admired, and so too was Wordsworth despite his 'place in the Excise' (Dedication, 5). When Julia prompts in Juan feelings that he does not yet understand, he takes to wandering in the cork forests, and throwing himself down in those 'leafy nooks' where poets go to 'find material for their books'. 'Every now and then' those books may find a reader '[u]nless, like Wordsworth, they prove unintelligible'. But in the very next stanza Byron reveals that, despite all his taunting, he is a reader of Wordsworth himself, and an unusually sensitive one:

> He Juan, (and not Wordsworth), so pursued
> His self-communion with his own high soul.   (I, 91)

The pastiche of Wordsworth's manner is admiring as well as amused. In the Dedication, the primary charge against the Lakers is not that they have 'turned out' Tories at the last – Byron never held Walter Scott's politics against him – but their claim that 'poesy has wreaths for [them] alone' (Dedication, 5).

Henry Pye, Southey's predecessor as poet laureate, puts Byron in mind of the pie in which 'four and twenty blackbirds' were baked, and that pie makes nonsense of Southey's claim to be 'the only blackbird in the dish'. The field of poetry is 'universal and allows / Scope to all such as feel the inherent glow' (Dedication, 7). The Lakers are charged with a failure to recognise their 'brethren', with their refusal to grant poets such as Scott, Rogers, Campbell, Moore, and Crabbe their right to the title. One reason that Byron names so many poets in his poem is to point out how far he differs from them, so far that, however much he may disapprove of them as men, he will not dispute even the right of the Lake Poets to a place on Parnassus:

> You're shabby fellows – true – but poets still
> And duly seated on the immortal hill.   (Dedication, 6)

Don Juan is a porous poem.[42] Byron opens it up to other poets, not just to their names but also to their words. As he acknowledges, 'I like so much to quote' (II, 17).[43] Poets very often echo one another, or steal from one another, but it is surprisingly rare for them to quote one another. It happens from time to time. Pope begins one of his imitations of Horace with a couplet quoted directly from Thomas Creech's translation. But the device was rare enough for Byron to have remarked it. Pope quotes Creech, and Byron quotes him doing so:

> 'Not to admire is all the art I know
>   (Plain truth, dear Murray, needs few flowers of speech)
> To make men happy, or to keep them so'
>   (So take it in the very words of Creech) –
> Thus Horace wrote we all know long ago;
>   And thus Pope quotes the precept to re-teach
> From his translation.   (V, 101)

He quotes Shakespeare more than anyone, but, as Jane Austen remarks, Shakespeare had long been 'part of an Englishman's constitution'.[44] The Latin tags, too, most of them from Virgil and Horace, that are sprinkled liberally throughout *Don Juan*, came to mind easily for those of Byron's sex and education. Byron quotes poets he admires, and he quotes poets he does not. He quotes four lines from Campbell's *Gertrude of Wyoming*, complaining only that the second of them, 'Where transport and security entwine', is 'twisted to a phrase of some obscurity' (I, 88). He smiles companionably at Moore for describing Hyde Park, where fashionable women form their 'slight acquaintance with fresh air', as a 'bower' (XI, 66), and at Walter Scott for reviving in his *Lay of the Last Minstrel* the word 'warison', and in doing so providing Byron with a rhyme for 'comparison'

(XV, 59). But he is almost as ready to quote his literary enemies, even his chief enemy, Southey:

> 'Go, little book, from this my solitude!
>   I cast thee on the waters – go thy ways!
> And if, as I believe, thy vein be good,
>   The world will find thee after many days.'
> When Southey's read, and Wordsworth understood,
>   I can't help putting in my claim to praise –
> The four first rhymes are Southey's every line:
> For God's sake, reader! take them not for mine.   (I, 222)

He quotes Scott's claim that 'Love ruled the camp, the court, the grove', but doubts whether 'courts and camps be quite so sentimental' (XII, 13). The misquotation from Scott is slight and surely unintentional, but Byron's misquotations may be pointed. Spenser had promised to 'moralise his song' with 'fierce warres and faithfull loves'. Byron remembers him differently: '"Fierce loves and faithless wars" – I am not sure / If this be the right reading' (VII, 8). In Addison's *Cato*, Cato's son makes a noble commitment to the cause of virtue: ''Tis not in mortals to command success, / But we'll do more, Sempronius; we'll deserve it.' Byron revises the sentiment to suit more modern times: 'But do you more, Sempronius – don't deserve it' (XIII, 18).

Byron quotes other poets so often to mark his difference from the Lakers and their absurd claim to be the only blackbirds in the pie, but he quotes, too, as a way of reminding his readers that poems, like other kinds of writing, occupy a place within the publishing industry. Poets, like every other kind of manufacturer, need raw materials. They are apt to wander through forests, because it is in such places that they find 'materials for their books' (I, 90). When the sale of those books is 'not so fleet', a cloud passes over the brow of their publishers, 'Longman and John Murray' (VII, 26), and the cloud darkens if a book is proscribed, as *Don Juan* was, by women, by those, that is, 'who make the fortune of all books', 'the bluecoat misses', the '[b]enign Ceruleans of the second sex' (IV, 108–9). Byron quotes so many poets as a way of reminding us that poets wear a 'motley mantle' (XV, 24). They too are public entertainers, however much they may deny it, and occupy a place in 'the literary *lower* Empire' together with all the other kinds of writer (XI, 62).

In *Don Juan*, Byron's interests extend throughout that literary empire. He is almost as fascinated by newspapers as by novels and poems. He takes as much interest in the 'twice ten hundred thousand daily scribes' who furnish the nation with its reading matter in the shape of 'pamphlets, volumes, newspapers' as in the more celebrated writers that he addresses so grandly, 'O, ye great authors, luminous, voluminous!', before admitting that he has forgotten what he wanted to say to them (IX, 35–6). In the poem it is Aurora Raby whose eyes gaze 'more on books than faces', and who values even wisdom more highly if it is inscribed 'upon a printed page' (XV, 85). Aurora's devotion to print is a measure of her detachment from the world, but it is quite otherwise for Byron. His interest in print, in print of all kinds, is a measure of the interest he takes in every aspect of the world around him. Poems and newspapers ought to mark the two extremes of the literary spectrum. Poems aspire, as Byron puts it in *English Bards*, to occupy the attention for 'a thousand years', newspapers only for the day of their publication. The disgrace that threatens the poet is that his work becomes throwaway, like a newspaper, which is why Hazlitt contrasts the true poet who 'can wait patiently and calmly for the award of posterity' with the poet willing to 'mortgage' his fame for 'a newspaper puff'.[45] The fate that attends newspapers is reserved by Dryden and Pope for the poets they despise, those whose works are valuable only for lining baking tins or being used as toilet paper, 'Martyrs of Pies, and Reliques of the Bum' (Dryden, *Macflecknoe*, 101). But Byron imagines it as a fate that his own second canto might share (II, 16), and he extends his fears to the whole poem, which may end up with 'the oblivious cooks, / Those Cornish plunderers of Parnassian wrecks' (IV, 108). His consolation is that even if they are only used to 'line portmanteaus, / Trade will be all the better for these cantos' (XIV, 14). He acknowledges the danger wryly rather than despairingly, partly because he knows that no poet can be confident that his work will survive, but also because he knows that newspapers, although they may be thrown away the day after they are published, are items at least as important as poems in the print culture of his nation.[46]

England had become a 'newspaper' country (XII, 65). That may, as Byron intimates, make it a 'low' country, but the habit of reading newspapers extends to the highest in the land. It is the *Morning Post* that offers the fashionable the 'sole record' of their adventures and misadventures (XI, 80). Lord Henry and Lady Adeline rely on it to report their movements: 'Departure, for his country seat, today, / Lord H. Amundeville and Lady A' (XIII, 51). To appear in its pages is the only route to 'modern fame', which is fame of a paradoxical, Warholian kind: 'it takes no further hold / Than an advertisement', it fades 'ere the ink be dry' (XIII, 51). At Norman Abbey the more elderly of the guests would never get through the day without the 'morning papers' (XIII, 102). Juan proves himself a naturalised Englishman when, unable to sleep (he has just seen a ghost), he takes up 'an old newspaper' and reads an advert, 'a long eulogy of "patent blacking"' (XVI, 26).[47] The one advantage that Byron claims for *Don Juan* over more traditional epics is that his 'story's actually true', for confirmation of which he points to 'history, tradition, and to facts', before extending his appeal to the evidence of 'plays in five, and operas in three acts'. In their proper place, in between history and the opera, come the 'newspapers, whose truth all know and feel' (I, 203). It is, as Byron must have known, the proper place for his poem too. Much of Byron's time in the last weeks of his life at Messolonghi was taken up by Leicester Stanhope, the 'typographical Colonel', who thought that the Greek cause would best be served by setting up newspapers (newspapers in English), the *Greek Telegraph*, and the *Athens Free Press*. Byron laughed at Stanhope, but he would have understood him.

In the war cantos, VII and VIII, Byron is particularly interested in one kind of newspaper, the Gazette, the journal of record, the newspaper of the Crown. When a major battle took place, the Gazette reported the action, named those who had distinguished themselves, and printed a casualty list in a Gazette Extraordinary like no. 17028, the despatch that gave the first authenticated account of the Battle of Waterloo. Byron detects an unholy conspiracy between the poet and the Gazetteer. The two cooperate in maintaining the cult of military heroism. 'Heroes are but made for bards to sing' (VIII, 14), and the *Iliad* is only Homer's 'Greek gazette of that campaign' (VII, 80). Poems and Gazettes both promise to memorialise a nation's heroes by setting their names in print. But in the case of the Gazette, the attempt is manifestly futile. The Gazette is, after all, a newspaper, no sooner glanced at than disposed of: 'Of all our modern battles, I will bet / You can't repeat nine names from each Gazette' (VII, 34). The *London Gazette* is glanced through and quickly forgotten. Homer's 'Greek gazette' by contrast has endured for millennia. Newspapermen write for today, poets for all time. But, as Byron is anxious to remind us, Homer is the exception rather than the rule. Of all the poets, how many do we remember? 'Not a hundred' (XII, 19).

Byron's animus against the Lake Poets was fuelled by their claim not to write for any existing readership. They reserved their 'laurels for posterity', but, as Byron points out, the outcome of 'an appeal to the unborn' can only be 'dubious': 'odds are that posterity will know / No more of them,

than they of her, I trow' (XII, 18). The Lakers' campaign to extend
copyright – Wordsworth thought even a period of thirty years 'no adequate
test for works of Imagination, even from second or third-rate writers, much
less from those of the first order, as we see in the instances of Shakespeare
and Milton'[48] – was evidence not so much of their respect for intellectual
property as of their egotism. Byron did not share their interest in the
verdict of posterity. It is all one to him whether his name will die with him
or endure for 'some centuries': 'The grass upon my grave will grow as
long, / And sigh to midnight winds, but not to song' (IV, 99). Insouciance
comes easier to him than the Lakers, because, unlike them, he has scaled
the pinnacle of literary success in his own lifetime, and at a time when he
was best fitted to enjoy it, when he was young: he has 'succeeded in [his]
youth / The only time when much success is needed' (XII, 17). Even if *Don
Juan* has been his Moscow, he can claim that for a few years at least he had
been the 'grand Napoleon of the realms of rhyme' (XI, 56), or, as he puts it
less grandiloquently, he had for a time been the fashion. The years of his
fame were the years in which, partly because of his own status, writers
became 'of the *Beau Monde* a part potential', occupying a rank that put
them almost on a par with boxers (XIV, 20). The first cantos of *Childe
Harold* and the Eastern tales that followed had made Byron into a literary
celebrity, the like of which Britain had never before known. But it is in *Don
Juan* that he begins to think searchingly about what it means when poetry,
which was once 'but passion', changed its character and 'grew a fashion'[49]
(IV, 106). Even the very greatest of poets cannot resist the sway of fashion.
Shakespeare himself is so much spoken of not for his genius but because
Shakespeare 'just now is much in fashion' (IX, 16). The materials out of
which Byron made those early poems of his became hackneyed almost at
once by virtue of being so much imitated. In *Don Juan*, Byron complains
that he can no longer write about jasmine and orange bowers: 'of late your
scribblers' have cultivated 'whole hotbeds' of oriental flowers 'in their
works / Because one poet travell'd 'mongst the Turks' (V, 42). He finds
himself in the position of the character based on Beau Brummel in Thomas
Lister's novel *Granby*, who abandons his interest in fashion when he sees
a cut of waistcoat that he had only recently adopted 'adorning the person of
a natty apprentice'.[50]

  Don Juan is written from the perspective of a once fashionable poet, of
a poet who has had his day and must now yield place to the Reverend
George Croly and the like, and is for that reason peculiarly well-qualified to
trace what the consequences might be when the literary sphere becomes
a satellite of the world of fashion. Fashion is a self-renewing system. An

item, a cut of waistcoat for example, becomes fashionable when enough people choose to wear it, and unfashionable when still more people follow suit and the number becomes big enough to include even the 'natty apprentice'. This seems the opposite of a literary system that defines the masterpiece as a work that has the power to transcend time, a work that remains a wonder for a thousand years. Hazlitt reports that when Wordsworth was asked how long Byron's reputation would survive his death, he replied, 'Not three days, Sir'.[51] For Wordsworth, Byron was a phenomenon in the world of fashion rather than the world of literature, and in *Don Juan* Byron seems to accept as much himself. He is 'a wanderer from the British world of fashion' where, 'like other dogs', he has had his day (II, 166). *Don Juan* is a poem in which Byron very often refers to poems and very often refers to newspapers, but its peculiarity is that it puts in question the difference between them. Newspapers, once read, serve only to line portmanteaus, but that is the fate of poems too, at any rate of most of them, and in *Don Juan* Byron seems to embrace rather than to resist that fate. He allows newspaper stories to infiltrate the poem, scandalous newspaper stories in particular, stories of Queen Caroline's improper relationship with an Italian servant (V, 61), or of the Bishop of Clogher discovered in a compromising situation with a Grenadier guardsman (VIII, 76). Newspapers, unlike poems, focus on individuals, their stock in trade is proper names, and in *Don Juan* Byron reveals himself as, alongside Dante, the great poet of proper names, from Thomas Gurney, the shorthand writer (I, 189) and 'Mr. Mann, of London', manufacturer of ships' pumps (II, 29), to Byron's banker, Ransom of Ransom & Co (XV, 8), and Lord Charles Kinnaird, elder brother of Byron's friend, Douglas Kinnaird (IX, 2), to a fashionable dandy such as Long Pole Wellesley (XI, 78). The focus on proper names is one aspect of a larger project. *Don Juan* is a poem that busies itself unpicking the distinction between the subject matter of newspapers and the subject matter proper to poetry.

Don Juan was published serially (long before the Victorian novelists contracted the habit): its first two cantos on 15 July 1819; Cantos III, IV, and V on 8 August 1821; three instalments one after the other in 1823, on 15 July, 29 August, and 1 December; and the final two cantos on 25 March 1824. It was an epic poem published in a way that disguised it as a periodical. The disguise was the more effective because Byron had so scandalously associated himself with a periodical, the short-lived *Liberal*, and because the final eleven cantos were published by John Hunt, who was known not as a publisher of poetry but of periodicals, of *The Liberal*, *The Yellow Dwarf*, and, most importantly, *The Examiner*, the weekly edited by his brother, Leigh. But the manner of its publication allowed Byron an opportunity afforded to few poets before him, and to none of those who had aspired to write epics. He was able respond to the poem's critics in the poem itself. Hazlitt thought it 'the business of poets to watch poets, not of poets to watch reviewers'.[52] Byron thought differently. He seized the opportunity to engage in a dialogue with his reviewers. It was Byron who instigated the dialogue. He claimed to have 'bribed' his 'grandmother's review – the British' to give a favourable notice of the poem: 'I sent it in a letter to the Editor / Who thank'd me duly by return of post.' With that insurance he feels able, he claims, to defy '[a]ll other magazines of art or science', including even 'the Edinburgh Review and Quarterly' (I, 209–11). He was delighted when William Roberts, the editor of the *British Review*, took him seriously, and ponderously rebutted the charge in the columns of his journal.[53] When Byron was writing the third canto of the poem, he took the opportunity to respond to reviews of the first two cantos. He presented the 'Ave Maria' stanzas, the stanzas in which he celebrates the 'hour of twilight' in the Ravenna pine forests, that time when all is silent save for the cicalas and the 'vesper's bell', as his response to all those 'pleased to say / In nameless print that I have no devotion' (III, 104). In the *Eclectic Review*, Josiah Conder refused to notice the first two cantos (he was far from alone in this), but included in the review of *Mazeppa* a reference to Byron's 'last *reputed* production'. It was poetry, he remarked, 'such as no brother could read aloud to his sister, no husband to his wife; – poetry in which the deliberate purpose of the Author is to corrupt by inflaming the mind, to seduce to the love of evil which he has himself chosen as his good'.[54] The *Eclectic* was a periodical written by and for the Dissenting community, but, even so, the notice of Byron's unnamed poem is extraordinary. His response was temperate, even good-humoured. So stern a moralist as the reviewer, he suggested, leads one to suspect him to be a 'rake turned methodistic or Eclectic / (For that's the name they like to pray beneath)' (III, 66). In the *Edinburgh*, Jeffrey hid his notice of the first two cantos of *Don Juan* in a review of *Cain, Sardanapalus*, and *The Two Foscari*,[55] and Byron's response is even more friendly. He quotes Jeffrey's verdict that his 'abuse of Southey . . . does no honour either to the taste or the temper of the noble author', but for all that Jeffrey remains '[d]ear Jeffrey' (X, 11 and 16). Byron chooses to ignore the more wounding charge that, however understandable it might be for Byron to respond in kind to Southey's attacks on him, it was 'cruel, coarse, and unhandsome' to extend the attack to Southey's wife (Jeffrey has in mind Byron's jibe that Southey and Coleridge had married 'two partners (milliners of Bath)' (III, 93). He ignores, too, Jeffrey's more general objection to the poem. Jeffrey was dismayed, as so many early reviewers were, by Byron's swift transitions, by his tendency to make such close neighbours of sentiment and cynicism. The effect, according to Jeffrey, is that 'our notions of right and wrong are at once confounded – our confidence in virtue shaken to the foundations – and our reliance on truth and fidelity at an end for ever'. But not even this disturbs Byron's benignity: 'However, I forgive him and I trust / He will forgive himself – if not, I must' (X, 11). In his responses to his reviewers, Byron bears out his claim that his 'natural temper's really aught but stern, / And even [his] Muse's worst reproof's a smile' (XI, 63). 'There never was an author so universally and warmly applauded' as Byron had been, Jeffrey had insisted, but when he 'took leave of Childe Harold to ally himself to Don Juan', he suffered a 'decline in popularity'; his reputation suffered 'a stain upon its lustre'. It was a view widely shared amongst the poem's reviewers, and Byron, rather surprisingly, chooses to incorporate it rather than rebut it. It has come to his notice, he notes in the fourth canto, that 'several people take exception / At the first two books', and his publisher (who may have read the *Eclectic*'s verdict that it is a poem a brother could not read to his sister nor a husband to his wife) has reported that '[t]hrough needles' eyes it easier for the camel is / To pass than these two cantos into families' (IV, 97). He is even happy to accept Jeffrey's view that *Don Juan* has dealt a mortal blow to his reputation: 'Juan was my Moscow' (XI, 56).

Byron seized the opportunity that the serial publication of *Don Juan* afforded him to respond to his reviewers, but his references to the reviews supplement references to almost every other kind of printed material: novels, poems, newspapers, even advertisements, like the 'long eulogy of "patent blacking"' that Juan reads to distract him from his ghostly visitation (XVI, 26), or the advertisement that persuaded Byron that Donna Inez was surpassed in virtue only by 'thine "incomparable oil," Macassar' (I, 17). The shoe polish advertisements were in rhyme, rhyme supplied, or so it was rumoured, by Byron himself. He reports in an appendix to *The Two Foscari* that he had been accused of having received 'five hundred pounds for writing advertisements for Day and Martin's patent blacking!' The exclamation mark registers astonishment rather than outrage. In *Don Juan* Byron does not just reflect on how the age in which he lives is an age of print, and on all the different kinds of print publication produced by the 'twice ten hundred thousand daily scribes' who enlighten the reading public in 'pamphlets, volumes, newspapers' (IX, 35). He understands that there is no secure distinction between all those daily scribes and those like himself, allowed their place of honour amongst the 'great authors, luminous, voluminous' (IX, 36). *Don Juan* is a poem so much concerned with print, and with printed material because Byron's ambition is to write the poem of the age, and he recognises that his own age is best characterised as an age of print, and of print of all kinds, from the most exalted to the humblest. *Don Juan* is the first major poem in English so fully to recognise that it does not just have a place in the history of literature; it has a place too in the history of the publishing industry, which is why in *Don Juan*, the epic poem of the age of print, Byron set himself to chronicle that industry so richly.

CHAPTER 4

The Gate of Life and Death

Don Juan is a heterosexual poem, scandalously so for some of its readers. It celebrates 'Philo-genitiveness', a word, Byron remarks, 'quite after my own heart / Though there's a shorter a good deal than this' (XII, 22). In 1987, Susan Wolfson already felt the need to argue that the poem offers antidotes to its 'conventional masculinism'.[1] Its hero is, after all, a young man with a 'half-girlish face' (I, 171), 'feminine in feature' (VIII, 52), a man who dresses as a woman in the poem's fifth canto and maintains the disguise all through the sixth, someone whose quickness of feeling puts one in mind of 'Ovid's Miss Medea' (I, 86). All poets have feminine muses, but Byron's muse (or one of them, for he has 'more than one Muse at a push' (X, 5)) is more feminine than most, a modest, inoffensive young woman who 'drops a brief and modern curtsy / And glides away, assured she never hurts ye' (XI, 63). But Juan, however convincing he may be in drag, is always more Charley's Aunt than RuPaul. He is reassuringly 'awkward' when he puts on a dress, tripping over his petticoat. His clumsiness is a way of reminding the reader that, however feminine his features, the 'effeminate garb' that he is obliged to don is foreign to his nature. His soul 'loathes' it (V, 76–8).[2] All through the poem Juan seizes every opportunity to display his masculine credentials, pummelling Don Alfonso, Julia's husband, when he bumps into him in the passage, facing down, armed with a pair of pistols, the tars intent on pillaging the foundering ship's store of grog (II, 35), cutting down the foremost in the 'file of pirates' summoned by Lambro to seize him (IV, 48), proving himself 'a broth of a boy' in the attack on Ismail (VII, 24), and responding when threatened by Tom the highwayman by firing a bullet into his assailant's 'pudding' (XI, 13). Even when he agrees to dress as a woman he takes care to remind Baba, the Sultan's eunuch, of the weight of his arm, which is not 'quite so light' as Baba may think (V, 82).

Byron's 'homosexuality', Wolfson suggests, is integral to the poem: it is what enables him to maintain a critical distance from the poem's 'hetero-sexual politics'. But there is little fellow-feeling in the reference to Percy

Jocelyn, Bishop of Clogher. On Friday, 19 July 1822, Jocelyn was detected in flagrante with a young guardsman in a private room of the White Lion, just off the Haymarket. The incident is recalled in *Don Juan* but elicits only a snigger: being 'taken by the tail' is, we are told, 'a taking / Fatal to bishops as to soldiers' (VIII, 76).[3] It is Byron's age rather than his orientation that allows him to view his hero's erotic shenanigans with a wry detachment. His hair, already grey at thirty ('I wonder what it will be like at forty?' (I, 213)), is a reminder that his 'days of love are over' (I, 216). The poem is a product of the most barbarous of all the middle ages, 'the middle age / Of man', a time when it is 'late to wive; / And as for other love, the illusion's o'er' (XII, 1–2).

Louis Crompton, who has done more than anyone to focus attention on Byron's relationships with young men, acknowledges that in the years in which he wrote *Don Juan* Byron's 'passion for boys seems to have been in abeyance'. After he left England in 1816 the 'passion for women predominated',[4] and continued to do so for seven years, until the last weeks of Byron's life, the weeks that he lived in Messolonghi, when he had suspended work on *Don Juan* and his emotional life came to centre on his unrequited love for the fifteen-year-old Lukas Chalandrutsanos. Seven years earlier, when he began his period of self-imposed exile, he had made a conscious decision no longer to pursue such relationships. The resolution was prompted no doubt by the rumours circulating during the long and painful separation crisis during which he and his wife became the subject of common gossip. 'As to "pages" – there be none such – nor any body else', he assured his half-sister, Augusta, in 1816, after he had taken up residence on Lake Geneva, in the Villa Diodati.[5] When Byron first left England in 1809, he had been accompanied by the youthful Robert Rushton, the son of one of his Newstead tenants, who served as his page. In 1816, he was determined not to repeat the experiment, and that determination is reflected in *Don Juan*. He allows Juan a young companion when he travels to London from Catherine the Great's court in St Petersburg, but the companion is a girl, the ten-year-old Leila, whose life had been saved by Juan during the Russian assault on Ismail. Byron's letters from Venice to his male friends are insistent on a 'passion for women', which, he assures James Wedderburn Webster, may be indulged in Venice at less expense than elsewhere. It is true that of the 5,000 sterling that he has spent thus far 'more than half was laid out on the Sex', but he has had 'plenty for the money – that's certain – I think at least two hundred of one sort or another – perhaps more'.[6] He will not allow his literary earnings to be used to liquidate his English debts. 'What I get by my brains', he tells Hobhouse and Kinnaird, 'I will spend on my b[olloc]ks – as long as I have a tester or a testicle remaining'.[7] In Venice, his social life, as he describes it to Kinnaird, was varied. He took lessons in Armenian, there was the theatre and the opera, he attended the Venetian salons, '& indulge[d] in coition always'.[8] He took to boasting of his sexual stamina. He had contrived an introduction to one Venetian noblewoman, 'fucked her twice a day for the last six', and has no plans to make the seventh a day of rest.[9] When he reports to Hobhouse his triumph in a swimming contest from the Lido all the way up the Grand Canal, he is careful to add that he had taken '*a piece*' before and after.[10] But there are other than biographical reasons that the masterpiece of Byron's years of exile should be so flagrantly heterosexual a poem as *Don Juan*.

Don Juan is a public, not a private poem. The reader it invokes so often is not the intimate friend that Wordsworth addresses in *The Prelude* but the anonymous representative of the early nineteenth-century reading public. It is admittedly a reader able to relish teasing references to Byron's private life, and in particular to his marriage, a reader aware of his wife's short stature ('I hate a dumpy woman' (I, 61)), even of her favourite dress material ('her morning dress was dimity' (I, 12)), but the separation scandal had opened up Byron's private life to the general public. His marriage had become the subject of newspaper reports, his intimate life the material of gossip, and not just English gossip. He told Lady Byron that their domestic affairs 'have now – I think – nearly made the tour of Europe – and been discussed in most of its languages'.[11] As Louis Crompton shows, even in private letters to close friends references to same-sex relationships, as opposed to relationships with women, were veiled. Writing from Falmouth to his friend Charles Skinner Matthews in 1809 Byron reported that in that seafaring town he and Hobhouse were 'surrounded by Hyacinths & other flowers of the most fragrant [na]ture'. He went on to report that he had 'some intention of culling a handsome Bouquet to compare with the exotics' he hoped 'to meet in Asia'. In his reply Matthews congratulated Byron on his 'first efforts in *the mysterious*', and recommended that Hobhouse refrain in future from calling attention to his own 'mysterious significances' by putting 'a *dash*' underneath them.[12] The lyrics to Thyrza that Byron published with the first two cantos of *Childe Harold* offer a more plangent instance of 'mysterious' writing. Byron disguises his grief at the death of John Edleston, the Trinity College choirboy, by representing the poems as elegies for a young woman, in which guise they were widely admired. Knowledge of the true object of Byron's grief was confined to the closed circle of initiates. Byron told one of his Harrow friends, 'pray, keep the subject of my "*Cornelian*" a *Secret*'.[13] R. C. Dallas was outside the circle, and Byron wrote to him denying that a stanza in *Childe Harold* commemorating Edleston's death was inspired by 'any *male* friend'.[14] Coded forms of address are quite foreign to Byron's practice in *Don Juan*, a poem in which he cultivates a manner that is open, unbuttoned, extravagantly indiscreet.[15]

Don Juan is a heterosexual poem too because it is a poem organised by difference, and all of the differences that organise the poem are emblazoned in the difference between men and women. It is a difference that the poem invites us to brood upon: 'What a strange thing is man! and what a stranger / Is woman!' (IX, 64). Man's love is of man's life a thing apart', Julia writes to Juan in her farewell letter, "Tis woman's whole existence' (I, 194). Men cry just as women do, but Juan is differentiated from the Sultana Gulbeyaz even by his tears: 'A woman's tear-drop melts, a man's half sears, / Like molten lead' (V, 118). In a fallen world women are '[c]ondemn'd to child-bed', but men too must accept their share of the primal curse. They are obliged to shave, although Byron may be alone in judging this an irritation that 'in the aggregate / May average on the whole with parturition' (XIV, 23–4). It is because the poem is organised by sexual difference that its narrative centres on the series of encounters between Juan and the eight women who figure in his interrupted amatory career, nine if we include the Romagnole chained to Juan on the pirate vessel whose eyes, '[b]right – and as black and burning as a coal', are wasted on Juan who cannot rid his mind of thoughts of Haidée ('Perhaps his recent wounds might help a little'(IV, 94–5)), and ten if we add Juan's young companion, Leila, who, despite her age (she is only ten), is so beautiful that the English matrons worry whether Juan will be able to 'command / Himself for five, four, three, or two years' space' (XII, 29).

Towards the end of the third canto, Byron makes one of his mock apologies:

> But let me to my story: I must own,
> If I have any fault, it is digression;
> Leaving my people to proceed alone,
> While I soliloquize beyond expression.   (III, 96)

It is a fault he often acknowledges. Just a few stanzas later he is reminded by the vesper bell of the unknown hand that laid flowers on the tomb of Nero, and at once checks himself:

> But I'm digressing; what on earth has Nero,
> Or any such like sovereign buffoons,
> To do with the transactions of my hero.   (III, 110)

Ten cantos later he is just as prone to be distracted from his characters and their doings, this time by thoughts of how Cervantes had, it may be to the detriment of the nation, 'smiled Spain's chivalry away':

> I'm 'at my old Lunes' – digression, and forget
> The Lady Adeline Amundeville. (XIII, 12)

Byron expects his readers to enjoy his digressions, of course. His sheepish apologies ('I feel this tediousness will never do – / 'Tis being *too* epic' (III, 111)) are only feigned – except that the poem would not work unless it succeeded in prompting a desire in the reader to get back to the transactions of its hero, or, in the thirteenth canto, to the situation of the most fascinating of the poem's several heroines, Lady Adeline Amundeville, the 'fair most fatal Juan ever met' (XIII, 12). One reason that even the ablest continuations of *Don Juan* – the third cantos written by Lady Caroline Lamb and William Hone, for example – fall so far below the original is that they fail to match the narrative interest that Byron sustains even though he is, as he admits, so prone to forget his story and surrender to soliloquy.

Byron ends the eighth canto with a summary of the poem's plot:

> Reader! I have kept my word, – at least so far
> As the first Canto promised. You have now
> Had sketches of love, tempest, travel, war – (VIII, 138)

And, as he reminds us, these are the materials from which all epic poems are made, the only difference being that his sketches are 'plain truth', taken from the life, '[a]ll very accurate'. But the tempest is confined to the second canto, and war to Canto VIII. Love and travel on the other hand are topics dispersed through all sixteen cantos of the poem. But although love and travel both run all the way through *Don Juan*, they do so to very different effect. Juan is not, like Odysseus, engaged in a quest to return home, nor, like Aeneas, is he charged with a mission, to travel to Italy and found a new Troy. Travel in *Don Juan* is panoramic, not purposive. Byron, he tells us, enjoys the experience of 'going at full speed – no matter where its / Direction be', and that is what the poem offers its readers. To read through the poem is to enjoy the 'pleasure in arriving / At the great end of travel – which is driving' (X, 72). Travel gives the poem its variety, but, because it has no goal, it cannot lend it narrative momentum. For that the poem relies on the fourth of its epic topics, love. When one of the poem's women makes an appearance, the poem's narrative concentrates itself around her. The narrator may still feel the gravitational pull of his 'old Lunes', but, when one of the poem's women is in the offing, it is a pull that he yields to

only briefly. Lady Adeline Amundeville is too fascinating a personage for
Byron's attention to be distracted for any longer.

Don Juan is a poem with a masculine hero, a young man who, for all that
he is 'feminine in feature', cannot, even when dressed as a woman, disguise
his 'somewhat manly majesty of stride' (V, 91), and the poem has
a masculine narrator, a man with grizzled hair who looks back on his
youth from the 'half-way house' of life, that 'horrid equinox' (XII, 1). The
relationship between hero and narrator, which is a little like the relationship forged in the Ismail cantos between Juan and his English near
namesake John Johnson, is the one stable relationship in the poem. But
at the poem's centre is the sequence of women that attract Juan's erotic
attention. At the centre of the poem is woman, or rather a woman's part. In
the sixth canto Byron raises an expectation that the part will be named
only, on this occasion, to leave the reader comically disappointed:

> I love the sex, and sometimes would reverse
>   The tyrant's wish, 'that mankind only had
> One neck, which he with one fell stroke might pierce:'
>   My wish is quite as wide, but not so bad,
> And much more tender on the whole than fierce;
>   It being (not *now*, but only while a lad)
> That womankind had but one rosy mouth,
> To kiss them all at once from North to South.   (VI, 27)

The anticlimax is mitigated in the following stanza when Byron claims that
he would be ready to change places with Briareus, who had 50 heads and
100 arms, provided that he could have 'all things multiplied / In such
proportion' (VI, 28).

Male members proliferate in *Don Juan*. Catherine the Great demands
that the men she chooses meet her own exacting requirements. She
measures them 'as you would do a steeple' (VII, 37), and her preoccupation
with men's appendages permeates all her other interests. She looks on war
as if it were 'a main of cocks', that is, a cock fight, '[w]herein she liked her
own to stand like rocks' (IX, 29). Byron is just as interested in the absence
of the male appendage as in the case of Baba, the sultan's eunuch, or the
'intellectual eunuch Castlereagh' (Dedication XI). But it is the female part
rather than the male that presides, and rightly so in a poem in which the
hero is always subordinate to the heroines. *Don Juan* is a poem that clings
to the traditional view that women are more centred in their bodies than
men: 'Men with their heads reflect on this and that – / But women with
their hearts or heaven knows what!' (VI, 2). When the scene shifts to the

Russian court at St Petersburg, Catherine the Great is revealed as that what's its name's 'grand Epitome' (IX, 57). Catherine, in a pun that Byron repeats several times in the poem, is 'this great whole' (IX, 58). The relationship between Catherine and a woman's part is metonymic, a jibe that gains added point because Byron wrote the Russian cantos in the months in which the trial of Queen Caroline seemed to reveal that, although Caroline had none of Catherine's autocratic power, the two queens were similar at least in their sexual appetites.[16] Byron, according to Thomas Moore, made the same joke about both women: 'He called Queen Caroline, the *Quim*, and has several coarse jests thereon.'[17] Byron's pun when he describes Catherine as 'this great whole' seems a jest of exactly this kind. But in *Don Juan* dirty jokes do not just appear in close neighbourhood with weighty philosophical reflections, the two kinds of remark are often hard to distinguish. The part which Byron names Catherine's 'great whole' is also the part that 'causes all the things that be' (IX, 57). It is the part that should be recognised, to borrow the title of Courbet's audaciously voluptuous rendering of it, as 'L'Origine du monde'. When Byron notes that '[s]ome heathenish philosophers / Make Love the Main Spring of the Universe' (IX, 73), he has in mind Lucretius in particular. Near the end of the poem's sixteenth canto, he acknowledges that even though she has 'played us many tricks / Still we respect thee, "Alma Venus Genetrix!"' (XVI, 109).[18] Venus, the mother goddess, the goddess of generation, is the deity who presides over *Don Juan* as well as *De Rerum Natura*. Byron offers his devotion to the mountains and the ocean,

> Earth, air, stars, – all that springs from the great Whole,
> Who hath produced, and will receive the soul. (III, 104)

William Roberts, editor of 'my grandmother's review – the British' (I, 209) – understood the lines as Byron's confession of his pantheistic tendencies, asking 'what or who may be the "Great Whole" to whom this saintly person addresses himself?'[19] Blessings on his innocence.

Byron and his friends were amused by Regan's way of asking Edmund whether he has had sex with her sister: 'But have you never found my brother's way / To the forfended place?' (V, i, 10–11). It became a running joke between them. In a letter to Hobhouse, Byron referred to Scrope Davies as 'the "forefender"'.[20] It seems no more than the locker-room talk of young men who knew their Shakespeare, although Byron was not averse to intimately salacious gossip of a less literary kind, as when he reminded Hobhouse that the clitoris of Lady Westmorland ('the Sapphic Westmoreland') 'is supposed to be of the longest'.[21] But in his very next

letter Byron tells Hobhouse that he had visited the anatomical waxworks in
the Museo della Specola at Bologna, a museum that fascinated him, even
though, or perhaps because, as he acknowledged to his half-sister, some of
the exhibits were 'not the most decent'. He mentions the waxworks in
three of his letters. What struck him in particular were what he calls 'the
parts of shame', which were modelled with exquisite fidelity. The parts of
both sexes were exhibited, he tells Murray, 'all made & moulded by
a *female* Professor whose picture & merits are preserved & described to
you'.[22] His interest, despite his suspicion that the display may be indecent,
seems serious rather than simply salacious. In just the same way the stanzas
in which Byron makes his direct address to Catherine's 'great whole',
although they certainly encourage the reader to snigger, invite a snigger
that is oddly compounded with serious regard, even with a certain awe. It is
worth noticing that Byron translates the epithet that Horace attaches to the
female part 'teterrima' as the 'worst', disinfecting it of all the disgust with
which the Latin word is loaded:

> Oh, thou 'teterrima Causa' of all 'belli' –
>   Thou gate of Life and Death – thou nondescript!
> Whence is our exit and our entrance, – well I
>   May pause in pondering how all souls are dipt
> In thy perennial fountain: – how man *fell*, I
>   Know not, since Knowledge saw her branches stript
> Of her first fruit, but how he falls and rises
> *Since, thou* hast settled beyond all surmises.
>
> Some call thee 'the worst Cause of war,' but I
>   Maintain thou art the *best*: for after all
> From thee we come, to thee we go, and why
>   To get at thee not batter down a wall,
> Or waste a world? Since no one can deny
>   Thou dost replenish worlds both great and small:
> With, or without thee, all things at a stand
> Are, or would be, thou Sea of Life's dry Land.   (IX, 55–6)

Byron never names the body part that he is addressing. When he quotes
Horace's phrase 'teterrima causa belli', 'the worst cause of war', he omits
the word 'cunnus', with which Horace specifies exactly what it is he has in
mind.[23] The word, or rather its English cognate, is registered in Byron's
stanzas only as an absence, a gap, or, in the terminology that Byron favours
in the poem, a 'hole'. The word is veiled from the reader, concealed, as it
were, beneath a petticoat of verbal decorum. The conceit is Byron's, for
whom the petticoat 'holds a treasure, like a Miser's hoard'. It is a garment

that 'more attracts by all it doth conceal' (XIV, 27). The word achieves a special prominence by being hidden or excluded, rather in the way that Murray, whether intentionally or not, drew readers' attention to the passages he had excised from the first two cantos of the poem by replacing them with asterisks. When Keats uses the word in a letter to his brothers, he follows a polite convention by allowing the first and final letter to enclose a vacancy. At a drunken dinner party he and his friends had discussed 'the derivation of the word C – t'.[24] Byron follows the convention himself in a verse letter that he sent Murray from Venice early in 1818:

> Now I'll put out my taper
> (I've finished my paper
> For these stanzas you see on the *brink* stand)
> There's a whore on my right
> For I rhyme best at night
> When a C – t is tied close to *my Inkstand.*[25]

But he follows the convention here because he is imagining the poem, as he almost always imagines his poems, as it might appear on the printed page. He is far too much the aristocrat to share Keats's middle-class pudeur when he is writing letters to close male friends. Just the year before he had written to Douglas Kinnaird when Kinnaird was about to give his maiden speech after his election as an MP. The speech, he told Kinnaird, would be a 'Spinning-house Maidenhead if you recall that *Cant* – or rather *Cunt* term of our Alma Mater'.[26] The joke seems trivial enough, a casual obscenity of the kind used by Byron, as it has been used by so many young men, to signal his intimacy with the male friend he is addressing. But when Byron began to write *Don Juan*, 'cant' and 'cunt' were revealed as the twin poles around which his whole enterprise pivoted. All through the poem, as David Woodhouse points out, the word cant gains 'an extra potency' by 'the shadow of a pararhyming monosyllable'.[27] When he considered abandoning the poem after the reception of its first two cantos it seemed like the victory of the first term over the second: 'I had such projects for the Don – but the *Cant* is so much stronger than *Cunt* – nowadays, – that the benefit of experience in a man who had well weighed the worth of both monosyllables – must be lost to despairing posterity.'[28] Cant is Byron's term for mauvaise foi, for all the fictions that we perpetuate in order to avoid the discomfort of confronting who we really are. When it stands in opposition to cant, cunt functions as its antithesis. It betokens a truth that cannot be gainsaid, a ground zero of reality. The one word is intimately associated with

England, the country never far from Byron's mind no matter where his
hero may be:

> The truth is that in these days the grand 'primum mobile' of England is
> *Cant* – Cant political – Cant poetical – Cant religious – Cant moral – but
> always *Cant*.[29]

He ends his preface to the third instalment of the poem in the hope, a futile
hope as he well knew, that the poem's critics would 'abate a little of the
Cant which is the crying sin of this double-dealing and false-speaking
time.' Byron associated the other term with Italy, the country where his
poem was written, and in particular with Venice, the city in which it was
begun. Douglas Kinnaird understood Byron's point very well. His only
objection was that in his depiction of Catherine, Byron had come close to
making common cause with the purveyors of cant. He wrote to Byron on
15 October 1822, after reading the third instalment of the poem (Cantos VI,
VII, and VIII):

> With regards to the new Cantos I am delighted with them – the political
> reflections, the address to Wellington & the Preface are admirable – but why
> call the Katherine a whore? – She hired or whored others – She was never
> hired or whored herself – why blame her for liking fucking? If she canted as
> well as cunted, then call her names as long as you please – But it is hard to
> blame her for following her natural inclinations.[30]

Cant is opposed to cunt, and it is opposed too to the cantos of Byron's
poem, the first instalment of which, just like the latter of those two words,
proved no more able to pass into families than a camel to pass through the
eye of a needle (IV, 97).[31] The circulation of Byron's cantos was blocked by
'all this cant', by all those eager to denounce *Don Juan* for its indecency
even though they made no objection to 'Smollett, Prior, Ariosto, Fielding'
(IV, 97–8). Cant is at bottom a way of speaking rather than of behaving: it
is 'a thing of words – without the smallest influence upon human
actions'.[32] It may be a specialised jargon like the thieves' cant spoken by
Byron's highwayman, Tom, but for Byron it is more importantly the word
that refers to all those things we say we believe because we think it is
expected of us, and because everyone else pretends to believe them. Byron
hugely admired '[r]ough Johnson, the great moralist' (XIII, 7), and it was
Johnson who bade Boswell clear his mind of 'cant': 'you may *talk* in this
manner; it is a mode of talking in Society; but don't *think* foolishly'.[33] Cunt
is cant's antithesis in part because it is a word that is not used when people
are talking in society, a word debarred from the ordinary social vocabulary.

But that in itself serves only to bring it in close neighbourhood with Byron's poem, which, despite its huge sale, scarcely figured in the cultural conversation in the five years over which it was first published. It was noticed, as I have already pointed out, in neither of the great reviews, as if the *Edinburgh* and the *Quarterly* judged *Don Juan* a title no more fit to enter cultural discourse than was the word cunt to be introduced into polite conversation.

When Byron addresses the cunt in two octaves without once using the word, he playfully mimics that prohibition. He makes his address to 'thou nondescript'. The part he is addressing is nondescript because it is a word that cannot be written down, a word banished from print. That, it may be, is one reason why Byron, as Jane Stabler points out,[34] applies the very same epithet to his own poem: *Don Juan* is '[a] non-descript and ever-varying rhyme, / A versified Aurora Borealis' (VII, 2). But it is not the principal reason. *Don Juan* is a nondescript poem because it will not stay still long enough to be described, and in this too the poem finds its proper analogy in the sequence of women who one after the other act to concentrate Juan's and Byron's attention on their persons, and to concentrate it in particular on that part of their persons that most powerfully incarnates the female power to attract male attention. Englishwomen, according to Byron, have 'romantic heads' rather than romantic hearts, but, provided it leads to 'the place for which you start / What matters if the road be head or heart?' (XI, 33–4). Hobhouse wrote to Byron on 15 July 1819, the day on which the first two cantos of the poem were published, and accurately predicted that *Don Juan* would exert just as potent a power of fascination on the public as cunts do on the poem's hero and its narrator. The absence of either the author's or the publisher's name from the title page, like the absence of the word 'cunnus' from Byron's quotation from Horace, would titillate readers: it would 'irritate public pruriency to a complete priapism'.[35]

Byron was as fond of double entendres as an end-of-the-pier comedian (or Shakespeare). An epigram on Sir Humphrey Davy's wife ends:

> And the *Strength* of her *parts* has already been shewn
> For last night she found out the *'Philosopher's Stone'*.[36]

After telling Murray that he is 'in the estrum & agonies of a new intrigue' with a blue-eyed Italian woman who is 'insatiate of love', he remarks that 'like Augustus – I would rather die *standing*'.[37] It is a fondness that he brought with him when he began to write *Don Juan*, which is one reason why William Jerdan felt able to dismiss the third instalment of the poem, Cantos VI, VII, and VIII, as 'brothel chants', cantos in which a British peer had adopted 'the style of a porter in which to utter the sentiments of a bagnio'.[38] But Byron did not confine his predilection for double entendre to his ribald productions. Very early in his career, in 1808, he ends a lyric in which he bids a sentimental adieu to his first love, Mary Chaworth (now married) – 'And I must view thy charms no more' – with lines that even he admits 'are a little too much on the "Double Entendre:"'[39]

> I cannot view my *Paradise*
> Without a wish to *enter there.*

Charles Matthews objected to Hobhouse's habit of underlining expressions that carried a double meaning. Readers of Byron's letters may sometimes feel a similar objection to Byron's use of italics. Byron found it impossible to refrain from double meanings even in contexts when the habit seems scarcely appropriate, in *Marino Faliero*, for example. Hobhouse objected to Lioni's description of Venetian noblewomen dressed for a masked ball, a passage in which he detected 'sensualities':

> the thin robes,
> Floating like light clouds 'twixt our gaze and heaven;
> The many-twinkling feet so small and sylphlike,
> Suggesting the more secret symmetry
> Of the fair forms which terminate so well.   (IV.i, 57–61)

He thought it too easy to supply a physical referent for the 'heaven' and the 'secret symmetry' that Lioni is tempted to imagine. They seemed to Hobhouse 'unworthy' of the play 'either as prettiness or as impurities',[40] but they were isolated lapses in a production that he was happy to read aloud to 'half a dozen girls from 15 to 25'. He would not have read them *Don Juan*. In *Don Juan*, double entendre is endemic rather than casual and often much too coarse to be comfortably shared with an audience of young women. Hobhouse was unsure whether the passage in *Marino Faliero* should be charged with prettiness or impurity. In *Don Juan*, references to male and female pudenda are not so ambivalent. After a woman has had one lover, love grows a habit, '[a]nd fits her loosely – like an easy glove' (III, 3). Marriage is like a padlock, except that a marriage, if it is 'pick'd' is good for nothing, 'Spoilt, as a pipe of claret is when prick'd' (V, 171). In an Italian convent 'all the passions have, alas! but one vent' (VI, 32), which the knowing reader will not take to be devotion. But in *Don Juan* double entendre is much more than a stylistic tic. It is the principal device through which Byron expresses his conviction that prettiness must not be allowed to sever its connection with sensualities any more than the soul, in this world at any rate, should be credited with an existence independent of the body. 'What nonsense it is to talk of Soul', he had written years before, 'when a cloud makes it *melancholy*'.[41] In the diary that he began to keep in the new year of 1821, Byron noted 'the complete inertion, inaction, and destruction of [his] mental faculties' brought on by an indigestion that he blamed on 'a dish of boiled cockles'. 'And this is the Soul!!!' he commented. He would 'believe that it was married to the body, if they did not sympathise so much with each other'.[42] Soul and body are married to one another in *Don Juan,* but they are joined in the kind of marriage that Byron contemplates all through the poem, fractious, distant unions of ill-assorted couples, marriages in which the two parties are brought together with a jolt, like the two meanings, one of them serious, the other salacious, in double entendre, the figure of speech so prevalent in the poem.[43]

Catherine the Great is not the first to be described as the 'great whole'. Towards the end of Canto III, Byron takes issue with all those critics of his who had accused him of irreligion by asking which of them has found 'the shortest way' 'of getting into Heaven'. He is, he admits, no churchgoer:

> My altars are the mountains and the ocean,
> Earth, air, stars, – all that springs from the great Whole,
> Who hath produced, and will receive the soul.   (III, 104)

But this 'great Whole' and Catherine's are closely associated. How could it be otherwise in a poem in which the principal deity is Alma Venus Genetrix? Lucretius is the philosophical master of *Don Juan,*[44] and Plato is his great antagonist:

> Oh Plato! Plato! you have paved the way,
>   With your confounded fantasies, to more
> Immoral conduct by the fancied sway
>   Your system feigns o'er the controulless core
> Of human hearts, than all the long array
>   Of poets and romancers: – You 're a bore,
> A charlatan, a coxcomb – and have been,
> At best, no better than a go-between.   (I, 116)

It was a view he had long held. 'I am no Platonist', he had told Francis Hodgson in 1811.[45] Caroline Lamb had suggested after their affair had ended that she and Byron might remain friends, but he dismissed her *'platonic speculations'* as 'nonsense – we began in that way before – & they ended in – all this uproar'.[46]Plato is to blame because he fancies that the world of ideas and the material world are independent of one another, and that ideas might hold sway over matter. He believes that the body ought to recognise the suzerainty of the mind, a notion both fantastic and dangerous, fantastic because the body is not susceptible to the mind's control, and dangerous because those who do not recognise the just claims of the body are left with no defence against its importunities. The 'substantial company' at Lord Henry's public dinner might leave one wondering how '[s]uch bodies could have souls, or souls such bodies' (XVI, 90), but they at least make no claim to have subdued their appetites and won freedom from the flesh.

In *Don Juan*, the mind may be lord and master and the body its servant, but only if master and servant are understood as having a relationship rather like the relationship Byron enjoyed with his faithful lifelong servant William Fletcher. The body, like Fletcher, always remains splendidly insubordinate. When Juan embarks from Cadiz, sent off on his travels by a mother anxious to remove him from the scandal of his affair with Julia, Juan, rather self-consciously, takes formal leave of his native land:

> Farewell, my Spain! a long 'farewell!,' he cried,
>   'Perhaps I may revisit thee no more,
> But die, as many an exiled heart hath died,
>   Of its own thirst to see again thy shore.'   (II, 18)

Watching from the stern of the boat as the shoreline recedes, Juan fancies himself a Spanish Childe Harold:

> Adieu, adieu! my native shore
> Fades o'er the waters blue;
> The Night-winds sigh, the breakers roar,
> And shrieks the wild seamew.   (*Childe Harold*, I, 118–21)

But Harold is allowed to savour the experience, whereas Juan's soliloquy is rudely interrupted. He takes out Julia's letter of farewell to read it through once more:

> 'And, oh! if e'er I should forget, I swear –
>   But that's impossible, and cannot be –
> Sooner shall this blue ocean melt to air,
>   Sooner shall earth resolve itself to sea,
> Than I resign thine image, oh, my fair!
>   Or think of any thing excepting thee;
> A mind diseased no remedy can physic
> (Here the ship gave a lurch, and he grew sea-sick).
>
> 'Sooner shall heaven kiss earth (here he fell sicker),
>   O, Julia! what is every other woe?

(For God's sake let me have a glass of liquor;
    Pedro, Battista, help me down below.)
Julia, my love! (you rascal, Pedro, quicker) –
    O, Julia! (this curst vessel pitches so) –
Beloved Julia, hear me still beseeching!'
    (Here he grew inarticulate with retching.)   (II, 19–20)

The fine speech with which he was intent on marking the occasion is
sabotaged by the body's more pressing demands. Juan's seasickness offers
a lively demonstration of the truth that the mind cannot claim independence of the body, that it remains always at the body's mercy. Love may
conquer 'noble maladies' but it is helpless against 'vulgar illnesses', against
'nausea, or a pain / About the lower region of the bowels' (II, 22–3).
Seasickness offers one demonstration of that truth, hunger offers another.
After Juan and John Johnson are sold into slavery, Juan sees an opportunity
to escape, but Johnson dissuades him. For one thing he is unsure of their
chances:

> Besides, I'm hungry, and just now would take
> Like Esau, for my birthright a beef-steak.   (V, 44)

Even the most primal taboos are not proof against hunger, as the sailors
cast adrift in their longboat find when, after gently bleeding him to death,
they make their meal of Juan's tutor, Pedrillo. 'Three or four' of the sailors,
it is true, refuse to share the meal, as does Juan (II, 78), but Juan, it should
be remembered, had declined his portion when the crew killed his pet
spaniel, only the very next day, when hunger had begun to bite more
fiercely, gratefully to accept the forepaw grudgingly offered him '(though
first denied) / As a great favour' (II, 71). Still more commonly in *Don Juan*
it is the sexual appetite that exposes the folly of believing that the mind can
regulate the demands of the body. But the two kinds of appetite are closely
related. Juan, wandering through the forest in the first throes of his love for
Julia, may pore for so long over the leaves and the flowers that he misses his
dinner (I, 94), but that is because he is sixteen and has not as yet learned to
decipher his own feelings. By the time he arrives on Haidée's island he has
come to understand that even love 'must be sustain'd by flesh and blood', and
that Venus herself has no power unless Ceres helps matters along by offering
'a plate of vermicelli' (II, 170). Juan is roused from his first sleep on the island
not by thoughts of Haidée's beauty but because the smell of Zoe's cooking
wakes in him a 'most prodigious appetite' (2, 153). Double entendre in *Don
Juan* is the figure that marks comically incongruous conjunctions, and one of
these is the conjunction of food and sex. Hunger is the only craving even

more powerful than the sex instinct: the history of mankind has demonstrated that there is no virtue 'except Starvation / Could stop the worst of vices – Propagation' (VI, 18). 'Long banquets' may stifle desire, but '[a] slight repast makes people love much more', which is why Venus is indebted to Bacchus and Ceres to whom she owes 'the invention of champagne and truffles' (XVI, 86). But there is more to it than that, as Byron's descriptions of food make clear. One of the dishes offered at the elaborate dinner that the Lady Adeline offers her country neighbours is a French confection, 'Petits puits d'Amour', little wells of love, hollow pastries filled with jam:

> But even sans 'confitures,' it no less true is,
> There's pretty picking in those petits puits.   (XV, 68)

At the dinner Juan finds himself seated 'next an "à l'Espagnole,"' which, Byron has to remind us, is '[n]o damsel, but a dish', although it is 'so far like a lady, that 'twas drest / Superbly, and contained a world of zest' (XV, 74). The appetite for food reminds us just as forcefully as the appetite for sex that we are creatures of flesh and blood, bound inextricably to our bodies:

> I think with Alexander, that the act
> Of eating, with another act or two,
> Makes us feel our mortality.   (V, 32)

Byron is ready to agree that the 'noblest kind of love is love Platonical', but it is a kind of love to 'begin or end with'.[47] It is the love proper to moonstruck youths and to those so old that they are no longer vulnerable to the demands of the flesh. For all the rest of us 'there are those things which words name senses', the things which make 'all bodies anxious to get out / Of their own sand-pits'. It may feel as if what spurs us is the desire 'to mix with a goddess'. We feel an urge to escape from the sandpit of the real into an ideal realm, but that feeling is in truth nothing more than the sex instinct: 'What a curious way / The whole thing is of clothing souls in clay!' (IX, 74–6). Plato would have us all struggle to escape from the phenomenal world, in which everything is subject to change into a pure, immutable world of forms, blind to the evidence supplied by our senses that the mutability from which he seeks relief is one of the principles of life:

> Else how the devil is it that fresh features
> Have such a charm for us poor human creatures?   (II, 208)

It is the clash between the demand for constancy and the desire for change that makes the relationship between men and women into a sex comedy, and Juan acts out that comedy in the series of relationships with women that gives the sixteen cantos of Byron's poem their story.

The whole business is condensed into a handful of stanzas at the end of the second canto. They are spoken by a man who detests 'inconstancy' above all things, whose heart harbours only '[l]ove, constant love'. But just the night before, at a Venetian masked ball, a social occasion much more comfortably accommodated in *Don Juan* than *Marino Faliero*,

> I saw the prettiest creature, fresh from Milan,
> That gave me some sensations like a villain.   (II, 209)

'Philosophy' comes to his aid, bidding him think of 'every sacred tie'. 'I will', he says, 'But then her teeth, and then, Oh, heaven! her eye!' The dialogue between Philosophy and the susceptible narrator is the dialogue on which the whole poem turns, the dialogue that, in the more scabrous terms that Byron uses in his letters, pits cant against cunt. 'Stop', Philosophy repeats, 'Stop, so I stopp'd' (II, 210–11). But the narrator's attentions to the pretty Milanese are suspended only to make way for a brilliantly mischievous passage in which Byron effects a sly reversal of the Platonic hierarchies. It seems at first almost as if Byron has undergone a Damascene conversion to Platonism. The proper business of life, he now insists, is 'the perception of the beautiful', and the beautiful has its being beyond this mortal world. It can be perceived only when it is '[d]rawn from the stars, and filtered through the skies'. Beauty of this kind is, Byron accepts, 'Platonic, universal, wonderful', only to nonplus the reader by at once offering a very different account of beauty: 'In short, it is the use of our two eyes.'

> With one or two small senses added, just
> To hint that flesh is form'd of fiery dust.   (II, 212)

The reader tumbles from the stars and the skies to solid earth, ejected from Plato's world of forms into an empirical world in which the perception of beauty like perceptions of all other kinds is dependent on the senses. Byron accommodates the noumenal world that, according to Plato, the phenomenal world can only shadow, but only in order to reverse Plato's preferences. 'A lovely statue', Byron agrees with Plato, commands our admiration because it is a material embodiment of the 'beau ideal', but Byron's admiration is only heightened when it is extended to 'nature's rich / Profusion', that is, to all the beautiful women who catch the eye for a moment in just the way that the fair Milanese caught his eye at the

Venetian masked ball. Sculpture 'bodies forth that ideal beauty which is never to be found in actual Nature': or at least, as Byron at once added, that is 'the general opinion', but he is inclined to doubt it. He has been entirely satisfied with the beauty of natural women; 'the head of Lady Charlemont', 'an Albanian Girl' seen 'mending a road in the mountains', 'some Greek, and one or two Italian faces'.[48] As he puts it in the poem, adoration of ideal beauty is only a stepping stone, useful if it conducts us to the proper end of all aesthetic contemplation, which is the 'adoration of the real'. Earlier in the canto, after the glowing introduction of Haidée, Byron had upheld the same position more robustly. The sculptors whose work he admires in these stanzas had seemed to him then a 'race of mere impostors', their best work only a feeble imitation of flesh and blood beauty:

> I've seen much finer women, ripe and real,
> Than all the nonsense of a stone ideal.   (II, 118)

Byron was not at all like John Ruskin. He did not flinch from women's bodies. In a letter to Teresa Guiccioli, for example, he discusses her period, a little archly but without embarrassment.[49] In *Don Juan* he suggests that women's ages should not be reckoned 'by their Suns or Years, / I rather think the Moon should date the dears':

> And why? Because she's changeable and chaste.
> I know no other reason, whatsoe'er
> Suspicious people, who find fault in haste,
> May choose to tax me with.   (X, 10–11)

For Plato the phenomenal world is unsatisfactory because it is mutable, subject to change. But for Byron its mutability is an aspect of its beauty, and, what is even more important to him, it is because the world we live in is mutable that it is our proper home. Byron hated the very word 'invariable': 'What is there of human – be it poetry – philosophy – wit, wisdom – science – power – glory – mind – matter – life – or death – which is "invariable".'[50] The world is subject to change, and so are we:

> The heart is like the sky, a part of heaven,
> But changes night and day, too, like the sky.

The heart is governed by a changeable English weather. In England it is damp. Storms end in rain just as in our lives' stormy episodes end in tears, the sequence that best characterises 'the English climate of our years' (II, 214). Byron has some harsh things to say about that climate – 'The English winter – ending in July, / To recommence in August' (XIII, 42) – but he remains an Englishman for all that. To him 'vines, olives, precipices, / Glaciers, volcanoes, oranges, and ices' scarcely compensate for the chaster beauty that England has to offer, which is a beauty only made possible by that damp English climate. When his hero arrives in England he learns to appreciate the beauty of 'meadows, managed like a garden', the beauty of a 'green field' (X, 76). But the strongest evidence presented in *Don Juan* that the heart, like the English weather, is changeable is not the green grass of England, but the heart's 'inconstancy'. It might be very 'pleasant for the heart, as well as liver' 'if one sole lady pleased for ever' (II, 213), but the evidence supplied by Byron's experience, by the experience of l'homme moyen sensuel who is figured by Byron in the everyman figure who attends the masked ball and finds his eye taken by the beautiful young woman from Milan, is all against it, and that evidence is supported in the poem by the chorus line of women who one after another become the focus of Juan's attention.

The first of them is Julia, the twenty-three-year-old married friend of Julia's mother, who takes it upon herself to teach the sixteen-year-old Juan 'the rudiments of love', by which Julia means 'the seraph way of those above' ((I, 85). Julia has a confidence in the purity of her feelings that invites a knowing smile:

> And then there are such things as love divine,
>   Bright and immaculate, unmix'd and pure,
> Such as the angels think so very fine,
>   And matrons, who would be no less secure,
> Platonic, perfect, 'just such love as mine'.   (I, 79)

Thus Julia thought, '[a]nd so I'd have her think, were I the man / On whom her reveries celestial ran'. Her large, dark eyes flash, revealing

>   something in them which was not desire,
> But would have been, perhaps, but for the soul
> Which struggled through and chasten'd down the whole.   (I, 60)

Julia is so charming in her ignorance of her own motives that readers should feel tempted to resist the pun in the final word of the stanza, especially those readers aware that the same pun, later in the poem, will be applied to the egregious Russian empress, but to refuse the pun is to reveal oneself as a reader who has been infected by Julia's own naivety.

Julia diverts attention from the lower part of her body, from everything below the waist, and the poem slyly imitates her. She is introduced in two stanzas, the first of which (I, 60) focuses on her eye, and the second of which (I, 61) also restricts the reader's attention to her head – her 'glossy hair', her 'brow', her 'eyebrow', her 'cheek' – before taking note of her stature, which is 'tall – I hate a dumpy woman'. Gradually, as the canto proceeds, the gaze moves down her body. By stanza 71 it has arrived at her hand, which withdraws itself from Juan's leaving a 'little pressure' so 'slight' as to make one almost doubt that the two hands had touched. The world turns upon its axis, Byron remarks at the beginning of the second canto, '[a]nd all mankind turn with it, heads or tails' (II, 4). In the poem's first canto, the poem's focus gradually shifts from the one to the other, from heads to tails. When Juan walks through the cork forests his mind is occupied by philosophical speculations of the kind brought on by puberty until those thoughts are arrested by the thought of 'Donna Julia's eyes' (I, 92). But on the sixth of June ('I like to be particular in dates') it all changes. He sits with Julia in a garden bower as the sun sets and the moon rises, one of his hands playing with the tangles of her hair, while the other is clasped by Julia's 'with a pure Platonic squeeze' (I, 111), until the hand moves from her hair to her bosom, to her waist,

> And then – God knows what next – I can't go on:
> I'm almost sorry that I e'er begun.   (I, 115)

The poem decorously averts its eyes as Juan and Julia consummate their love, and rejoins them only in November, when Julia's maid, Antonia, interrupts the young couple as they lie together in Julia's marital bed to warn them that Julia's fifty-year-old husband Don Alfonso is knocking thunderously at the door with 'more than half the city at his back' (I, 117). Don Alfonso and his servants burst into the room and conduct a thorough search:

> Under the bed they search'd, and there they found –
> No matter what – it was not that they sought.   (I, 144)

A year after the canto was published Murray asked Byron if he remembered 'L'Avanture [sic] du pot de chambre'. He was referring to an incident that took place in Lady Oxford's boudoir, and had been, Byron recalled, 'very laughable at the time'. Queen Caroline, then the Princess of Wales, had tripped over a chamber pot as she came into the room ('a minute sooner she might have stumbled over something still more awkward'): 'How the *Porcelain* came to be there I cannot conceive – and remember asking Lady O[xford] afterwards – who laid the blame on the Servants.'[51] It may have been a memory of this episode that prompted Byron to have Alfonso's servants discover a chamber pot under Julia's bed. But in any case the two incidents are 'laughable' for the same reason, because the presence of the chamber pot acts as so lively a reminder that women cannot live, as Julia had aspired to do, a Platonic life of the mind. Women, just as much as men, have bodily functions that have to be attended to. As the bedroom is searched, Juan lies concealed beneath the bedclothes, squeezed between Julia and Antonia (Antonia is pretending that she had been sharing her mistress's bed), in a position that can only serve to reinforce his knowledge that women just as much as men have tails.

Juan and Julia discover each other's bodies, which they are only freed to do once they have recognised that their love for one another is not Platonic. It is a lesson that Juan and Haidée do not need. When Haidée finds Juan washed up on the beach of her father's island, he is, after all, quite naked, and although she is 'shock'd', compassion quickly overcomes pudeur. She cannot countenance the thought of a 'stranger dying with so white a skin' (II, 129). When Julia is first introduced the reader's attention never drops below her face, but Haidée is from the first represented at full length, from 'the auburn of her hair' (II, 116) to her toes – 'what was shocking, / Her small snow feet had slippers, but no stocking' (II, 121). Even when she is more formally dressed, her feet remain visible: her 'orange silk full Turkish trowsers' fall around 'the prettiest ancle in the world' (III, 72). The love between Juan and Julia is a comedy. It is even, at its climax, a bedroom farce. But the love that Juan and Haidée share is pastoral, which is why their love, unlike Juan and Julia's, can be consummated onstage. When they clasp each other in an embrace that ends 'in broken gasps', they are contemplated as if they were statues. They 'form a group that's quite antique, / Half naked, loving, natural, and Greek' (II, 194). They are presented as a sculptural group, which is to say they are represented as nude not as naked. The reader's gaze is cool and detached rather than voyeuristic. The stanza invites us to inspect the pair as if we were connoisseurs.

Don Juan celebrates difference, but in this episode the rule of difference is suspended.[52] Juan and Haidée are bound to each other by similarity: 'Each was the other's mirror.' When they gaze each in the other's eyes the spark of joy that they see belongs to either of them or both. The 'brightness was but the reflection / Of their exchanging glances of affection' (IV, 13). Men and women in *Don Juan* speak different languages, but language cannot separate Juan and Haidée because they have no language in common.[53] He speaks Spanish, she speaks Romaic, so that they can communicate with one another only by sound, in a language like birdsong (IV, 14), a language in which sound and meaning are one and the same. It is an Adamic language that by a benign magic has survived the fall, a language that is not founded, as all human languages are, on phonetic difference. Juan learns a little Romaic, but even on their last night together, when Haidée murmurs in her sleep, her speech remains for him a 'wordless music' (IV, 29).[54] In their love flesh and soul are joined in a marriage that seems quite immune from the cynicism with which, all through the poem, Byron views that institution. They remain tethered to the world of the poem by their circumstances. They owe their life of ease and plenty to the activities of Lambro, Haidée's piratical slave-trading father, and they live their life of love surrounded by a tribe of hangers-on who seem much the same as hangers-on anywhere, caring only that the 'capon's fat' and 'wash'd down' with good wine (III, 45). But they are tethered to the world still more tightly by the narrator, who locates the value of their love in its removal from the world that he and, he assumes, his readers inhabit. They offer a respite from an 'old world' grown 'dull', a world that has made us

> sick of its hack sounds and sights,
> Intrigues, adventures of the common school,
>   Its petty passions, marriages, and flights,
> Where Hymen's torch but brands one strumpet more,
> Whose husband only knows her not a wh – re.   (IV, 17)

They have read 'no novels', and so they enjoy by right of nature what in anyone else would be 'a factitious state, / An opium dream of too much youth and reading' (IV, 19). The thought absolves the lovers of bad faith only by convicting in their stead the poem's readers, that is, by convicting all of us who have been entranced by the tale of 'the faithful and the fairy pair' (IV, 18). Byron's only wish for Juan and Haidée is that they die young, and be spared a 'long and snake-like life of dull decay' (IV, 9), and in Haidée's case at least the wish is granted. Death frees her from the narrative circumstances that had tied her to a tawdry world. She survives as pure lyric, her name sighed over by 'many a Greek maid in a loving song' (IV, 73). Juan by contrast is shipped to Constantinople where he rejoins a world in which flesh and spirit are joined together in the kind of fractious marriage more typical of the poem. This is the world registered most sharply by double entendre. Dudu is put to bed with Juan, who has been introduced to the harem in his female disguise, and during the night the other women are woken by her scream. She had been disturbed, she explains, by a dream in which she bit into an apple from which '[a] bee flew out and stung her to the heart' (VI, 77). After hearing her explanation the Mother of the Maids classes the dream amongst all the other 'stories of a cock and bull' that she has heard (VI, 80). But it is when Juan travels from Petersburg to England, and finds himself in a country the inhabitants of which pretend that the mind and the body have nothing to do with one another, that double entendre becomes the verbal device that defines a nation.

The English cantos have three heroines, of which the least, 'her frolic Grace – Fitz-Fulke' (XVI, 123), has double entendre written into her very name. The second heroine, Aurora Raby, is immune from the device, quarantined from it by her unfeigned innocence. The poem's women are like the sexual act, thoughts of which they all of them inspire. Sex is at once repetitious and always different, and so is the sequence of Juan's women. Aurora, as Byron points out, is a repetition of Haidée. Both are innocent, which is why both are spared double entendre. 'Each was radiant in her proper sphere', but Haidée is the child of nature, Aurora of civilisation: 'the difference in them / Was such as lies between a flower and gem' (XV, 58). But Aurora is a repetition, too, of Juan's ten-year-old ward Leila, another character preserved from double entendre by her innocence. They have the same way of regarding the world, 'with small surprise', taking no undue interest in the 'novelties' that fascinate most 'people of condition' (XII, 27). Aurora is older, of course, already marriageable, but she is '[e]arly in years, and yet more infantine / In figure' (XV, 45). Her surname, as Lady Adelaide points out, rhymes with 'baby' (XV, 49). And Leila and Aurora are alike too in the attachment they feel for the religion in which they were raised. Aurora remains a Catholic because she 'deem'd that fallen worship far more dear / Perhaps because 'twas fallen' (XV, 46), and, despite Juan's hopes for Leila's 'salvation', '[t]he little Turk refused to be converted' (X, 55). It is the Lady Adeline Amundeville, the shadow of Juan's first love, Julia, who serves as the focus for the play of double entendre in the English cantos.

Adeline and Julia both succeed in disguising from themselves the nature of their feelings for Juan. Adeline 'knew not her own heart' (XIV, 91), which had been Julia's predicament too. Adeline, like Julia, is Juan's senior, if only by six weeks (XIV, 51), but she has been married for three years, which, she feels, gives her the right to offer Juan the benefit of her matronly advice. Adeline has an absolute trust in her own wifely honour: 'Chaste was she, to detraction's desperation, / And wedded unto one she had loved well.' Both she and her husband seem armoured against any hint of scandal, '[s]he in her virtue, he in his hauteur' (XIII, 14). Lord Henry is clearly older than his wife but there is no discrepancy in age of the kind that accounts for the susceptibilities of Julia, a woman of twenty-three, married

to Alfonso, a man of fifty. There is 'no great disparity of years' between
Lord Henry and his wife' (XIV, 87). Something, nevertheless, is missing
from the marriage:

> But there was something wanting on the whole –
>   I don't know what, and therefore cannot tell –
> Which pretty women – the sweet souls! – call *Soul.*
>   *Certes* it was not body; he was well
> Proportion'd, as a poplar or a pole,
>   A handsome man, that human miracle;
> And in each circumstance of love or war
> Had still preserved his perpendicular.   (XIV, 71)

Lord Henry's ability to sustain 'his perpendicular' and the fine proportions
of his pole only serve to alert the reader to the double meaning of the
'whole' that leaves Adeline feeling that there was something missing from
her marriage. Like all women she is in quest of a 'something all-sufficient
for the *heart*': 'But how to fill up that same vacant part? / There lies the rub'
(XIV, 74). Adeline is a delightful woman, 'the glass of all that's fair' (XIII,
13), the prototype of Trollope's Glencora Palliser. Byron's puns desecrate
her, like the 'huge tits' and 'fissured crotch' scrawled on the laughing girl
advertising 'Sunny Prestatyn' in Larkin's poem. But Larkin's graffito artist
'Titch Thomas' finds his only inspiration in vicious envy. Byron's smut is
less violent, and it is also more serious, because Byron is alert to the damage
women suffer when they allow themselves to believe that the only vacancy
they feel that needs filling is a vacancy in the heart. The rhyme that Byron
favours for 'whole' in *Don Juan* is 'soul'. He uses it twelve times in the
poem. It is a rhyme that encapsulates the contest between cant and cunt on
which the whole poem turns.

CHAPTER 5

Allusions Private and Inglorious

Byron's friends agreed that *Don Juan* was unpublishable. Hobhouse was with Scrope Davies when he read through the manuscript of the first two cantos, and every now and then one or other of them exclaimed, 'it will be impossible to publish this'. It was not that they thought ill of the poem. They were conscious of its 'extraordinary merit', at one in their admiration of its 'genius, wit, poetry, satire, and so forth'. Hobhouse even allowed that Byron might have discovered his 'real forte' in the 'singular style' of the new poem. But both men doubted whether 'any amputation' could render it fit for publication since 'the objectionable parts are in point of wit humour & poetry the very best beyond all doubt of the whole poem'. Douglas Kinnaird had at first seen no objection to publishing, but he soon came round to Hobhouse's and Scrope Davies's point of view. It was John Hookham Frere whose *Monks and Giants* had first suggested to Byron how the ottava rima of the burlesque Italian poets might be imported into English, but Frere agreed with Byron's other friends. The publication of *Don Juan*, Frere thought, would go far to destroy the literary reputation that Byron enjoyed. There were many objections to the poem. There was the 'indecency' ('a whole stanza on the origin of the pox') that would serve only to confirm 'all the idle stories' about the tenor of Byron's 'Venetian life'. There were 'the flings at religion'. The parody on the commandments ('Thou shalt believe in Milton, Dryden, Pope; / Thou shalt not set up Wordsworth, Coleridge, Southey' (I, 205)) was 'surely inadmissable' even though it was 'one of the best things in the poem or indeed in all that sort of poetry'. And it was in any case unworthy of Byron to engage in literary skirmishes with 'such wretched antagonists' as the Lake Poets. But there was one overriding objection to the poem. Hobhouse could not brook 'the sarcasms against the lady of Seaham', that is, against Annabella Milbanke, Byron's estranged wife. Annabella's family house was at Seaham in County Durham.[1]

The scandal of the publication of *Don Juan* was, as Clara Tuite points out, inseparable from the scandal of the breakdown of Byron's marriage.[2] In the first canto of the poem Byron held up to ridicule the woman he derisively referred to in his letters as the Princess of Parallelograms ('Her favourite science was the mathematical' (I, 12)).[3] When Hobhouse showed him the manuscript, Thomas Moore took the same view as Hobhouse. For all that it included 'some highly beautiful passages & some highly humourous ones' *Don Juan* 'as a whole' was clearly unpublishable:

> – Don Juan's mother is Lady Byron – and not only her learning, but various other points about her ridiculed – he talks of her favourite dress being *dimity* (which is the case) – dimity rhyming very comically to sublimity – & the conclusion of one stanza is 'I hate a dumpy woman' – meaning Lady B. again – This would disgust the Public beyond endurance – [4]

And so it did. The first canto, according to the *Edinburgh Monthly Review*, was 'scandalously directed against *her* towards whom, as he ought *ever* to have breathed the purest tenderness, he ought now to make his life a course of fond and affectionate reparation'.[5] J. G. Lockhart, writing in *Blackwood's*, doubted his readers would credit 'that the odious malignity of this man's bosom should have carried him so far, as to make him commence a filthy and impious poem, with an elaborate satire on the character and manners of his wife'.[6] Byron objected vociferously to such accusations. When Murray produced proofs of the first canto, Hobhouse added comments in the margins. 'This is so very pointed', he remarked when Inez 'call'd some druggists and physicians / And tried to prove her loving lord was mad' (I, 27). Byron crossed out Hobhouse's comment, and retorted, 'If people make applications it is their own fault',[7] and some years later he incorporated his objection in the poem itself. He protested against the habit of '[r]eaping allusions private and inglorious / Where none were dreamt of' (XIII, 25). His readers should recollect that 'the work is only fiction': 'I sing of neither mine nor me, / Though every scribe, in some slight turn of diction, / Will hunt allusions never *meant*.'[8] He is not given, he assures his readers, to making veiled remarks: 'when I speak, I *don't hint*, but *speak out*' (XI, 88). But Byron is never more disingenuous than when insisting on his own candour. Even he could scarcely pretend that when Lady Adeline wonders whether the young Miss Millpond might be a suitable match for Juan it had never crossed his mind how closely the name chimes with Miss Milbanke, the woman he had married:

> There was Miss Millpond, smooth as summer's sea,
>   That usual paragon, an only daughter,
> Who seem'd the cream of equanimity

> Till skimm'd – and then there was some milk and water,
> With a slight shade of Blue too it might be,
> 　　Beneath the surface; but what did it matter?
> Love 's riotous, but marriage should have quiet,
> And being consumptive, live on a milk diet.　　　　(XV, 41)

It might be objected that the personal allusions are merely local. After the first canto there is little to put the reader in mind of Lady Byron until this single stanza in the fifteenth. Byron had first chosen as the epigraph for the poem a phrase taken from Horace, 'domestica facta'. 'Do not have this motto', Hobhouse advised. Byron's first impulse was to defend his choice. The phrase, he told Hobhouse, 'merely meant – *common life* – which I presume was Horace's meaning'.[9] Byron was right, but Hobhouse was right too to anticipate how the phrase would be interpreted, and Byron conceded as much. 'Agreed', he wrote on the proof against Hobhouse's comment, and the epigraph was changed.[10] But, predictably, the alteration did nothing to discourage Byron's readers from understanding the poem in the light of the poet's domestic circumstances.

After the first canto, Donna Inez, Juan's mother, disappears from the poem, except for a brief appearance in Canto X, when she writes to Juan in St Petersburg, to advise him that he has a brother '[b]orn in a second wedlock', and to congratulate him on winning the favour of the Empress Catherine. Donna Inez trusts to the Empress's age and the icy Russian climate to guard against any scandalous rumour that Catherine might feel for Juan anything more than a '*maternal* love' (X, 31–3). But even in the absence of Donna Inez, all through the sixteen cantos of the poem the reader is reminded repeatedly of Byron's marital misfortunes. When Lambro returns home he has to make his way through a crowd of guests – his daughter, who believes him to be dead is giving a feast in Juan's honour – and as he enters his house the forgotten father morphs into the abandoned husband:

> To find our hearthstone turn'd into a tomb,
> 　　And round its once warm precincts palely lying
> The ashes of our hopes, is a deep grief,
> Beyond a single gentleman's belief.　　　　(X, 51)

'I'm a plain man, and in a single station', the narrator observes in the first canto, and the remark only serves to draw attention to Byron's own experiences of married life even without the celebrated couplet that it introduces:

> But – Oh! ye lords of ladies intellectual,
> Inform us truly, have they not hen-peck'd you all.　　　　(I, 21)

Just three weeks after his marriage Byron had fondly described himself in a letter to Lady Melbourne as 'chicken-pecked' (he had good-naturedly agreed to accompany his wife on a visit to her parents at Seaham).[11] In this case the letter came first, but it is sometimes the other way around. When Donna Inez leaves him, Don Jóse finds himself '[s]tanding alone beside his desolate hearth, / Where all his household gods lay shiver'd round him' (I, 36). It was shortly after he had written these lines that Byron recalled how, when his wife abandoned him and returned to her parental home, he had been left standing alone at 13 Piccadilly Terrace, in the house the newly married pair had shared, 'upon [his] desolate hearth, with [his] household gods shivered around [him]'.[12] The animus against his wife extended to his mother-in-law. A list of the 'paltry things' that test a man's patience begins with a 'scolding wife' and reaches its climax when Byron calls to mind '[a] bad old woman making a worse will, / Which leaves you minus of the cash you counted / As certain' (VI, 21).[13] It might even be that the very greatest poems, as Byron suggests not quite facetiously, have their origin in unhappy marriages: 'Dante's Beatrice and Milton's Eve / Were not drawn from their spouses, you conceive' (III, 10). It is presumptuous of Byron to compare his own poem with *The Divine Comedy* and *Paradise Lost*, except that all three are the work of poets 'hapless in their nuptials' (III, 10). *Don Juan* may be a poem of a kind quite different from *Paradise Lost*, but their poets have something at least in common, 'For the first Mrs. Milton left his house' (III, 91), just as Lady Byron had left Byron's. It is still more significant that Byron's focus all through the poem on the breakdown of his own marriage anticipates the great domestic epics that the novelists produced later in the century – *Madame Bovary*, *Middlemarch*, *Anna Karenina* – although in them it is true the character hapless in nuptials is more often a woman, like Donna Julia, or Gulbeyaz, or Lady Adeline Amundeville. As George Eliot remarks, the epic of the nineteenth century would be a 'home epic', and it would take as its epic action the slow progress of a marriage, 'the gradual conquest or irremediable loss of that complete union which makes the advancing years a climax, and age the harvest of sweet memories in common'.[14] *Don Juan* is the first such epic the century produced.

The first readers of *Don Juan* were so alert to the personal allusions in the poem because they took into account Byron's previous offences. On 2 April 1816, two poems by Byron, in one of which he bids a tender farewell to his wife and in the other launches an astonishingly virulent attack on her governess, were published in *The Champion* under the heading 'Lord Byron's Poems On His Own Domestic Circumstances'.

Byron had not authorised the publication, but he ought to have foreseen it. At his request Murray had printed off fifty copies of the poems and they had circulated widely. The mischief was exacerbated by William Hone, who reprinted both poems, padded out to a pamphlet by the addition of a few more of Byron's shorter pieces. Lady Blessington delivered her verdict on behalf of all women: Byron had chosen to make an appeal for 'public sympathy, by the publication of verses which ought only to have met the eye of her to whom they were addressed'. The publication of the poems was an outrage to 'that delicacy, that shrinks from and shuns publicity, so inherent in the female heart'.[15] In 'Fare thee well' Byron is artfully magnanimous, acknowledging his failings ('Though my many faults defaced me'), and confessing a love for his wife that remains undimmed even after she has vacated the marital bed and removed their infant daughter from his care. In 'A Sketch from Private Life', Mrs Clermont, loathed by Byron for encouraging his wife in her obduracy, is excoriated in fifty-two couplets magnificent in their sustained venom. Byron finds a place in *Don Juan* for his fury against Mrs Clermont as well as his resentment of his wife. He is against burning witches, but allows that 'b – ches – who create / Mischief in families, as some know or knew' should be, if not burned, at least singed, 'but slightly, let me state' (XVII, 7). Byron describes himself in 'Fare thee well' as 'disunited', by which he means separated from his wife and his child, but the two poems suggest a more radical disunion. It is not so much that he feels differently about the two women he addresses. It is rather that the difference between the poems allows him to register his own wildly divergent responses to the breakdown of his marriage. In one poem Byron responds with tender regret, in the other with an unchecked fury of rage and contempt. But the poems have in common a willingness to make public the kind of feelings to which most of us would allow only private expression. They are indecorous poems, and John Scott, the editor of *The Champion*, only drew attention to their indecorum when he laid them before the readership of a weekly newspaper, confident that his readers would take a lively if prurient interest in Byron's domestic mishaps. But it was Byron who had given him the opportunity to do so, and by publishing *Don Juan* he compounded the offence. As an early reviewer of *Don Juan* put it, one of the reasons that the publication of the poem was so regrettable was that it was a poem in which Byron had opened up to public scrutiny 'the privacy of his domestic life'.[16]

England, as Byron points out in *Don Juan*, is a 'newspaper' country, which means that it is also a 'low', 'humdrum', 'law-suit' sort of a place

(XII, 65). The scandal of Julia's affair with Juan and the divorce that followed were reported 'in the English newspapers, of course' (I, 188). Newspapers just as much as poems or novels gave the age its character, and one crucial aspect of that character was the dismantling of the distinction between the public and the private most luridly exemplified, as Byron notes, in the detailed reports in the English newspapers of divorce cases.[17] Byron was a victim of the new refusal to respect the boundaries separating the public from the private,[18] but he was also one of those principally responsible for dismantling that barrier, and never more outrageously than in the sly allusions that recur throughout *Don Juan* to the breakdown of his own marriage. In the preface to Cantos VI, VII, and VIII of his poem, Byron excuses his attack on Castlereagh by insisting, unconvincingly, that the stanzas had been written 'some time before his decease'. Furthermore, his attack, he insists, has to do only with the public man: 'That he was an amiable man in *private* life, may or may not be true, but with this the Public have nothing to do.'[19] Byron maintains here, or at least he claims to, the traditional distinction between the public and the private spheres, except that the attack on Castlereagh's ministerial misdemeanours reaches its crescendo when Byron turns his attention from Castlereagh's policies to his suicide. Had he been a radical and cut his throat he would have been buried at a crossroads with a stake through his heart: 'But the Minister was an elegant Lunatic – a sentimental Suicide – he merely cut the "carotid artery" (blessings on their learning) and lo! the Pageant, and the Abbey! and "the syllables of Dolour yelled forth" by the Newspapers.' Byron levels his attack, he might claim, not on Castlereagh for having killed himself but on the hypocrisy of the public response to his suicide. But any such claim would be disingenuous, as he reveals when he refers to 'that long Spout / Of blood and water, leaden Castlereagh' (IX, 50), and still more explicitly in the following canto when the late foreign secretary becomes '[c]arotid-artery-cutting Castlereagh!' (X, 59). But Byron's hatred for Castlereagh, who had been Secretary of State for Ireland during the 1798 rebellion, and who, together with Metternich, was the principal architect of the post-Napoleonic European order, was public in its origin even if it becomes uncomfortably personal in its expression.[20] The case is quite different with two other public figures held up to public contempt in *Don Juan*. Sir Samuel Romilly and Henry Brougham were both of them reforming Whigs, men that Byron might reasonably be expected to embrace as political allies. Romilly's wife died on 29 October 1818, and three days later, overcome by grief, Romilly took his own life. Like

Castlereagh, he cut his throat. He is commemorated in the first canto in a stanza that couples him with Donna Inez:

> Some women use their tongues – she look'd a lecture,
>   Each eye a sermon, and her brow a homily,
> An all-in-all sufficient self-director,
>   Like the lamented late Sir Samuel Romilly,
> The Law's expounder, and the State's corrector,
>   Whose suicide was almost an anomaly –
> One sad example more, that 'All is vanity,'
> (The jury brought their verdict in 'Insanity').   (1, 15)

It is not a casual comparison. Donna Inez shares her talent for looking a lecture with Lady Byron, and Sir Samuel Romilly had roused Byron's rancour by offering Byron's wife his legal advice even though, as Byron believed, he had secured Romilly's services himself. 'He was one of Miss Milbanke's advisers', and his death did nothing to assuage Byron's fury: 'I never would have forgiven him living & will not affect to pity him dead.'[21] His grudge against Brougham was even more bitter. Byron seems never to have discovered that Brougham was responsible for the scathing review of *Hours of Idleness*, which prompted Byron to write *English Bards and Scotch Reviewers*, but Brougham had, Byron believed, been a principal source of the 'vague and extraordinary reports' (in William Hone's phrase[22]) of Byron's behaviour that had circulated through London in the early months of 1816. Brougham had been visiting Geneva when Byron was living in the Villa Diodati in close neighbourhood with the Shelleys. His intimacy with Mary and Percy Shelley and Claire Clairmont prompted scandalous rumours amongst the expatriate community, and Byron believed that Brougham had carried those rumours home with him and spread them all over London. Byron always claimed whenever he thought of returning to England that a chief inducement was the opportunity it would afford him to issue a challenge to Brougham. He was persuaded to omit from the first canto seven stanzas of furious denunciation:[23]

> Bully in Senate, Skulker in the field,
>   The Adulterer's advocate, when duly feed,
> The libeller's gratis Counsel, dirty Shield
>   Which Law affords to many a dirty deed.

The adulterer that Brougham spoke for, it is worth noticing, was Princess Caroline, and the libeller that he defended free of charge was Leigh Hunt. Byron was sympathetic to Caroline, who had been kind to him in London when the two met, and he was sorry when she died.[24] He admired Leigh

Hunt so greatly as a man who had risked his freedom by publishing a vigorous attack on the Prince Regent that he visited him in prison.[25] But in his fury against Brougham all that friendship and admiration is swept aside. In the autumn of 1822, when he was at work on Canto X, Byron could restrain himself no longer:

> A legal broom 's a moral chimney-sweeper,
> And that's the reason he himself 's so dirty;
> The endless soot bestows a tint far deeper
> Than can be hid by altering his shirt.   (X, 15)

Byron claimed good authority for his outpourings of spleen. Like Johnson, 'the great moralist', 'he liked an honest hater'[26] (XIII, 7). But Byron's hatreds, unlike Johnson's, are oddly compounded of principle and pique. Moral indignation can scarcely be distinguished from personal resentment.

Don Juan was dedicated to Robert Southey in seventeen octaves that Byron was persuaded to omit when the first two cantos of the poem were published in 1819. In the event, the Dedication was not made public until 1832. Byron chose Southey as his principal target, because Southey was the poet laureate and hence the proper representative of the poets of the day ('BOB SOUTHEY! You're a poet – poet Laureate'), because he was a political turncoat, an 'epic renegade' who 'turn'd out a Tory at / Last', and because he was a leading member of the school of modern poets that Byron most despised, the Lakers, one of the triumvirate of poets who had chosen to keep themselves to themselves by taking up residence at 'Keswick'. But he was also chosen because Byron had a grudge against him. Byron had serious disagreements with Wordsworth's and Coleridge's poetic principles, but between him and Southey it was personal. Byron thought that Southey, like Brougham, had injured him, and in much the same way. In 1813, when he and Southey were first introduced, Byron had been impressed. 'His talents', Byron noted in his journal, were 'of the first order': 'he is the only existing entire man of letters'.[27] He was in addition 'the best looking bard' Byron had seen for some time.[28] But by 1818 he felt very differently. He explained the matter in a letter to Hobhouse:

> I will tell you why. – The Son of a Bitch on his return from Switzerland two years ago – said that Shelley and I 'had formed a League of Incest and practised our precepts with &c,' – he lied like a rascal – for they *were not Sisters* – *one* being Godwin's daughter by Mary Wollstonecraft – and the other the daughter of the present Mrs G[odwin] by a *former* husband.[29]

Byron's refutation of the charge is oddly legalistic, but the bitterness of his resentment is apparent. It extended even to Southey's family. Jeffrey, writing in the *Edinburgh*, granted Byron the right of retaliation against Southey, but adds, 'he had no right to say any thing of Mr Southey's wife'.³⁰ He was thinking of the stanza in Canto III, in which Byron recalls Coleridge's unfulfilled project to establish with Southey an ideal common-wealth, a pantisocracy, in America, on the banks of the Susquehanna, a project only feasible if the two poets had wives to accompany them. In pursuance of their scheme, as Byron puts it in the poem, 'he and Southey, following the same path, / Espoused two partners (milliners of Bath)' (III, 93). Sarah and Edith Fricker were neither of them milliners. They were educated young women, products of the school run by Hannah More, who had supported themselves after their father became bankrupt by working as seamstresses. But Jeffrey's point is that they were private citizens, and should not have been held up to public ridicule in the course of a literary squabble in which they had taken no part. In his preface to *A Vision of Judgement* Southey had categorised Byron, without naming him – he was referred to only 'by innuendo', as Jeffrey puts it – as an author who had by the publication of 'a lascivious poem' established himself at the head of a 'Satanic school' of poetry that threatened at once the political and the moral well-being of the nation. Byron, Jeffrey allowed, had a right to reply, but by implicating Mrs Southey in the dispute he had disgraced himself. Jeffrey's conclusion was withering, 'We rather think it had been better, after all, to be the founder of the Satanic School, than the Master of the John Bulls, Beacons, and Sentinels.'

John Bull, *The Beacon*, and *The Sentinel* were Tory weeklies.³¹ Byron risked being associated with them not because of their political complexion (although Jeffrey must have known that Byron would find it especially galling for his name to be coupled with Tory periodicals) but because they were scurrilous. They were publications that traded in 'personalities': that is, they extended their attacks on their political opponents from their political principles to their private lives, even to their personal appearance. They behaved, in other words, exactly as Byron had when he supplemented his attack on Coleridge and Southey as political apostates by ridiculing them for their choice of wives. Byron's second poetic commandment had forbidden the setting up of Wordsworth, Coleridge, and Southey as poetic idols, not just because they wrote in accordance with poetic principles that Byron rejected but because 'the first is crazed beyond all hope / The second drunk, the third so quaint and mouthey' (I, 205). All three charges, but the second in particular, the reference to Coleridge as a drunk, seem to warrant Jeffrey's charge that Byron had descended to personalities, and in doing so had expunged the distinction between poetry and gutter journalism. The man 'once hailed as the greatest of our living poets' had taken 'leave of Childe Harold to ally himself with Don Juan!'[32] By writing that poem Byron had put himself on a level with people like Theodore Hooke, editor of *John Bull*. But it was not *John Bull* or *The Beacon* or *The Sentinel* that Jeffrey had principally in mind. The publication most often denounced in 1822 for its resort to personalities was *Blackwood's Edinburgh Magazine*. Jeffrey refuses to refer to it directly because *Blackwood's* was a publication, Jeffrey had decided, that would never be named in the *Edinburgh Review*.[33]

The tactic was not lost on the magazine. Jeffrey's remarks were picked up in the issue for May 1822, in an episode of the *Noctes Ambrosianae*, the irregular series in which *Blackwood's* contributors and *Blackwood's* characters met together in the private room of an Edinburgh tavern to discuss the latest publications over supper and whisky punch.[34] Dr Wodrow welcomes Jeffrey's intervention:

> Well, now, I must say that I read that passage with delight: there is no doubt that Lord Byron is very much to blame, if it really be so, which I am no judge of, that he was the first who wrote in a personal manner. It was introducing a dangerous – a deadly trick.

Andrew Wylie is more sceptical: 'Does Mr Jeffrey really charge Lord Byron with being the author and instigator of the sin of personality?' Sir Andrew suspects that Byron may have had predecessors. In a recent issue the magazine had defended its own practice by appealing to the example of Dryden and Pope. In *Absalom and Achitophel* and *The Dunciad*, 'every verse . . . is a drop of the genuine aquafortis of personality'.[35] Milton might have been added to the list, the Milton of the prose essays with their furious attacks on Salmasius (in *Don Juan*, it is worth remembering, Byron had issued the commandment 'Thou shalt believe in Milton, Dryden, Pope' (I, 205)). But on this occasion Christopher North places Byron's personalities in a far longer tradition. It is a device, he points out, that was only inherited by Milton, Dryden, Butler, Swift, Pope, and Arbuthnot. It had passed down to them from Aristophanes, Horace, and Cicero. In Christopher North's account the history of personality becomes a complete history of satire, and a history of the better part of all literature, both classical and modern.

Byron admired *Blackwood's*, despite its Tory politics. He suggested to Murray that 'Augustus Darvell', his unfinished short story, might be published 'in the Edinburgh magazine', and he insisted that he liked and admired John Wilson, one of its leading writers, even when he thought Wilson responsible for the magazine's 'Remarks on Don Juan', a paper that incorporated a fairly comprehensive attack on Byron's moral character.[36] He was so indulgent, surely, because he recognised that *Blackwood's* responded more intelligently to *Don Juan* than any of the other periodicals. In 1821, J. G. Lockhart had published a pamphlet, *Letter to the Right Hon. Lord Byron by John Bull*, that summed up the magazine's complex and contradictory reaction to the poem. Lockhart's pamphlet was anonymous, and his authorship was not fully established until the twentieth century. Byron had three suspects, 'one is *Hobhouse* – the other – Mr. Peacock (a very clever fellow) and lastly Israeli', although he also thought it just possible that it had been written by Washington Irving. Byron's suspicions are oddly scattered. Isaac d'Israeli was a fervent admirer, Hobhouse was his closest friend, and Peacock had lampooned him as Mr Cypress in *Nightmare Abbey*. But in their diversity the cast of suspects rather accurately reflects the complexity of Lockhart's response to the poem. Byron's response to the pamphlet was enthusiastic: 'it is diabolically *well* written – & full of fun and ferocity – I must forgive the dog whoever he is'.[37] *Blackwood's* was so preoccupied with *Don Juan* because it saw in the poem its own reflection, and the tolerance with which Byron regarded the magazine's erratic and sometimes violent responses to his poem suggests that he too recognised in the magazine his own mirror image.

What Byron found there most obviously, of course, were personalities, attacks on the magazine's opponents that darted unpredictably between the personal and the principled. Two of the chief targets were Leigh Hunt and William Hazlitt. Hunt and Hazlitt were competitors, rivals of the magazine in the field of periodical literature, and they were ideological enemies, spokesmen for the political views that the magazine most reprobated. Hazlitt was attacked not just as a radical but as a man whose face was pimpled. Leigh Hunt was ridiculed not only for his politics but also for his enthusiasm for tea-drinking, his penchant for wearing yellow breeches, and (although the charge was only hinted) as a man unnaturally fond of his sister-in-law (the fury with which Lockhart denounces Hunt for having chosen in the *Story of Rimini* a plot that hinges on the incestuous relationship between Paolo and his sister-in-law becomes a good deal more pointed if one allows it a personal application). In much the same way Keats was held up to contempt both as an incompetent versifier and as a man who had been apprentice to an apothecary. The magazine was aware of the outrage that such attacks provoked: 'Were anyone, for instance, to drop a word about Hazlitt's face being as thick-studded with pimples as a tumbler of soda water is with air-bubbles, or to hint that John Keates was a smart hand at a glister, you have no notion what a lamentable squeaking would be sent forth.'[38] Hazlitt's pimples, like Hunt's yellow breeches, were inventions of the magazine, but it was of no avail to point this out because the magazine would claim in its defence that it was metaphorically if not literally true that Hunt wore yellow breeches and that Hazlitt's face was pimpled. No one understood the method better than Byron: 'And, after all, what is a lie? 'Tis but / The truth in masquerade' (XI, 37). When Byron read Friedrich Schlegel he was reminded of Hazlitt, and the Hazlitt he was reminded of was Hazlitt as he had been represented in *Blackwood's*: Schlegel is 'like Hazlitt, in English, who *talks pimples* – a red and white corruption rising up (in little imitation of mountains upon maps), but containing nothing, and discharging nothing, except their own humours'.[39]

   When Byron denies the *Blackwood's* charge that *Don Juan* begins with 'an elaborate satire on the character and manners of his wife', he does so very much in the *Blackwood's* manner. If he depicts a Corsair, Byron complains, the Corsair is taken for a self-portrait, and if 'a disagreeable, casuistical, and by no means respectable female pedant' appears in a work 'by no means ascertained to be [his] production', 'it is set down for [his] wife'. Byron begins by denying any resemblance, but goes on to admit that he has made use of 'real circumstances' in devising the plot of his poem, and even of events that have occurred 'in [his] own family'. Nevertheless, he insists, his characters are not family 'portraits': 'I never would introduce the likenesses of it's living members.'[40] Donna Inez rifles her husband's possessions in search of incriminating documents: she 'open'd certain trunks of books and letters'. It was, as Hobhouse knew, one of the charges that Byron had brought against his wife. 'There is some doubt about this', he wrote in the margin, and Byron replied that the incident was 'poetically true' whether or not it had actually taken place.[41] *Blackwood's* and Byron both delight in fostering a volatile relationship between statements of fact, which may be true or false, and poetic statements to which truth functions do not apply. In *Blackwood's* Hazlitt is at once a rival journalist and a character invented by the magazine, and something very similar might be said of Donna Inez in *Don Juan*, and of Bob Southey too. It is not just that *Blackwood's* and *Don Juan* both dabble in personalities, the personalities, both for the poem and the magazine, are essential to their success. Hazlitt in *Blackwood's* and Donna Inez in *Don Juan* are both fine comic creations, but the comedy would lose much of its zest if Hazlitt had no connection with the saturnine periodical writer who spent his evenings in London drinking in the Cider Cellar, and Donna Inez would not be nearly so funny if she were unrelated to the young mother who had left her poet husband and returned to her parents' house at Seaham. And there is a further point to be made. The magazine and the poem are not just reliant on personalities for their comedy: it is through their personalities that they achieve their timeliness. It is their personalities that establish them as the most complete expressions of the state of the nation at a particular juncture, in the closing years of the Regency and in the early years of the reign of George IV.

These were the years in which publishing became an industry, supplying, through circulating libraries, and the production of a rapidly increasing variety of newspapers, magazines, poems, and novels, the demands of a mass readership that had not existed in the previous century. For the writers of the eighteenth century, their readerships and their social circles were, if not identical, at least continuous one with the other. When, as they so often do, they pause to share their thoughts with their readers, they do so with the unironic intimacy of those confident that they know the kinds of people that they are addressing. The writers of the late Regency preserve the forms of address, but know full well that the literary culture that supported earlier writers in their use was now obsolete. The discrepancy between the intimacy of the address and the blank anonymity of the readership to which the address is made is often exploited in magazines for its comic potential. One of John Wilson's most brilliant papers for *Blackwood's* is entitled 'An Hour's Tete-a-Tete with the Public'.[42] The device was at once taken up in the *London Magazine*. Thomas de Quincey addressed his *Confessions of an English Opium-Eater* (the *Confessions* was first published over two issues of the *London Magazine*) to 'the public (into whose private ear I am confidentially whispering my confessions)', and Janus Weathercock (one of the pseudonyms of T. G. Wainewright), again writing in the *London*, advertised the imminent publication of 'Mr Weathercock's Private Correspondence, Intended for the Public Eye'.[43] In *Don Juan* a very similar paradox defines the poem's relationship with its reader. Byron addresses *Don Juan* to the 'gentle reader! and / Still gentler purchaser!' (I, 221), that is, to a reader with whom his relationship is social and intimate, and yet somehow also economic and anonymous.

Don Juan is addressed, as *Blackwood's* pointed out in its 'Remarks' on the poem, to 'those who are acquainted (as who is not?) with the main incidents in the private life of Lord Byron'.[44] The sentence neatly summarises the peculiar case of a man whose private life had become public property. The poem, as the magazine noticed, repeatedly engineers little collisions between private and public spaces, as when Byron invites the reader to assess the hardships that the shipwrecked Juan underwent by comparing them with 'those related in my grand-dad's Narrative' (II, 132). The phrase positions the reader as a friend of the family, someone acquainted with Byron's grandfather, or as anyone at all who happens to have read the *Narrative* that the Honourable John Byron published in 1768, giving a graphic account of 'the Great Distresses Suffered by Himself and His Companions on the Coast of Patagonia'. Even private reminiscences turn out, on examination, to be less private than might have been supposed. Juan was so good a swimmer that he could have crossed the Hellespont, 'As once (a feat on which ourselves we prided) / Leander, Mr Ekenhead, and I did' (II, 105). Byron had already published in the same volume with *Childe Harold* a poem, 'Written after Swimming from Sestos to Abydos', in which he commemorated his achievement, and attached to it a note describing how on 3 May 1810 he had accomplished the feat accompanied by Mr Ekenhead, a lieutenant serving under Captain Bathurst on the frigate the *Salsette*.[45] Private and public come together poignantly in a single line of the passage in Canto XI in which Byron offers his own brilliant variation of the ubi sunt motif. 'Where are the Lady Carolines and Franceses?' (XI, 80), he asks. Time takes away, and what it takes is never expressed more feelingly than in this line, in which two women that Byron knew well, one of whom, Lady Caroline Lamb, had been his mistress, and the other, Lady Frances Wedderburn Webster, might have been another if Byron had not chosen to spare her, are stripped of the individuality that made them such vivid presences in Byron's life. They become generic, their names reduced to metonyms for the class of women to which they belonged.

In Byron's line the Lady Carolines and Franceses seem interchangeable, but the cases of the two women were quite different. Byron's relationship with Lady Caroline Lamb was notorious, a matter of public scandal, and Caroline Lamb had herself ensured that the scandal reached far beyond the aristocratic circle to which she and Byron belonged, the circle that Byron denominated 'the twice two thousand people bred / By no means to be very wise or witty' (XI, 45). She had commemorated the affair in a novel, *Glenarvon*, making it available to every reader in possession of a ticket for a circulating library. Byron would not have been surprised. Nearly four years earlier he had imagined her publishing his letters to her: 'the Editor of any magazine will treat with her for them on moderate terms'.[46] The fate she chose is one of the many that Byron imagines for women disappointed, as almost all women are, in their marriages:

> Some take a lover, some take drams or prayers,
>   Some mind their household, others dissipation,
> Some run away, and but exchange their cares,
>   Losing the advantage of a virtuous station;
> Few changes e'er can better their affairs,
>   Theirs being an unnatural situation,
> From the dull palace to the dirty hovel:
> Some play the devil, and then write a novel.   (II, 201)

Byron was proud, although also perhaps a little regretful, that he had spared Lady Frances's virtue even though she was the wife of his particular friend, but had their unfulfilled romance been made public the consequences might have been grave. Byron imagined, with his usual bravado, that he would have had to answer James Wedderburn Webster's challenge. He described the crisis in the relationship in one of his fabulously indiscreet letters to Lady Melbourne: 'I must tell you the place of declaration however – a billiard room!' After confessing his passion he had taken 'a very imprudent step – with pen & paper – in tender & tolerably turned *prose* periods (no *poetry* even when in earnest)'. But that was in 1813. Ten years later, Byron's feelings for Lady Frances were rather less in earnest, and he felt free to make the incident public, although only, to quote Jeffrey, 'by innuendo', in the ottava rima of *Don Juan*:

> But great things spring from little: – Would you think,
>   That in our youth, as dangerous a passion
> As e'er brought man and woman to the brink
>   Of ruin, rose from such a slight occasion,
> As few would ever dream could form the link
>   Of such a sentimental situation?
> You 'll never guess, I 'll bet you millions, milliards –
> It all sprung from a harmless game at billiards.   (XIV, 100)

This was a little more than indiscreet: it was caddish. But it at least serves to show how Byron, not just here but throughout *Don Juan*, makes public the kind of material that codes of politeness demand should remain confidential, and he does so not just 'with pen & paper' but in the still more public medium of print.

Byron and Caroline Lamb may both of them have violated the boundary between what might properly be introduced into the public arena and what ought to remain private, but theirs was a transgression oddly common in the period. Another member of Byron's circle, John Polidori, who had been employed by Byron as his private physician, introduced his Gothic story *The Vampyre* with a first-hand account of Byron's relations with the Shelleys and Claire Clairmont, his neighbours during his residence at the Villa Diodati. Others were guilty of the same offence. In his review of *Biographia Literaria*, John Wilson reminded Coleridge that 'the true confessional is not the bar of the public'. But, as John Wilson well knew, the public thought differently. 'This is confessedly the age of confessions', Wilson was later to claim.[47] There was De Quincey, whose *Confessions* of his opium addiction made such a stir when they were first published in the *London Magazine* that Charles Lamb was prompted to re-publish his 'Confessions of a Drunkard'. It was a time when writers seemed recklessly willing to make public their most intimate secrets. In *Liber Amoris*, published, like nine of the cantos of *Don Juan*, in 1823, Hazlitt memorialised his frustrated passion for Sarah Walker, the daughter of the woman who kept the house in Southampton Buildings, Holborn, where Hazlitt lodged after the breakdown of his marriage. He records in excruciating detail his pursuit of the young woman and his humiliation when he found that she had transferred her affections to one of his fellow lodgers. Hazlitt published *Liber Amoris* anonymously. In the text the aggrieved lover is referred to only as 'H – ', an oddly transparent alias to have chosen. Hazlitt took no more care to preserve his anonymity than Byron when he published *Don Juan*, and his identity was at once exposed.[48] In the throes of his passion for Sarah Walker Hazlitt was under a compulsion not just to pursue the young woman but to reveal his infatuation to anyone he happened to meet. He explained the matter to his friend Bryan Procter (the poet who wrote under the name Barry Cornwall):

'I am a cursed fool' said he to me. 'I saw J – going into Will's Coffee-house yesterday morning; he spoke to me. I followed him into the house; and whilst he lunched I told him the whole story'. 'Then' (said he) 'I wandered into Regent's Park, where I met one of M – 's sons. I walked with him some time, and on his using some civil expression, by God! I could not help myself, I told him the whole story.' . . . 'Well, sir' (he went on) 'I then went to Haydon, but he was out. There was only his man, Salmon, there: but, by God! I could not help myself. It all came out: the whole cursed story! Afterwards I went to look at some lodgings in Pimlico. The landlady at one place, after some explanations as to rent, etc.said to me very kindly, "I'm afraid you are not well, sir?" – "No, ma'am", said I, "I am not well"; and on inquiring further, the devil take me if I did not let out the whole story, from beginning to end!'[49]

The publication of *Liber Amoris* was simply an extension of this pattern of behaviour. *Liber Amoris* may have been, as Jonathan Gross thinks, a 'pathological work',[50] but if so the pathology seems to have been widespread, cultural as much as individual. Caroline Lamb yielded to it when she published *Glenarvon*, as did Peacock when he alluded so pointedly in *Nightmare Abbey* to the romantic entanglements of his friend Shelley, and Byron yielded to it too, not just when he allowed himself to refer in *Don Juan* to the billiard room in which his relationship with Frances Wedderburn Webster came to a crisis, but more persistently when he chose in the first canto of the poem to hold up his estranged wife to public ridicule.[51]

It is as if there were two readerships, one of them continuous with the writer's social circle, which in Byron's case corresponded quite closely with the exclusive social group that he designates 'the twice two thousand', and another readership that was at once more heterogeneous and much more numerous. It was the second readership on which best-selling authors such as Byron and periodical writers such as Hazlitt relied for their earnings, and yet they were in the habit of addressing that readership in something approaching the extravagantly unguarded manner that Byron adopts in his letters to Lady Melbourne. A similar division characterised the political as well as the literary culture of the period. The government of the country remained the preserve of the twice two thousand, but their behaviour in office was exposed to the active scrutiny of the many thousands who kept track of their doings in the columns of their daily newspapers.[52] The disparity, in literary culture between the two readerships, and in political culture between the two constituencies, made both cultures volatile, unstable. Gossip, of the kind that Byron delighted in sharing with Lady Melbourne, 'that abominable tittle tattle' as he calls it in *Don Juan* (XII, 43), is harmless enough when confined to a closed social circle, but may become libellous if circulated more widely, and especially when circulated not in handwriting but in print. The most dramatic symptoms of this volatility were the duels of the period, the duel in which Castlereagh, the war minister, shot Canning, the foreign secretary, in the thigh, or the duel in which John Scott, editor of the *London Magazine*, suffered the wound from which he died. Scott had instigated the quarrel when he retaliated against *Blackwood's* by bringing to bear against it the magazine's own weapons. *Blackwood's* had denounced Leigh Hunt and Keats as members of the Cockney School of poetry and found itself denounced in its turn as the founder of the Reekie School of criticism.[53] Byron seems never to have fought a duel, but he very often threatened to. All through the years in which he wrote *Don Juan* he was toying with the possibility of returning to England to issue a challenge to Henry Brougham, because Brougham, he believed, had slandered him. Brougham might have thought that he had done no more than gossip. It had become hard to tell the difference.

It is often argued that in the Romantic period poets looked inwards to find their epic subject matter. Wordsworth spoke for them all when he took it as his epic task to venture into 'our Minds, into the Mind of Man'. It was a journey, he claimed, that dwarfed anything that had been attempted by any epic poet before him. He would be required to 'breathe in worlds / To which the heaven of heavens is but a veil', and to confront terrors that far outdid those 'scooped out / By help of dreams' from Chaos or the 'darkest pit of lowest Erebus' or 'aught of blinder vacancy'.[54] Byron, as I pointed out in Chapter 1, makes similar claims himself on occasion, as when he imagines how some 'Columbus of the moral seas' might discover new worlds in the human soul (XIV, 101–2), but it was an enterprise that Byron most often viewed with suspicion. It was a little too like Bishop Berkeley's project:

> What a sublime discovery 'twas to make the
> 　Universe universal Egotism!
> That all's ideal – *all ourselves*: I'll stake the
> 　World (be it what you will) that *that's* no Schism.　　(XI, 2)

It may be, as Berkeley claims, that it is impossible to prove the existence of anything outside the mind, and yet 'who can believe it!' (XI, 1). Byron has too much respect for the external world, a world 'which at the worst's a glorious blunder' (XI, 3)), he finds it far too interesting, readily to accept the proposition that everything is '*ourselves*'. Goethe was not familiar with *Don Juan*, Eckermann recalls, but he did know *Beppo* and he found the poem too empirical ('zu viel Empirie'). Eckermann on the other hand knew *Don Juan* well, and the empiricism that Goethe disapproved of excited him. He was particularly struck by the London cantos. Byron 'is not very scrupulous whether his objects are poetical or not; but seizes and uses all just as they come before him; even the wigs in the hair-cutter's window, and the men who take care of the street lamps'.[55] Eckermann has in mind a stanza in the canto introduced by Byron's reflections on Bishop Berkeley. Juan is arriving in London:

> Through coaches, drays, choked turnpikes, and a whirl
> 　Of wheels, and roar of voices and confusion;
> Here taverns wooing to a pint of 'purl,'
> 　There mails fast flying off like a delusion;

    There barber's blocks with periwigs in curl
      In windows; here the lamplighter's infusion
    Slowly distilled into the glimmering glass
    (For in those days we had not got to gas); –   (XI, 22)

Juan's London is lit with oil-lamps, but Byron is writing for a gas-lit city, a 'modern' world (he uses that word twenty-six times in the poem), and for Byron the modern world is simply too various to be subordinated, as Goethe and Wordsworth would have preferred, to an idea. It is too stubbornly, too excitingly, empirical.

The world, as Byron represents it in *Don Juan*, is a public space, but a space patrolled by private individuals. Wordsworth had taken it as his task to celebrate '[h]ow exquisitely the individual Mind' is fitted to 'the external World'. It could hardly be otherwise as far as he was concerned, Byron might have retorted, since Wordsworth scarcely allows the external world an existence independent of the mind, a state of affairs he safeguards by having as little to do with the world outside himself as possible, preferring to spend his time, like Juan when he is falling for Julia, in 'self-communion with his own high soul' (I, 91). Wordsworth and his fellow Lakers, Byron complains, by choosing to live in places such as Keswick have hidden away from the world. They have chosen 'a long seclusion', preferring their own to any 'better company' (Dedication, 5). Mind and world for Wordsworth are married. His is 'the spousal verse / Of this great consummation'. The marriage is rather like Wordsworth's own: it is happy but far from equal. It is a marriage in which, as he puts it in *The Prelude*, the masculine principle, the mind, is 'lord and master' (XII, 271). In *Don Juan* marriages are very different. For one thing they are fractious. It is a poem interested in all those bruises produced when husband and wife, the self and the world, the private and the public, collide, and they collide most spectacularly in the poem's private allusions. In the first canto the account of the erotic adventure of a sixteen-year-old Spanish youth is founded on an anecdote told Byron by an Italian friend. Juan's escapade was 'none of mine'. It had all 'happened some years ago at Bassano with the Prefect's wife' when Byron's friend, a man called Parolini, had been only a boy, 'and was the Subject of a long cause ending in a divorce or separation of the parties'.[56] It is a comic anecdote, but the anecdote is given a special charge when Byron incorporates within it a caricature of his own wife. Similar collisions take place throughout the poem, compressed, it may be, into a single line ('Where are the Lady Carolines and Franceses?' (XI, 80)), and it is through those collisions that Byron explores one of the poem's chief

interests. For Byron the great theme left the modern poet, the theme that
he takes up in *Don Juan*, is the antithesis of Wordsworth's: it is the lack of
fit between individual mind and the external world.

Don Juan flits restlessly between the first person and the third.[57] The
poem moves forward by alternating between the two: 'So on I ramble, now
and then narrating, / Now pondering.' 'It is time we should narrate', he
decides, but on this occasion he cannot even complete the octave before the
first person yet again interrupts the third (IX, 42). That rhythm defines the
whole poem. Throughout it Byron allows himself to be diverted from his
characters, leaving them 'to proceed alone' while he surrenders to his
tendency to 'soliloquize beyond expression' (III, 96). *Don Juan* is
a narrative poem. ''Twas on a summer day – the sixth of June' (I, 103), as
Byron puts it in one of the poem's several beginnings. But it is a poem in
which the narrative is repeatedly interrupted by lyric interludes: 'No
more – no more – Oh! never more on me / The freshness of the heart
can fall like dew' (I, 214). It is the poem of a poet '[a]t once adventurous and
contemplative' (IV, 107). On the face of it, it is the narrative, the third
person, that predominates. Byron, he often claims, is distinguished from
his peers by his respect for facts. Epic poets have a tendency to 'embellish',
whereas 'this story's actually true' (I, 202). 'This is a fact and no poetic
fable', he insists, when introducing an especially plangent episode (V, 33).
He is Homer's equal, '[i]f not in poetry, at least in fact, / And fact is truth,
the grand desideratum' (VII, 81). He is prepared to tolerate all manner of
lapses, '[s]o that I do not grossly err in facts' (VIII, 74), for, after all, 'the
fact's a fact – and 'tis the part / Of a true poet to escape from fiction'. It is
a foolish convention that allows verse more freedom 'from the restriction /
Of truth than prose' (VIII, 86). Byron 'by no means deals in fiction',
choosing rather to gather 'a repertory of facts' (XIV, 13). His descriptions of
'love, tempest, travel, war' differ from those to be found in other epic
poems in being 'all very accurate' (VIII, 138). One of Byron's verbal tics in
Don Juan is the repeated use of the phrase 'in fact', employed on no less
than thirty-four occasions. The reverence for fact, like all the poem's other
postures, may be play-acted – Byron rarely fails to give an impression that
he is acting a part even when extolling the virtues of 'plain truth' – but that
does not, for Byron, undermine his claim to be of all poets the 'most sincere
that ever dealt in fiction' (XVI, 2), and the sincerity he claims has a lot to do
with a respect for facts, with his acknowledgement of a world that refuses to
be subordinated, as Wordsworth and Coleridge thought that it might be,
to the poetic imagination.

Byron associates fact with prose. It is the poets who have a tendency to deal in fiction. He is unusual among poets in insisting on his respect for prose, and one reason he respects it so highly is that the prose writer is obedient, as the poet is not, to the world of fact. The respect for prose is most evident in the account of the shipwreck and in the war cantos, in both of which he closely follows prose sources. He acknowledges his debt for details of the shipwreck to his 'grand-dad's "Narrative"', but he was still more indebted to *Shipwrecks and Disasters at Sea*, a compendium of marine mishaps edited by Sir J. G. Dalyell. It was the prose source that gave Byron the confidence to claim of his account of the wreck of the *Trinidada* that there was not 'a *single circumstance* of it – *not* taken from *fact*'.[58] In the poem's first canto Byron imagines what he might write if ever he should 'condescend to prose' (I, 204), but in the cantos on the Siege of Ismail there is no condescension. Rather, Byron presents himself as the humble servant of 'the author (to whose nod / In prose I bend my humble verse)' (VIII, 104). He follows his source so faithfully that McGann feels the need in his edition of the poem to re-print lengthy extracts from Castelnau's *L'Histoire ancienne et moderne de la nouvelle Russie* in an appendix. The prose sources allow Byron in the shipwreck and the war cantos to understand the world as an engineer rather than a poet. When their boat springs a leak, the sailors stir themselves: 'The stronger pump'd, the weaker thrumm'd a sail' (II, 38). A Greek military engineer, a 'new Vauban', is responsible for Ismail's formidable defences: 'Two batteries, cap-a-pée, as our St. George, / Casemated one, and t'other "a barbette"' (VII, 12). Byron uses a specialised vocabulary, but not a vocabulary of the kind that is 'sometimes called poetic diction'. Poetic diction frees its exponent from 'the restriction / Of truth', but for engineers 'the fact's a fact' (VIII, 86): their jargon honours facts by allowing them to be named more precisely.

In *Don Juan*, the third person alternates with the first but the world of fact is not subordinated to a world of feeling or vice versa. Rather, the one is forever being interrupted by the other. Byron wrote the poem in the years when he was also writing his memoir, the story of his own life that he gave to Thomas Moore and that Moore burned after Byron's death, spurred on by Hobhouse, in John Murray's fireplace in Albemarle Street. The first person interludes often summon memories, the 'boy feelings' bred in him by his childhood in Scotland that lend a special resonance to 'Scotch plaids, Scotch snoods, the blue hills, and clear streams, / The Dee, the Don, Balgounie's Brig's *black wall*' (X, 18). The memory may be triggered by a name. The view over the Bosphorus had charmed Mary Wortley

Montagu, and just to speak her name is enough to make Byron feel all over again the intensity of his boyhood devotion to Mary Chaworth:

> I have a passion for the name of 'Mary,'
>   For once it was a magic sound to me;
> And still it half calls up the realms of fairy,
>   Where I beheld what never was to be.   (V, 4)

Mary Chaworth was Byron's first love. Julia, Juan's first love, was as dear to him as a particular spot in the churchyard of St Mary's had been to Byron when he was a Harrow schoolboy, as dear to him as the younger boys he had taken under his protection:

> Dear the helpless creature we defend
> Against the world; and dear the schoolboy spot
> We ne'er forget, though there we are forgot.   (I, 126)

There is a public world in *Don Juan*, a world of facts, a world of pumps and barbettes and periwigs, and a private world of feeling, the door to which can never quite be opened to the reader, only left ajar, and what most interests Byron about those two worlds is how different they are.

In the fifth canto, just after Baba has completed his purchase of Juan and John Johnson in the slave market, there is an episode that has fascinated many of the poem's readers. It is an interruption rather than a digression. On 8 December 1820, Byron was living in Ravenna, and making a fair copy of the fifth canto of *Don Juan* when something happened that struck him so forcibly that it was not enough to give an account of it in letters, to Thomas Moore, to Murray, to his wife, to Augusta.[59] He had to find a place for it within the poem.

> The other evening ('twas on Friday last) –
>   This is a fact and no poetic fable –
> Just as my great coat was about me cast,
>   My hat and gloves still lying on the table,
> I heard a shot – 'twas eight o'clock scarce past –
>   And running out as fast as I was able,
> I found the military commandant
> Stretch'd in the street, and able scarce to pant.   (V, 33)

Byron had him taken up and brought into the house. His wounds were tended, but there, in the bed on which Byron's servants had laid him, he died, as the 'rough faces' of the men he had commanded gazed on him for the last time and Byron gazed with them. It is one of the rare occasions when the time of the poem's narrative intersects with the time of its composition, rather like the episode in *The Prelude* when Wordsworth recalls how disappointed he had been to find that he had crossed the Alps without knowing it. It is only as he recounts the story that he realises its true significance. It is not a tale of disillusionment, he now sees, but a testimony to the power of the human imagination that can figure to itself mountains in comparison with which any actual mountain will seem paltry. The new understanding serves to confirm Wordsworth in his faith that '[o]ur destiny, our nature, and our home / Is with infinitude, and only there, (Book VI, 538–9). In *Don Juan* the experience is a good deal less uplifting. Byron watches as the commandant died: 'such things claim / Perhaps even more attention than is due / From me.' He watches '[t]o try if [he] could wrench aught out of death / Which should confirm, or shake, or make a faith' (V, 38). But it is to no avail. It all remains 'a mystery', and Byron is left only with the puzzle that consciousness can cease so abruptly, that '*We*, whose minds comprehend all things', might all at once be transformed by 'five bits of lead' into a dead body, something incapable of consciousness. As he stands over the body he confronts the mystery of a living being metamorphosed into a thing. There is no conclusion to be drawn, and there is very little to be said. All that can be done is to move on: 'But let us to the story as before' (V, 39).

The commandant's men gather round the bed to gaze once more on a man whose word they had waited on, a man they had worshipped. They gaze on 'the commanding clay' (V, 37), a phrase that rather wonderfully captures the moment at which the living man deadens into an object, the point at which consciousness becomes clay. *Don Juan* is a poem full of things. It is rather like the room in which Gulbeyaz receives Juan, a room in which '[o]bject on object flash'd so bright and fast' that the eye can scarcely take it all in (V, 93). Byron is fond of catalogues. When Adeline gives a public dinner the menu spreads over a dozen octaves. Or there is Lambro, a taciturn man, who can speak his love for his daughter only in the long list of items that he selects for her from the ships' cargoes that he plunders:

> French stuffs, lace, tweezers, toothpicks, teapot, tray,
>   Guitars and castanets from Alicant,
> All which selected from the spoil he gathers,
> Robb'd for his daughter by the best of fathers.
>
> A monkey, a Dutch mastiff, a mackaw,
>   Two parrots, with a Persian cat and kittens,
> He chose from several animals he saw –
>   A terrier, too, which once had been a Briton's.   (III, 17–8)

Almost as many things crowd into the eight lines as we encounter in
the whole of *The Prelude*. Byron is conscious of this tendency of his,
anxious that he has described Norman Abbey, Lord Henry's country
estate, so minutely that he will be taken for an 'auctioneer', and
playfully comparing the catalogue he has produced with Homer's
'Catalogue of Ships' (XIII, 74). But Byron's description of the Abbey,
like Lambro's collection of objects that he will present as gifts to his
daughter, does not expand because Byron is interested in the things in
themselves. He does not take a miser's interest in the contents of the
Abbey and its fixtures, although he understands the miser's feelings very
well: 'How beauteous are rouleaus! how charming chests, / Containing
ingots, bags of dollars, coins' (XII, 12). He describes Norman Abbey
and its contents at such length because the description allows him to
remember Newstead Abbey and how much it had meant to him. The
things here, and all the way through the poem, are important as an
index to the feelings, even if they remain stubbornly separate from
them. But feelings in *Don Juan* are of two kinds. There is the kind
visible on the 'rough faces' of the commandant's men, communal
feelings, feelings of the kind that binds the men together in their
grief, and there is the emotion that the same event prompts in
Byron, a feeling which is his alone, and so private that it scarcely
admits being put into words.

Epics are poems that give voice to a world, but what sort of epic would it
have to be to give voice to a world the distinguishing characteristic of which
was that its inhabitants were no longer sure that they held it in common,
a world in which people felt that the crucial experiences, the experiences
that made them who they were, were private rather than shared? In *Don
Juan* Byron allows private lyric episodes to perforate the epic. In these
episodes Byron summons feelings, like that sense of time past, of lost
youth, that permeates so much of the poem, or the feelings prompted by
those special sites, like that spot in the Harrow churchyard, that have
a consecrated place in the memory, or he might simply summon names,
Mary, it may be, or Lady Frances, that mean something to Byron that they
cannot mean for the rest of us. Often the poem leaves the reader unsure
quite how to understand its language, unsure whether it is written in
a language that we all share, or in a language that can only be rightly
understood through its relationship with the particular individual who
framed it. It is a problem splendidly if spitefully raised in the first canto in
the person of Donna Inez. Donna Inez is at once the brilliant comic
creation that Byron devises as the mother of his hero and an outrageous

lampoon in which Byron seizes the opportunity publicly to humiliate his wife. After Inez makes her first appearance in the poem every reference to the married state leaves the reader wondering whether it voices the common human experience, or whether it would be better understood as voicing the particular resentments of a wounded man. The love of Juan and Haidée, Byron's Greek island idyll, is offered to all of us who have found that our 'old world grows dull':

> And we are sick of its hack sounds and sights,
> Intrigues, adventures of the common school,
> Its petty passions, marriages, and flights,
> Where Hymen's torch but brands one strumpet more,
> Whose husband only knows her not a wh – re.
>
> Hard words; harsh truth; a truth which many know.   (IV, 17–8)

But how many exactly? Is it one of those harsh truths borne out by our common experience, or is it a conviction born of a far more individual, and perhaps a far more bitter experience? 'I'm a plain man, and in a single station', the narrator confides (I, 22), shortly after introducing Donna Inez. The remark is a wink to the reader. It extends an invitation to understand the whole poem as the vehicle that allows a husband who thinks himself wronged to give voice to his resentment. The Countess of Blessington first met Byron when she called on him in Genoa on 1 April 1823, as Byron was completing the sixteenth canto of *Don Juan*. By then his relationship with Teresa Guiccioli had lasted for almost three years, almost three times as long as he had lived as a married man, but what struck Lady Blessington was that he could not stop talking about his wife. Her failure to offer any adequate explanation of why she had left him continued to play on Byron's mind: she 'occupies his attention continually', his thoughts 'revert continually to her and his child'.[60] Whether we believe her or not, it is certainly the case that references, open or covert, to his marital circumstances recur all through *Don Juan*. Juan's sadness as he stands on deck and watches the Spanish coast recede is explained because he is leaving behind '[h]is mother, and a mistress, and no wife' (II, 15). Byron offers it as a general truth that 'love and marriage rarely can combine':

> Marriage from love, like vinegar from wine –
> A sad, sour, sober beverage – by time
> Is sharpen'd from its high celestial flavour
> Down to a very homely household savour.   (III, 5)

It is a general reflection but by this point the reader is alert to the possibility that it is a general reflection founded on a very particular experience. Dante and Milton were both 'hapless in their nuptials', and the case of a third poet crosses the reader's mind even before Byron offers the suggestion that in the character of Beatrice Dante may have '[m]eant to personify the mathematics' (III, 10–11). It is a husband's rather than a father's plight that the reader is reminded of when Lambro returns home, finds the daughter who thinks him dead feasting with her young lover, and experiences 'a deep grief / Beyond a single gentleman's belief' (III, 51). It is bitter personal experience, too, the reader understands, that persuades the narrator that the Muslim's entitlement to take four wives is less a sin than 'a *bore*':

> Most wise men with *one* moderate woman wed,
> Will scarcely find philosophy for more.   (VI, 12)

Soldiers advance to the front as eagerly as a bridegroom to a wedding feast, a 'metaphor' that Byron defends '[s]ince there is discord after both at least' (VII, 49). Suwarrow, a canny general, hates 'recruits with wives', as likely to be less willing to surrender their lives than single men, but he excepts from his distrust all those who have been 'wed a year' (VII, 70). When Juan finds himself separated from his comrades in the assault on Ismail, Byron is prompted to remark that in battle '[w]arrior from warrior' is often divided, '[l]ike chastest wives from constant husbands' sides / Just at the close of the first bridal year' (VIII, 27). Even in the heat of battle, as he is describing the assault on Ismail, he pauses to speculate that the Houris who welcome Muslim martyrs into Paradise might be especially pleased to congratulate the newly married man who dies before 'dull Repentance hath had dreary leisure / To wish him back a bachelor now and then' (VIII, 113), and it is the same private experience that gives so acerbic an edge to the denial that Heaven is Love: 'Heaven is not Love, 'tis Matrimony' (XII, 14). Even in the fifteenth canto Byron is still presenting himself as a disillusioned husband, as a man who would have expected to have made 'a decent spouse / If [he] had never proved the soft condition' (XV, 24). A painter might make his reputation by picturing 'the dance / Of marriage', he thinks, just as Holbein had with his 'Dance of Death', but then it occurs to him that the two dances are, in fact, one and the same (XV, 39). *Don Juan* is the epic poem of the nineteenth century, and the poem of a poet who cannot throughout its sixteen cantos rid himself of the memory of his unhappy marriage, and it is the one precisely because it is the other. It is the epic poem of an age when what united people was the knowledge that the experience that best defined them was private. The epic poem of the nineteenth century could only be written by a poet like Byron, a poet scandalously willing to run the risk that poems on his most intimate domestic affairs might appear in the columns of a weekly newspaper, by a poet ready to make the bar of the public his confessional. Disraeli's Contarini Fleming understands that he has ever lived in 'two worlds, a public world and a private world'.[61] It is the perception on which the Victorian novel is founded. The true epic of the nineteenth century, it may be, could only be produced by someone prepared to begin his poem with 'an elaborate satire on the character and manners of his wife'.

CHAPTER 6

Taking Another Tack

Byron had no end in view when he wrote *Don Juan*, and not just because it promised to be a never-ending poem. 'Few mortals know what end they would be at' (I, 133), and Byron makes no claim to be one of the few. 'Men should know why / They write, and for what end', he allows, but he cannot claim as much for himself: 'I never know the world which will come next':

> So on I ramble, now and then narrating,
> Now pondering.   (IX, 41–2)

As I noted in Chapter 5, the transitions between narrating and pondering, between the third person and the first, give the poem its distinctive rhythm, which is why Byron makes a habit of pointing them out.[1] 'But to our tale', he announces when he has been distracted from his hero's doings by memories of the women of Cadiz (II, 8). Later in the canto Juan's longing for a beef-steak reminds Byron how much he misses a pot of English beer. But beer, he admits, 'being far / From this my subject, has no business here', and he returns to his story: 'But to resume' (II, 156–7). Ten stanzas later he is once again distracted, this time by memories of how he had once been feted in 'the British world of fashion', a world that now seem as insubstantial as a dream, and again he pulls himself up short: 'Return we to Don Juan' (II, 167). In the next canto it is Wordsworth and his 'drowsy frowzy poem, call'd the "Excursion"', that distract:

> But let me to my story: I must own,
>   If I have any fault, it is digression;
> Leaving my people to proceed alone,
>   While I soliloquize beyond expression.   (III, 96)

The evening hour, when the vesper bell sounds as if in mourning for the death of the day, prompts the thought that no one, not even the emperor Nero, dies unmourned. Flowers were scattered on his grave by some unknown hand. It is an affecting thought from which Byron brusquely recalls himself:

> But I'm digressing; what on earth has Nero,
>   Or any such like sovereign buffoons,
> To do with the transactions of my hero.   (III, 110)

There are digressions within digressions. When Juan takes Haidée as his bride (she is 'Nature's bride' (III, 202) even though there has been no marriage ceremony), it prompts a digression on inconstancy ('But Juan! had he quite forgotten Julia?' (III, 208)), which in its turn prompts the narrator to recall an encounter with 'the prettiest creature, fresh from Milan' (III, 209), from which he recalls himself to his digression on inconstancy: 'But to return' (III, 211). That phrase became a defining signature of the new manner, as Lockhart registers when he attempts the style himself in 'The Mad Banker of Amsterdam' (Lockhart credits Byron's predecessor John Hookham Frere as its inventor):

> But to return – (in this new style of Frere's
> A phrase which oft hath been, and oft must be.)[2]

By 1823, when the thirteenth canto of *Don Juan* was published, it was a style that had become all Byron's own:

> I'm 'at my old Lunes' – digression, and forget
>   The Lady Adeline Amundeville;
>   The fair most fatal Juan ever met.   (XIII, 12)

By now the story seemed to interrupt the digressions rather than vice versa. The fear of heights, the fear that overtakes us when we look down from a precipice, is born not so much from a fear of falling as a frightened recognition of an urge to jump. 'But what's this to the purpose? you will say', Byron asks, and answers simply, ''tis my way':

> I write what's uppermost, without delay;
>   This narrative is not meant for narration,
> But a mere airy and fantastic basis,
>   To build up common things with common places.   (XIV, 7)

But even in 1819 when the first two cantos of the poem appeared readers took the new manner in their stride. It was after all, as almost all the reviewers pointed out, the manner of *Beppo*:

> To turn, – and to return; – the devil take it!
> This story slips for ever through my fingers.   (*Beppo*, 63)

And in a sense it had been the manner of *Childe Harold*, too, a poem that moves forward, like *Beppo* and *Don Juan*, by following a process of association, even though Byron does not call attention to the procedure as he does in the comic poems. The sites at which the Childe pauses prompt digressions. They license Byron to 'write what's uppermost'. They open up the poem by giving him the opportunity not just to describe what he sees around him but to record whatever comes most immediately to mind, so that standing on the Bridge of Sighs he thinks of Venice, and then of his exile from England, and of his 'hopes of being remembered in [his] line / With [his] land's language', and Venice reminds him too that such ambitions are precarious, a chastening thought for him, and a thought that ought to chasten the pride not just of the poet but of the nation he has left behind him. Byron's reputation as the first English poet of the age rested on *Childe Harold*, on its third and fourth cantos in particular, and *Beppo* too had been popular. The poem's story, Jeffrey pointed out, occupied only about twenty of the ninety-five stanzas: 'The rest is made up of digressions and dissertations at the author's discretion; and these form unquestionably by far the most lively and interesting part of the work.'[3] But although he clearly understood the manner very well, Jeffrey did not applaud when Byron deployed it again in *Don Juan*. He found the new poem so offensive that he refused to review any of its instalments in the *Edinburgh*. Jeffrey admired *Childe Harold* and he enjoyed *Beppo*, but he could not stomach *Don Juan*. In *Don Juan* Byron speaks of 'love, patriotism, valour, devotion, constancy, ambition' as if he was 'among the most devoted of their votaries' only to cast off the character 'with a jerk', as if intent on demonstrating that it is possible to have 'all fine and noble feelings, or their appearance, for a moment, and yet retain no particle of respect for them – or of belief in their intrinsic worth or permanent reality'.[4]

Jeffrey, it seems, could enjoy both *Childe Harold* and *Beppo* even though the two poems were written in very different manners. He could not tolerate *Don Juan* because in *Don Juan* Byron repeatedly moves from the manner of one poem to the manner of the other 'with a jerk'. Many of the poem's first readers shared Jeffrey's reaction. For the *British Review Don Juan* was a poem that 'delights in extracting ridicule out of its own pathos': 'With a melancholy sweep of his lyre [Byron] dissolves the soul into tenderness and pity, and then, profanely sporting with the feelings he has excited, resumes, with an apparent alacrity, the levity of his habitual manner.'[5] The 'finest sentiment', a reviewer in the *Literary Chronicle* complained, 'is rapidly succeeded by the broadest humour'.[6] Even Leigh

Hunt, one of the poem's most sympathetic readers, found the manner disconcerting: Byron has a habit of 'turning to ridicule or hopelessness all the fine ideas he has excited, with a recklessness that becomes extremely unpleasant and mortifying'. Hunt was left 'startled and pained by the sudden transitions from loveliness or grandeur to ridicule or the mock-heroic'.[7]

Just a year after Byron's death the poet George Darley pointed out that if Byron resembled Shakespeare 'in any particular', it was 'in the faculty of passing from the solemn to the ludicrous, of dropping from the empyreal heights of fancy to the low concerns of reality – in one stroke of the wing'.[8] Jeffrey's 'jerk' has become for Darley the beat of a bird's wing: he celebrates the very device that had persuaded Jeffrey that *Don Juan* was beneath his notice. It was the ability that put Byron on a level with Shakespeare. By then John Scott, the *London Magazine*'s first editor, was five years dead, killed in a duel brought on when he had launched an attack on *Blackwood's Edinburgh Magazine* in the columns of the *London*. In a piece published just before he died he had responded to Byron's manner very differently. He agreed with Jeffrey:

> the quick alternation of pathos and profaneness, – of serious and moving sentiment and indecent ribaldry, – of afflicting, soul-rending pictures of human distress, rendered keen by the most pure and hallowed sympathies of the human breast, and absolute jeering of human nature, and general mockery of creation, destiny, and heaven itself, – this is a sort of violence the effect of which is either to sear or to disgust the mind of the reader – and which cannot be fairly characterized but as an insult and outrage.[9]

'This is not an English fault', Scott went on to remark. There had been earlier examples of it, he admitted, but they were to be found 'in foreign literature'. To William Roberts, too, Byron's new manner seemed foreign. In his review of *Beppo*, he associated Byron's swift transitions with 'French ridicule', which, he suggested, could only be resisted by the cultivation of 'very decided national habits and character'.[10] The Byronic manner that struck John Scott and William Roberts as foreign, 'an insult and an outrage', a few years later seemed to George Darley quintessentially English, Shakespearean.

As I pointed out in Chapter 1, the *Blackwood's* writers responded to *Don Juan* so perceptively because they recognised that in *Don Juan* Byron had re-made English poetry in much the same way that the *Blackwood's* writers had re-made the magazine. Magazines had always been miscellaneous. The *Blackwood's* innovation was to allow the magazine's miscellaneous contents

to jostle against one another, to collide, an editorial policy to which the
magazine drew attention by noticing (in verse) the objection of a doubtless
fictitious reader, a Berkshire rector, who complained that the magazines
'quick transitions' seemed to him 'derangement'. The editors replied that
they liked 'different things in the same page to see':

> A sonnet there, a good grave essay here,
> Chalmers, Rob Roy, Divorce law, the New Play.[11]

Thomas Chalmers, the Church of Scotland minister, had an interest in
social reform that made him a frequent butt of the magazine, in the pages
of which he jostled with notices of Scott's new novel, and a dozen other
things. The 'derangement' of which the Berkshire rector complains is at its
most extreme in the magazine's most celebrated series of papers, the *Noctes
Ambrosianae*. In an instalment that first appeared in 1827, the Shepherd
(that is, James Hogg, impersonated on this occasion by John Wilson)
points out to Christopher North, the magazine's fictitious editor, how
Blackwood's has transformed the publishing world:

> Afore ye and her cam out, this wasna the same warld it has been sin syne.
> Wut and wisdom never used to be seen linkin' alang the gither, han' and
> han' as they are noo, frae ae end o' the month to the ither, – there was
> naprented a byuck that garred ye break out at ae page into grief, and at
> anither into a guffaw.[12]

But *Don Juan* had been just such a book, and the *Blackwood's* writers knew
it. The fourth episode of the *Noctes*, written by Lockhart, appeared in 1822.
It did not, like most instalments of the series, record a night spent by the
Blackwood's men in Ambrose's tavern in Edinburgh, but was transferred
'by poetic licence' to Pisa, where Byron and Morgan Odoherty, the
magazine's resident Irishman, converse as they share a table at a local
taverna.[13] Odoherty introduces *Blackwood's* to Byron as 'a real Magazine
of mirth, misanthropy, wit, wisdom, folly, fiction, fun, festivity, theology,
bruising, and thingumbob'. *Blackwood's* 'unites all the best materials of the
Edinburgh, the Quarterly, and the Sporting Magazine – the literature and
good writing of the first – the information and orthodoxy of the second,
and the flash and trap of the third'.[14] He is, as he very well knows,
recommending *Blackwood's* as the magazine equivalent of Byron's own
Don Juan, a poem of which, he tells Byron, he thoroughly disapproves,
before admitting that he 'would rather have written a page of Juan than
a ton of Childe Harold'. Ironically, the magazine's proprietor, William
Blackwood, had objected so strongly to the moral tone of *Don Juan* that he

refused to stock the poem in his Edinburgh shop (his moral objection to the poem was certainly sharpened by a feud with John Murray instigated when Murray withdrew from his agreement to act as the London distributor for *Blackwood's*). The irony was not lost upon the magazine's contributors. John Wilson reviewed Lockhart's *Letter to Lord Byron* in *Blackwood's* in characteristic manner. He signalled his intimacy with the author by dismissing the pamphlet as 'trash' delivered in a style that could only be described as 'absurd', but he was careful to quote Lockhart's observation that the *Blackwood's* men were given to directing 'furious paragraph after furious paragraph . . . against a book nearly as clever as if they had written it themselves'. Wilson and Lockhart both knew very well that if Byron had happened to offer *Don Juan* to the magazine, Christopher North would at once have 'smiled a sweet smile, and desired the right honourable guest to ascend into the most honourable place of his upper chamber of immortality'.[15]

John Scott saw that the manner Byron cultivated in *Don Juan* and that John Wilson and Lockhart practised in *Blackwood's* was marked by its 'quick transitions', but it was a manner that remained alien to him. It was 'not an English fault'. Its only precedents were in 'foreign' literature. There are moments in *Don Juan* when Byron seems to accept as much himself. Readers in 'our sober clime', he grants, are likely to find his poem 'exotic'. Its manner is Italian rather than English: 'Pulci was sire of the half-serious rhyme' (IV, 6).[16] But there was another possibility. English literary history might be re-written in a way that represented it as a literature best characterised by exactly the quick transitions that had struck John Scott as so viciously foreign. Shortly after the appearance of the second instalment of *Don Juan*, *Blackwood's* published a paper denying that Byron had any claim 'to the merit of originating the serio-comic style, or even of introducing it first to English literature'. The credit for that should go to Chaucer, who exhibits in all his poems the 'sudden quirks and changes' that readers had found so striking in *Don Juan*. The conversations in *Troilus and Criseyde* between Pandarus and Troilus are 'quite in the dialogic style of Beppo'.[17] The paper naturalises the manner shared by *Don Juan* and the magazine. It presents it not just as a native manner, but as the manner that best defined the national literature, its true originator the founding father of English poetry, 'Dan Chaucer, well of English undefyled'.

Byron's quick transitions disconcerted Jeffrey and John Scott because they seemed to reveal Byron's insincerity. Even for Lockhart in his first response to the poem it had been 'a sad and an humiliating thing to know, that in the same year there proceeded from the same pen two productions, in all things so different, as the Fourth Canto of Childe Harold and this loathsome Don Juan'.[18] He already recognised the greatness of *Don Juan*, but had not yet reconciled himself to its quick transitions. 'As a piece of terrible painting' the shipwreck in Canto II outdoes the *Aeneid*, and yet even here, when Byron is at his most sublime, the mood is repeatedly interrupted by a 'demoniacal laugh', by 'odious sarcasms' of which the most innocent is:

> They grieved for those who perish'd with the cutter,
> And also for the biscuits casks and butter.   (II, 61)

Like other reviewers Lockhart admired the 'beautiful letter' in which Julia bids Juan farewell, 'They tell me 'tis decided; you depart', and he quotes most of it, but he quotes too the stanza that follows:

> This note was written upon gilt-edged paper
>   With a neat crow-quill, rather hard, but new;
> Her small white fingers scarce could reach the taper,
>   But trembled as magnetic needles do,
> And yet she did not let one tear escape her;
>   The seal a sunflower, '*Elle vous suit partout,*'
> The motto cut upon a white cornelian;
> The wax was superfine, its hue vermilion.   (I, 198)

Julia takes her leave of Juan nobly, generously, and in the next stanza Byron reveals that even as she does so she maintains a fastidious concern for appearances. For Lockhart, 'contemptuous coldness' glints from the stanza, the coldness with which women are so often spoken of by 'such people as the author of Don Juan'. Lockhart knew too that for all its beauty the fate of Julia's letter was to become a prop in the poem's broad comedy. As his ship sails away from Spain, Juan 'drew / Her letter out again, and read it through' (II, 18). 'Sooner shall earth resolve itself to sea, / Than I resign thine image', he declares, only for the ship to 'give a lurch', and force on him the discovery that love, though proof against all kinds of disaster, is snuffed out all at once by seasickness. Lockhart knew too that Julia's letter survives Juan's malady only to meet a yet ghastlier end. After the shipwreck, when the castaways decide to draw lots to decide which of them will be sacrificed to appease the hunger of the others, they find that they have no paper, and 'took by force from Juan Julia's letter' (II, 74).

Such sequences left many readers, Jeffrey and John Scott amongst them, feeling cheated, as if Byron is mocking them for having allowed themselves to be moved by the letter on its first appearance in the poem. Leigh Hunt, too, as I have pointed out, found Byron's habit of 'turning to ridicule or hopelessness all the fine ideas he has excited' disconcerting.[19] When she is parted from Juan, Haidée withers away and dies, taking with her into the grave her unborn baby. The island on which she is buried is no longer inhabited: 'no dirge, except the hollow sea's / Mourns o'er the beauty of the Cyclades' (IV, 72). Haidée's story comes to its sad close, and Byron at once announces his decision to take 'another tack': 'I don't much like describing people mad / For fear of seeming rather touch'd myself' (IV, 74). Forward movement in *Don Juan* is zig-zag, like a boat's when it sails against the wind. The poem moves like that, Byron tells us, because that is how we all of us live our lives: we 'live and die, make love and pay our taxes, / And as the veering wind shifts, shift our sails' (II, 4). The poem too repeatedly shifts its sails, and often at what seem the most inopportune moments, as when in Canto VII, for example, Byron chooses to end his vivid evocation of all the horrors of war with a joke as tired as it is feeble. Despite all their other excesses the Russian soldiers raped very little, and 'the buxom middle-aged' were left wondering '[w]herefore the ravishing did not begin!' (VIII, 132).

For Jeffrey it followed that none of Byron's principles, not even his contempt of military glory, had for him any 'permanent reality'. Some early reviewers entered a psychological defence on Byron's behalf. His cynical wit should be understood as a defence mechanism. It was the carapace that Byron had grown to protect a soul only too tremblingly sensitive to the wounds that it had suffered. A reviewer in the *Literary Speculum*, for example, understood the whole poem as a symptom of the emotional wounds inflicted on Byron by the break-up of his marriage.[20] The poem's jerks, its abrupt transitions between 'serious and moving sentiment' and 'indecent ribaldry', are defensible, as far as these readers are concerned, if they can be understood as the expression of a unitary self. Byron is capable of offering a very similar defence on his own behalf: 'And if I laugh at any mortal thing, / 'Tis that I may not weep' (IV, 4). But it is not a case that he is particularly anxious to press. When Jeffrey read *Don Juan*, he began to doubt whether Byron believed in anything. In the final cantos of the poem the 'vivacious versatility' of the Lady Adeline Amundeville, the most fascinating of the poem's several heroines, prompts very similar misgivings in her young friend Don Juan. When Juan sees her perform her social role so perfectly, 'as though it were a dance', he 'began to feel / Some doubt how much of Adeline was *real*' (XVI, 96). But Byron offers his assurance that the skill with which Adeline 'acted, all and ever part / By turns', is not a proof of her insincerity, ''tis merely what is called mobility',

> And false – though true; for surely they're sincerest
> Who are strongly acted on by what is nearest.   (XVI, 96–7)

In this she is just like the poem in which she appears. *Don Juan* is a mobile poem, a poem always most responsive to the demands of the moment, a poem very like Lady Adeline, always most strongly acted on by what is nearest.

Byron is no more committed than Lady Adeline to the idea of a single self. At most he half believes it, but, then, *Don Juan* is all the way through a poem of half belief. It is a poem, one might even say, that believes in halves. It is a 'half-serious rhyme' (IV, 6), a product of 'that hateful section / Of human years', life's 'half-way house' (X, 27). There is no poem in English that makes more play with a word that it finds sixty-six occasions to use. Adeline herself is 'half a poetess' (XVI, 39), which is just as it should be (Byron sometimes liked to claim that he was no more than half a poet himself). She is a favourite character of Byron's because she does everything by halves, but, then, so do most of the other characters in the poem. In the first canto Julia sits with Juan 'half embraced / And half retiring' from his 'glowing arm' (I, 115). When her husband begs her pardon, it is 'half withheld, and then half granted' (I, 180). Gulbeyaz too is a woman of halves, '[o]f half voluptuousness and half command' (V, 108). For Byron things seem more rather than less intense if they come by halves, like the name Mary, which for him has a sound so magical that 'it half calls up the realms of fairy' (V, 4). Juan and Haidée's embrace is most highly charged when they are '[h]alf naked' (II, 194). Ovid is somehow more rather than less rakish because only 'half his verses show him' so (I, 42). Byron, he tells us, owes 'half' his philosophy to Diogenes (XV, 73), but it would be truer to say that his was a philosophy of halves, which is fitting for a poet who describes himself as 'half a Scot' (X, 17), and for that matter 'half English' (XI, 12). Byron thinks in halves of necessity, because he is in two minds about everything:

> whene'er I have express'd
> Opinions two, which at first sight may look
> Twin opposites, the second is the best.

But he is in two minds even about that, and he is also in two minds about whether he only has two minds: 'Perhaps I have a third, too, in a nook' (XV, 87). In *Don Juan* Byron, like Lady Adeline, does everything by halves.

It is a poem that is not, and could not be, the product of a unified self, because it is the product of a poet always conscious that he is 'disunited', that he is best characterised by his self-divisions. And for that very reason it is a poem able to represent the world as it is, for 'if a writer should be quite consistent, / How could he possibly show things existent?' (XV, 87). For Jeffrey, Byron's quick transitions are his way of denying the 'permanent reality' of the world, but for Byron those quick transitions are exactly what allows his poem to encompass reality as he understands it, a reality which is not single but multiple, and not permanent but fleeting. The poem sets things side by side. Its most distinctive punctuation mark is the dash – was there ever a poem with as many dashes in it as *Don Juan*? Byron had always been fond of dashes. In a review of *The Corsair* he was already being warned against the habit. The reviewer complained of the 'frequent omissions of the necessary conjunction'. Byron had fallen into the habit of offering 'linear conjunctions', 'mysterious dashes', in place of the 'more intelligible connections which language and grammar afford'.[21] But by the time he came to write *Don Juan,* he had come to think that the dash was the punctuation mark best adapted to the way things were. He had come to the conclusion that only the dash, the disjunctive conjunction, could mark the connections that obtained in the world as he had come to understand it.

The sixteen cantos of *Don Juan* are spread over five years. In the first canto Juan is a stripling, a youth of sixteen. When he accepts Lord Henry's invitation to Norman Abbey he is a worldly young man of twenty-one. The Juan who sits beside Julia, half embracing her with an arm that 'trembled like the bosom where 'twas placed' (I, 115), is not the man who, even after Dudu wakes all the women of the harem with a piercing scream, remains as fast asleep 'as ever husband by his mate / In holy matrimony snores away' (VI, 73), still less the man who does not so much fall in love with Catherine the Great as succumb to 'self-love' (IX, 68). During his residence at the Russian court Juan becomes 'a very polished Russian' (X, 21). Very soon after he arrives in England, '[a] little "*blâsé*" (XII, 81), '[a] little spoilt, but by no means so quite' (XIV, 41), he contrives to make himself into a finished English gentleman, effortlessly displaying all the expected social graces. He is, for example, an accomplished flirt, urbanely replying, when Lady Adeline advises him to marry, that he would happily 'wed with such or such a lady / If that they were not married all already' (XV, 30). Juan has the gift of being all things to all people, a little like the turncoat poet of Canto III, who would write a chanson in France, a 'six canto quarto tale' in England, and a 'ballad or romance' in Spain (III, 86), and a little like Byron himself.

Byron traces Juan's development from callow youth to self-possessed young man, but *Don Juan* is not a bildungsroman, not a poem primarily concerned to map the process by which a boy grows up to be a man. It is a poem organised in space rather than in time. The scene shifts from Seville to '[o]ne of the wilder and smaller Cyclades' (II, 127), to Constantinople, to Ismail or Izmail on the Danube, and to 'Petersburgh', before arriving at that 'mighty mass of brick, and smoke, and shipping' that is 'London Town' (X, 82). The poem is driven forward by ships, by 'the most holy "Trinidada"' in which Juan sails from Cadiz, and the galliot that transports him to the slave market of Constantinople, and by carriages, the kibitka in which he jolts his way from Ismail to Petersburg, and the fine barouche in which he crosses Europe, accompanied by Leila, and his collection of pets, '[a] bull-dog, and a bull-finch, and an ermine' (X, 50), travelling through Poland, Prussia, and down the Rhine to Holland, before making the short crossing to Dover. *Don Juan* is organised by movement through space rather than movement through time, and one of the ways that it signals as much is by being a poem so much less concerned with marking continuities than with tracing patterns of difference.

The first episode of *Oliver Twist* appeared in 1837, just fourteen years after Byron left off writing *Don Juan*. By then Dickens knew just as well as Byron how to tell a story in a sequence of quick transitions. It was a technique he had learned, as Byron may have too, from the theatre, from melodramas like Maturin's *Bertram*, a wild success in 1816 when it was staged at Drury Lane on Byron's recommendation. In melodrama, according to Dickens, the tragic and the comic scenes succeed one another 'in as regular alternation, as the layers of red and white in a side of streaky bacon', and these 'sudden shiftings of the scene' are, Dickens suggests, not so unnatural as they may seem: 'The transitions in real life from well-spread boards to death-beds, and from mourning weeds to holiday garments, are not a whit less startling.' Dickens, like Byron, thinks of real life spatially: he thinks of it spread out before him, like the city, London, that he knows so well, its prosperous enclaves in such close neighbourhood, as the crow flies, to its wretched hovels, the houses next door to one another, it may be, in one of which a family shares a comfortable meal, while in the other it groups around the bed where a mother or a father or a child lies dying. Such 'rapid changes', Dickens advises, are by many 'considered as the great art of authorship'.[22] Dickens is teasing, of course, but he is serious too. Those who walk past Newgate 'with a light laugh or a merry whistle' little think how close they may be to the condemned cell. They may be 'within one yard of a fellow-creature' whose life 'will shortly terminate in a violent and shameful death'.[23]

He knows that it is the ability to make those rapid changes that allows him to represent life in the way that he understands it, and in this the Byron of *Don Juan* is one of Dickens's precursors.[24]

John Murray showed the first two cantos of *Don Juan* to Francis Cohen (he later changed his name to Palgrave) before they were published, and forwarded Cohen's response to Byron. Like Darley, Cohen thought the ease with which Byron moves between the grave and the gay Shakespearean, but Byron, he thinks, takes it all too far:

> Lord B. should have been grave & gay by turns; grave in one page & gay in the next; grave in one stanza, & gay in the next. And not grave & gay in the same page, or in the Same stanza, or in the Same line.

He welcomes 'a ready transition from fun & drollery to sublimity & pathos', but 'they must not be mixed up together'. They must be 'kept distinct though contemplated jointly'.[25] Cohen's complaint provoked one of Byron's more magnificent retorts:

> His metaphor is that 'we are never scorched and drenched at the same time!' – Blessings on his experience! – did he never play at Cricket or walk a mile in hot weather? – did he never spill a dish of tea over his testicles in handing the cup to his charmer to the great shame of his nankeen breeches? – did he never swim in the sea at Noonday with the Sun in his eyes and on his head – which all the foam of ocean could not cool? did he never draw his foot out of a tub of too hot water damning his eyes & his valet's? did he never inject for a Gonorrhea? – or make water through an ulcerated Urethra? – was he ever in a Turkish bath – that marble paradise of sherbet and sodomy? – was he ever in a cauldron of boiling oil like St. John? – or in the sulphureous waves of hell? (where he ought to be for his 'scorching and drenching at the same time') did he never tumble into a river or lake fishing – and sit in his wet cloathes in the boat – or on the bank afterwards 'scorched and drenched' like a true sportsman? – 'Oh for breath to utter'.[26]

For Byron as for Dickens rendering the real meant finding a way to record its 'rapid changes'. For Jeffrey, reality was 'permanent'. It was defined by its persistence through time. When Byron voices a sentiment at one moment only to cast it off 'with a jerk' the next, he reveals, as far as Jeffrey is concerned, that all his sentiments are factitious, assumed rather than real. But for Byron reality is discontinuous, and the jerks from one episode to another, from the death of Haidée and her unborn baby to the jaunty conversation with which the opera buffo entertains Juan on the galliot carrying the two of them to the Istanbul slave market, only bring his poem closer to the reality of life as we experience it. Byron's is a reality in which we are forever being drenched and scorched at the same time. 'How odd are the connections / Of human thoughts, which jostle in their flight!', Byron remarks (IX, 65), and *Don Juan* is a poem intent on tracking all those thoughts as they jostle so uncomfortably one against the other.

The first readers of *Don Juan* were surprised that Byron should have occupied himself so busily in the poem ridiculing Wordsworth and his associates. J. H. Frere advised Hobhouse that Byron was 'too great a man to descend into the arena against such wretched antagonists', and an early reviewer agreed: Byron pursued Wordsworth 'with an inveteracy of ridicule, somewhat hard to account for'.[27] Byron was the best-selling poet of the day. *The Corsair* had sold 10,000 copies on the day of its publication, 'a thing perfectly unprecedented'.[28] In the same year Longman published Wordsworth's *Excursion* in an edition of only 500, which had still not sold out twenty years later.[29] Wordsworth's reputation was more ambivalent than these sales figures would suggest. In 1818, when Leigh Hunt wrote that Wordsworth was 'generally felt among his own profession to be at the head of it', his was a distinctive rather than a wildly eccentric opinion.[30] But it still seems odd that Byron should have allowed Wordsworth such prominence in *Don Juan*, a poem in which he is referred to by name on twelve occasions, almost twice as often as Castlereagh (although Castlereagh, it is true, is also twice referred to as Londonderry). It raises the possibility that Byron came to understand his own poem in part by thinking about his differences from Wordsworth, and in particular of the difference between *Don Juan* and Wordsworth's longest poem ('I think the quarto holds five hundred pages' (Dedication, 4)), his 'drowsy frowsy poem, call'd the "Excursion," / Writ in a manner which is my aversion' (IV, 94).[31]

In *The Excursion*, as in all Wordsworth's poems, it is persistence through time that gives things their substance. In the first book Margaret's cottage and her garden gather their significance as the pedlar visits them again and again, all through the 'nine long years' (1, 872) that Margaret lingers after her husband has left her. In those years the cottage and the garden are marked more and more deeply by Margaret's neglect. They fall into decay, and so does Margaret, their tenant, but it is the long lapse of time, those 'nine tedious years', that confer on the cottage and the woman their human weight. Don Juan, unlike the pedlar, once he has visited a place never returns, and as he moves about the globe he scarcely seems to carry his past with him. Remembering and making poetry are for Wordsworth activities so nearly allied that it becomes hard to tell them apart. In *Don Juan* Byron chooses a hero more remarkable for his talent for forgetting. When Juan sits at table with Haidée, Julia is not a spectre at the feast. As Juan sailed away from Spain, it had seemed to him 'impossible' that he would ever forget her:

> Sooner shall this blue motion melt to air,
> Sooner shall earth resolve itself to sea.   (II, 19)

But the feeling does not last. Not once during his sojourn on the Greek island does she cross his mind. It is true that memories of Haidée strengthen Juan in his resolve to spurn Gulbeyaz's peremptory advances: 'However strange, he could not yet forget her.' But if, as we are told, 'he had got Haidée into his head' (V, 124), she seems not to stay there very long. Even before the interview with Gulbeyaz is over he finds his virtue leaking, like Bob Acres's valour, through his palms (V, 142), and no memories of Haidée come to his rescue in the harem that night when he is put to bed with Dudu. When Juan leaves her court Catherine's only hope is that 'Time the comforter will come at last', and, sure enough, Time makes his appearance 'four-and-twenty hours' later, when Catherine begins to busy herself in choosing Juan's successor (X, 48). Juan is not so brutal, but Haidée crosses his mind only once again before the poem ends, when he thinks how much she differs from Aurora Raby despite all the similarities between them:

> Yet each was radiant in her proper sphere:
> The Island girl, bred up by the lone sea,
> More warm, as lovely, and not less sincere,
>   Was Nature's all: Aurora could not be
> Nor would be thus; – the difference in them
> Was such as lies between a flower and gem.   (XV, 58)

The comparison seems cool, connoisseurial rather than impassioned, and Byron easily returns to his narrative via a sly remark on the triteness of his 'sublime comparison' between the flower and gem.

Wordsworth delights in days that are 'bound each to each'. The thought comes to him when he reflects how all his life long his heart has lifted when he has seen a rainbow in the sky. The colours of the rainbow, like the days of his life, are continuous. They merge into one another. And the arch of the rainbow makes it a proper emblem of a life in which the adult man still feels his connection with the child that he once was. Unlike his hero, Byron remembers all through his poem. He remembers his Scottish upbringing, his schooldays at Harrow, his youthful infatuation with Mary Chaworth, the student

slang he picked up at Cambridge, he remembers the year after the
publication of the first cantos of *Childe Harold* when he found himself
so suddenly famous, most feelingly of all he remembers his wife and the
breakdown of their marriage. But memories do not complete him as
they complete Wordsworth. He stumbles across them. He barks his
shin against them. There is a rainbow in *Don Juan* too, but it is
a rainbow very different from Wordsworth's. To the seafarers cast
away in their long boat it feels like hope, a deceptive hope as it turns
out for all but one of them. But when it first appears, bursting through
the clouds and resting 'its bright base on the quivering blue' of the sea,
it is a glorious sight,

> Brought forth in purple, cradled in vermilion,
>   Baptized in molten gold, and swathed in dun,
> Glittering like crescents o'er a Turk's pavilion,
>   And blending every colour into one,
> Just like a black eye in a recent scuffle,
> (For sometimes we must box without the muffle).   (II, 92)

Byron's rainbow, unlike Wordsworth's, arches above a discontinuous
world. The rainbow may be transient, but for Wordsworth it is something
he has seen all through his life. For Byron, the rainbow's impermanence is
its essence: 'It changed, of course.' It is 'a heavenly cameleon', its special
attribute that its colours are unfixed. For both men rainbows are like
poems, but they are like poems of a very different kind. Byron's rainbow
is a poem like *Don Juan*, a 'versified Aurora Borealis', by which he means
a 'non-descript and ever-varying rhyme' (VII, 2), and he signifies as
much when he describes the rainbow in an exotically picturesque simile,
'[g]littering like crescents o'er a Turk's pavilion', and at once and, as Jeffrey
would say 'with a jerk', offers as a substitute a simile that is aggressively and
vulgarly native, '[j]ust like a black eye in a recent scuffle'. The rainbow is
'[q]uite a celestial kaleidoscope'. The kaleidoscope had only recently been
patented by the Scottish scientist Sir David Brewster ('This is the patent-
age of new inventions' (I, 132)), and had at once become the most fashionable of adult toys. Murray sent one to Byron early in 1818 through his
solicitor, John Hanson. Byron was not particularly grateful. He complained to Hobhouse that Hanson had only brought with him 'a damned –
(Something) – SCOPE', instead of the books he wanted, and he had
broken the glass and cut a finger in his attempt at 'ramming it
together'.[32] But by the end of the year, when he was writing the second
canto of *Don Juan*, he had come to see that the kaleidoscope had given him

a metaphor not just for a rainbow but for his whole poem. *Don Juan* moves forward, just like the succession of images in a kaleidoscope, in a discontinuous sequence, scene succeeding scene with a jerk.[33]

Juan grows up as the poem proceeds, but he does not really develop. Instead he undergoes a sequence of costume changes. In his most striking appearances in the opening cantos, when he flees 'naked, favour'd by the night' from Julia's marital house (I, 188), and when Haidée finds him washed up on the beach of her island home and is overcome with pity for a 'stranger dying, with so white a skin' (II, 129), Juan is wearing no clothes at all. But once he has made himself at home with Haidée he adopts an extravagant and extravagantly exotic Greek or Albanian costume, 'a shawl of black and gold', 'a white baracan' so transparent that the gems he wore beneath it were clearly visible, a 'turban, furl'd in many a graceful fold', and an 'emerald aigrette' that had as its clasp 'a glowing crescent' (III, 77). The dress with which Baba provides him for his introduction to Gulbeyaz is almost as elaborate, but feminine, 'A pair of trowsers of flesh-colour'd silk', and 'a slight chemise as white as milk' fastened with 'a virgin zone' (V, 77). In Petersburgh he is placed in the hands of 'an Army tailor', and transformed into a regimental Cupid, 'Love turned a lieutenant of Artillery!' (IX, 44):

> His Bandage slipped down into a cravat;
>   His Wings subdued to epaulettes; his Quiver
> Shrunk to a scabbard, with his Arrows at
>   His side as a small sword, but sharp as ever,
> His Bow converted into a cocked hat.   (IX 45)

And in England he becomes almost as soon as he disembarks at Dover so much the finished English gentleman that it takes an encounter with a ghost for him to permit himself to appear in public with his neckcloth tied '[a]lmost an hair's breadth too much on one side' (XVI, 29). He becomes a dandy, but a dandy after the model of Beau Brummell. For Brummell to dress perfectly was to dress so well that it will scarcely be noticed. In England, Juan dresses just as he danced,

> without theatrical pretence
> Not like a ballet-master in the van
> Of his drill'd nymphs, but like a gentleman.   (XIV, 38)

Juan spends the poem travelling from country to country, and he is a different person in every country that he visits. His days, unlike Wordsworth's, are not bound each to each: they are fragmented. All through the poem Byron represents time as discontinuous, defined by change. It is because English weather is so changeable that Byron can speak of 'the English climate of our years' (II, 214). The poet is not, as Wordsworth would have it, the man who reacts to the rainbow now just as he had when he was a boy: rather, he is one of those who 'partake all passions as they pass', and so does the poem that he writes. It may not be very proper to represent passions as passing, but to pretend otherwise would not only be untrue to our experience, it would also go far to spoil 'a very pretty poem' (IV, 107). Wordsworth rejoices that the years have left him unchanged, but for Byron, as John Johnson explains to Juan, life is self-renewing. It '[c]asts off its bright skin yearly like a snake', except that it does so much more often than once a year. The new skin may only last for 'a week or two' (V, 21–2). London is the world's chief city, one reason for which is that London is a city that does not persist through time. London is 'Freedom's chosen station', as Juan understands when he walks its streets for the first time, and one of the reasons that Freedom takes its stand in London has nothing to do with the British constitution. London is forever being re-born: 'resurrection / Awaits it, each new meeting or election' (XI, 9). It is a city that persists through time only by continually re-making itself. The people who inhabit it are much the same, which is why no portrait of them can be true:

> A picture is the past; even ere its frame
> Be gilt, who sate hath ceased to be the same.   (XVI, 19)

It is entirely appropriate that Georges Cuvier rather than Erasmus Darwin or any of the evolutionists should be the patron scientist of *Don Juan*, because for Cuvier history is discontinuous: the present replaces the past by destroying it. One day we will think of thrones and of those who occupied them '[a]s we now gaze upon the Mammoth's bones, / And wonder what old world such things could see' (VIII, 137). In the following canto Byron had been about to impart a particularly valuable thought, but finds, when he finally gets round to it, that he has forgotten what it was. He is not much worried:

> But let it go: – it will one day be found
>   With other relics of 'a former world,'
> When this world shall be *former*, underground,
>   Thrown topsy-turvy, twisted, crisped, and curled,
> Baked, fried, or burnt, turned inside-out, or drowned,
>   Like all the worlds before, which have been hurled
> First out of, and then back again to chaos,
> The Superstratum which will overlay us.   (IX, 37)

'So Cuvier says', and Byron is happy to agree with him. Cuvier had been the first to recognise extinct species like the dinosaurs, and Byron imagines the body of George IV being excavated in some future age by his puny descendants, and its huge bulk contemplated with the same awe with which we contemplate the remains of mammoths (IX, 39).[34] The world we live in, like all the worlds before it, will be buried, but buried things do not stay buried for ever. From time to time they come to the surface, and then we trip over them, as Byron so often all through the poem trips over his memories, with the result more often than not that he suffers a painful bruise.

Sartor Resartus first appeared in 1833, just ten years after Byron left off writing *Don Juan*. It was a decade, according to Carlyle, in which Byron had become 'obsolete', and he bids his reader, 'Close thy *Byron*; open thy *Goethe*'.[35] But in *Sartor Resartus*, Carlyle expounds the science of clothes. It is, he acknowledges, a science of the superficial, and that makes it particularly relevant to *Don Juan*, which is a poem very like its hero: both are 'a little superficial' (XI, 51). It is another of Byron's differences from Wordsworth. Wordsworth offers his poems as 'meditations passionate from deep / Recesses in man's heart' (1805 *Prelude*, I, 231–2). He ventures far into internal spaces, '[i]nto our Minds, into the Mind of Man – / My haunt, and the main region of my song'. He is an explorer of inner depths. The meanest flower that blows inspires in him 'Thoughts that do often lie too deep for tears'. For Wordsworth the wide spaces are within us, as the boy discovers when he is waiting for the owls to respond to his call and the voice of mountain torrents is carried 'far into his heart'. The Wye valley, when it is remembered, gives sensations that are felt 'along the heart', as if the heart were itself a landscape as wide and solemn as the landscape through which the Wye flows. Byron offers in place of Wordsworth's aesthetics of depth an aesthetics of surfaces. His boast is that he ranges wider than Wordsworth, which is what makes him wish that the Lake Poets would change their lakes for ocean (Dedication, 5), but he has no Wordsworthian ambition to plunge into the depths. He 'would skim / The Ocean of Eternity' (X, 4). *Don Juan* moves like Katinka, the Georgian in the Sultan's harem, whose feet 'skim the earth' (VI, 41), or like Juan himself, who when he danced was like Pope's Camilla: he 'scarce skimm'd the ground' (XIV, 39). Haidée, as she watches Juan sleeping, understands that he has sunk in his sleep into the depths of his being – as he sleeps he is '[h]ush'd into depths beyond the watcher's diving' (II, 197), and Byron has no more ambition than Haidée to dive so deep down that he can explore those depths. Wordsworth may sink deep and ascend high, but Byron, or so he claims, travels further. He is the 'Columbus of the moral seas' (XIV, 101), and Columbus could travel so far, he goes on to remind us, because he travelled lightly, 'in a cutter, / Or brigantine, or pink, of no great tonnage' (XV, 27). He might say as much for his own poem, which, as Byron insists, is so much easier going than *The Excursion. Don Juan* is like the turnpike roads that Byron finds so delightful. It offers the reader the pleasure of dashing along its surface, '[s]o smooth, so level, such a mode of shaving / The earth' (X, 78). He makes no claim to rival Walter Scott – who could, he asks, except Shakespeare and Voltaire (a rather odd pairing)? His ambitions are different: 'in my slight way I may proceed / To play upon the surface of Humanity' (XV, 59–60). He can afford the modesty, because by then his readers will have learned that human surfaces are just as interesting as human depths. Poetry, Byron tells us, is a bubble, a bubble that the poet blows 'just to play with, as an infant plays' (XIV, 8). He is perfectly ready to admit that poetry may be a bubble of the South Sea kind, too, a confidence trick, but his primary meaning is that poetry, like a bubble, is all surface. Its iridescence, its rainbow play of colour, has nothing at its centre – pop it, and it disappears – which is what brings poetry so close to life.[36] Our lives, just like poems, are 'bubbles on the ocean / That Watery Outline of Eternity' (XV, 2). They appear for a moment and then they burst.[37] The world too is a bubble, or if not a bubble a globe of glass, which is almost as fragile as a bubble, and is unlikely to last much longer. Still more to Byron's point, it is just like a bubble in being all surface:

> 'Where is the world?' cries Young, at *eighty*? Where
>   The world in which a man was born? 'Alas!
> Where is the world of *eight* years past? *'T was there* –
>   I look for it – 't is gone, a Globe of Glass!
> Cracked, shivered, vanished, scarcely gazed on, ere
>   A silent change dissolves the glittering mass.
> Statesmen, chiefs, orators, queens, patriots, kings,
> And dandies, all are gone on the wind's wings.   (XI, 76)

In dedicating *Peter Bell* to Robert Southey, Wordsworth explained that he was only now, in 1819, publishing a poem that 'first saw the light in the summer of 1798'. In the intervening years 'pains have been taken at different times to make the production less unworthy of a favourable reception; or, rather, to fit it for filling *permanently* a station, however humble, in the Literature of my Country'. The poem did not impress Byron, nor did the other poem that Wordsworth brought out in 1819, *Benjamin the Waggoner*: '"Pedlars," and "boats," and "waggons!" Oh! Ye shades / Of Pope and Dryden, are we come to this?' (III, 100). But just as interestingly he emphatically disclaims Wordsworth's ambition that his poem should outlive its time. He is not like Wordsworth a poet who 'reserves his laurels for posterity' (Dedication, 9). Men 'write, speak, preach, and heroes kill' for fame, but what is fame?: ''tis but to fill / A certain portion of uncertain paper' (I, 218). If he sees his fame eclipsed in his own lifetime, or if it survives 'some centuries',

> The grass upon my grave will grow as long,
> And sigh to midnight winds, but not to song.　　　(IV, 99)

He has had his days of fame, and he has had them when they meant the most, when he was young. In comparison, the 'appeal to the unborn' that supports the pretensions of poets such as Wordsworth seems flimsy (XII, 17–8). 'The loftiest minds outrun their tardy ages' (Byron's examples are Pythagoras, Locke, and Socrates), Byron agrees, but he does not claim himself to be an 'intellectual Giant' like them: he is content, or so he pretends, to be one of the little people (XVII, 9–10). He had not always taken that position. He published the fourth canto of *Childe Harold* just a year before the first two cantos of *Don Juan*, and he had not thought it then an unworthy ambition to win a place in 'the temple where the dead / Are honoured by the nations': 'I twine / My hopes of being remembered in my line / With my land's language', he had admitted, and it had been a proud admission (*Childe Harold*, IV, 9–10). Many early readers of *Don Juan*, as Byron well knew, thought it a poem that he had degraded himself by writing. In the most scathing notice of the poem that ever appeared in *Blackwood's* the reader is invited to wonder that the same poet should have been responsible for 'two productions in all things so different as the Fourth Canto of Childe Harold and this loathsome Don Juan'.[38] But Byron did not share that view. He was proud of *Don Juan*. Canto IX is introduced by twenty-one intricately rambling stanzas. They end when Byron explains his reputation for misanthropy – it is 'Because / *They hate me, not I them*' – before he turns once again to his story:

> 'Tis time we should proceed with our good poem,
> 　For I maintain that it is really good,
> Not only in the body, but the proem,
> 　However little both are understood.　　　(IX, 21–2)

By then Byron knew very well that his hopes of being remembered in his line with his land's language rested principally on *Don Juan*, which makes it seem at first sight odd that he should use the poem to make fun of poets like Wordsworth who had chosen to make their 'appeal to the unborn' rather than address their actual readers. Lucy's body in Wordsworth's great lyric is '[r]olled round in earth's diurnal course / With rocks and stones and trees'. She is dead, but she has found in the grave the permanence, the power to withstand time, that she shares with the rocks and stones and trees that are rolled around with her, and shares too, as the two centuries that have passed since it was written have shown, with the poem that remembers her. But that is not the kind of poem that can represent the world as Byron understands it in *Don Juan*, a world like 'a globe of glass', a world '[c]racked, shivered, vanished, scarcely gazed on, ere / A silent change dissolves the glittering mass'. In *Don Juan*, Byron's refusal to appeal to posterity is one aspect of his commitment to the cracked world, a world from which Wordsworth and his fellow Lakers, who have kept their own company '[a]t Keswick' (Dedication, 5), have chosen to seclude themselves. Pythagoras, Locke, and Socrates were ill used by their contemporaries, and that should be, Byron suggests, a lesson to us. 'We little people in our lesser way' should learn from their example to put up with 'Life's small rubs' (XVII, 10). It is winning of Byron to class himself amongst the little people and we may doubt how much he means it, but it is one instance of a crucial rhetorical strategy in *Don Juan*. Throughout the poem Byron insists that, however different they may be, he and his readers share a single space, that they inhabit the same world, and this, as he recognised, made him very different from Wordsworth.

    For Byron, *The Excursion* was Wordsworth's 'new system to perplex the sages'. 'System' was an important term for him.[39] He associated it with the philosophers. Berkeley has his 'system', and it is impossible to disprove it: 'And yet who can believe it!' (XI, 1). Plato has his system, too, but it is just as fantastic as Berkeley's in its claim that the mind can exercise perfect control of the body. 'O Plato! Plato!' Byron exclaims, you have been responsible for more

> Immoral conduct, by the fancied sway
>   Your system feigns o'er the controulless core
> Of human hearts, than all the long array
>   Of poets and romancers.   (I, 116)

In his preface to *The Excursion* Wordsworth had announced his ambition to write 'a philosophical poem'. Byron would not have been reassured when Wordsworth added that it was not 'the Author's intention formally to announce a system'. When Leigh Hunt had shown him *The Story of Rimini* Byron had told him that it was 'good poetry at bottom, disfigured only by a strange style', and Hunt had answered that 'his style was a system, or *upon system*, or some such cant; and, when a man talks of system, his case is hopeless: so I said no more to him, and very little to any one else'.[40] Byron's objection is that system makers do not enter into conversation with the rest of us. They ask only to be believed. Wordsworth and his 'drowsy, frowzy poem' do not have readers, they only have 'followers, like / Joanna Southcote's Shiloh, and her sect' (III, 94–5). Joanna Southcott had died in 1814, but before then her claim to be pregnant with the Messiah (she was sixty-four) had been widely credited amongst her 100,000 followers. She had mistaken, in Byron's words, a dropsy for a pregnancy. When Byron compares her to Wordsworth he means to be rude, but he is also making a serious point: the two are alike in that they both attract disciples. In *Don Juan* Byron cultivates a quite different relationship with his readers.

One of his habits in *Don Juan* is to offer similes not singly but in bunches: as McGann puts it, he 'gathers his similes in a heap'.[41] It is a habit that he shares with Shelley, but he deploys it quite differently.[42] In his 'Essay on Love', Shelley explains that for all of us the true love object is an idealised mirror image of ourselves. We travel the world looking for some perfect embodiment of this image, and, unsurprisingly, given that it is an image of ourselves, we fail to find it. But though this may seem sad, it is a failure that, Shelley argues, should be celebrated, because it produces in each one of us a want or lack that 'urges forth the powers of man to arrest the faintest shadow of that without the possession of which there is no rest nor respite to the heart over which it rules'. It is precisely because we are unable to find the perfect love object that we are freed to recognise 'the faintest shadow' of that ideal object everywhere, freed to spend our lives passing from one object to another, accommodating every possible object within a capacity for love that is never exhausted because it never meets an object that fully satisfies it.[43] The thought finds its most finished poetic expression in *Epipsychidion*, in which Shelley's love object is a young Italian woman of his acquaintance called Emilia Viviani. No comparison is adequate to Emilia, the woman to whom the poem is addressed, and so each simile is offered only to be replaced by another, which also proves to be inadequate, in a process that has no necessary end, and that does in fact occupy more than a 100 lines of the poem. Emilia is

An image of some bright Eternity;
A shadow of some golden dream; a Splendour
Leaving the third sphere pilotless; a tender
Reflection of the eternal Moon of Love
Under whose motions life's dull billows move;
A Metaphor of Spring and Youth and Morning;
A Vision like incarnate April, warning,
With smiles and tears, Frost the Anatomy
Into his summer grave.   (115–23)

'Ah, woe is me', Shelley continues, a gloominess that comes to him, one
suspects, because he has run out of breath, or, to use more elevated terms,
because it is beyond his mortal powers to prolong that play of substitution
for the eternity that would alone be adequate fully to express the infinite
beauty of Emilia. The poem is propelled forward by its own inadequacy, by
Shelley's failure to find a figure of speech adequate to Emily's ineffable
beauty. Even when Byron seems to be doing something similar, as when he
searches for a simile adequate to the beauty of the women of Cadiz, the
effect is very different:

An Arab horse, a stately stag, a barb
New broke, a cameleopard, a gazelle,
No – none of these will do.   (II, 60)

It is not so much that the women's beauty is unspeakable, more that the
linguistic resources of the orientalist poet are so limited. Byron's similes often
multiply not because the object that they seek to describe is transcendental
but because he is more interested in difference than similarity. His rainbow is
like the crescents over a Turk's pavilion and like a black eye in a recent scuffle
(II, 92), not because its beauty is unspeakable but because Byron wants to
jerk his readers in a single octave from the Ottoman empire to 13 Bond
Street, where Gentleman John Jackson had established the academy in
which he taught young noblemen like Byron to box. Byron's similes are
inadequate like Shelley's, but not because they attempt to describe some
object that transcends the phenomenal world. They are inadequate because
in this world things are different from one another. There are rainbows and
Turkish crescents and black eyes, and the differences between the three items
seem much more striking than the similarities. When Baba inspects the
merchandise displayed in the slave market, we are told,

No lady e'er is ogled by a lover,
Horse by a blackleg, broadcloth by a tailor,
As is a slave by his intended bidder.   (V, 26–7)

In three lines Byron summons four gazes, and the effect is to invite the reader to think about the differences between them. When the Sultan's women reach the sanctuary of their harem, they are '[l]ike birds, or boys, or bedlamites broke loose', or like '[w]aves at spring-tide', or they are just like themselves, like 'women any where / When freed from bonds', or they are 'like Irish at a fair', who enjoy themselves with the recklessness of people granted a brief release from the irksome superintendence of their English governors (VI, 34). The similes do not help us to imagine the women's relief so much as the range of experience that Byron brings to bear on his poem. It is the same when Byron refuses to speculate on what has kept Lady Adeline Amundeville chaste all through the three years of her marriage. He will not examine her motives, because "Tis sad to hack into the root of things':

> I hate a motive, like a lingering bottle
>   Which with the landlord makes too long a stand,
> Leaving all claretless the unmoistened throttle,
>   Especially with politics on hand;
> I hate it, as I hate a drove of cattle,
>   Who whirl the dust as Simooms whirl the sand;
> I hate it, as I hate an argument,
>   A laureate's ode, or servile peer's 'content.'

It is a generous selection of hatreds, a testament to how full a life the poet has lived. The sinking of the spirit that we feel when a happy day comes to an end prompts another sequence:

> The evaporation of a joyous day
>   Is like the last glass of champagne, without
> The foam which made its virgin bumper gay;
>   Or like a system coupled with a doubt;
> Or like a soda bottle when its spray
>   Has sparkled and let half its spirit out;
> Or like a billow left by storms behind,
> Without the animation of the wind;
>
> Or like an opiate, which brings troubled rest,
>   Or none; or like – like nothing that I know
> Except itself; – such is the human breast;
>   A thing, of which similitudes can show
> No real likeness.   (XV, 9–10)

Similes fail because for Byron it is the differences between things that are interesting, not their similarities. If this passage disappoints, it disappoints because the flat champagne is not different enough from the decarbonated soda water. Wordsworth's poems are written out of an interiority so deep that difference is erased, erased so completely that it would be inappropriate even to ask if the 'thoughts too deep for tears' that bring the 'Immortality Ode' to a close are sad thoughts or happy thoughts. As Elizabeth Bowen puts it, 'the fact is, people are much the same if one goes down deep'. 'All the variety', she adds, 'seems to be on the surface',[44] which is why Byron prefers in his slight way to 'play upon the surface of Humanity'. On the surface of things it is the differences that matter. On the surface, as he puts it when he wants to describe what the end of a happy day feels like, things are revealed as not really being much like anything except themselves.

Byron's world, in comparison with Wordsworth's, is highly differentiated. Just as important it is not a world that is presented by the poet to his readers: rather, it is a world that he invites his readers to share. Lady Adeline is like a volcano in which the lava bubbles under a mantle of snow, until it strikes Byron that he should 'let the oft-used volcano go':

> Poor thing! How frequently, by me and others,
> It hath been stirred up till its smoke quite smothers.
>
> I'll have another figure in a trice: –
> What say you to a bottle of champagne?
>
> (XIII, 36–7)

On Haidée's isle the waves fall so gently on the shore that their foam '[s] carcelyo'er passed the cream of your champagne / When o'er the brim the sparkling bumpers reach' (II, 178). In Canto XV, the end of a joyous day leaves you feeling a bit flat, like a glass of champagne that has lost its bubbles. But here the claim, surely false, is that the 'liquid glassful' that remains if the rest of the bottle's contents are frozen into 'a very vinous ice' offers the very essence of champagne, champagne at its strongest and purest. Byron offers the simile to the reader who recognises how hackneyed volcanoes have become. It presents itself to him 'in a trice', evidence of an inventiveness that is inexhaustible. But, as Byron well knows, it is untrustworthy evidence, because he has not come up with the simile himself. He has borrowed it from his 'buon camerado' Walter Scott. Scott had imagined a 'heart ardent at the call of freedom or of generous feeling' that belied at 'every moment the frozen shrine in which false philosophy had incased it', a heart 'glowing like the intense and concentrated alcohol, which remains one single but burning drop in the centre of the ice which its more watery particles have formed'. The reader who remembers the passage will have the added pleasure of recalling that the ardent heart that Scott has in mind is Byron's: Scott coined the simile in his review of the fourth canto of *Childe Harold*.[45] Byron had been pleased by Scott's review. It was, as he remarked to Murray, 'the review of one poet on another – his friend',[46] and when Byron borrows the simile he does so as a way of acknowledging Scott as a fellow poet and as a way of offering his assurance that the friendship Scott had shown for Byron is returned. Byron regularly opens up *Don Juan* to other poets – he does not share Southey's ambition to 'be the only Blackbird in the dish' (Dedication, 3) – and still more importantly he opens it up to his readers. One of the inmates of the harem looked as she slept 'as marble, statue-like and still', as 'cold and pure, as looks the frozen rill', or

> the snow minaret on an Alpine steep,
> Or Lot's wife done in salt, – or what you will; –
> My similes are gathered in a heap,
> So pick and chuse – perhaps you'll be content
> With a carved lady on a monument.   (VI, 68)[47]

Readers ought to rest satisfied with the carved lady: it is after all a simile that Byron has borrowed from Shakespeare. Wordsworth and his confrères do not accept the claims of other people to be poets. Poetry, they believe, has 'wreaths for [them] alone', and they are just as unwilling to recognise their readers. Byron offers *The Excursion* as Wordsworth's 'vasty version' of his 'new system', which, like all other systems, is closed, which is one of the chief things that Byron has against it. Wordsworth will not enter into conversation with his readers: he simply offers them his system. Leigh Hunt told Byron that he had written *The Story of Rimini* according to a system, and 'when a man talks of system, his case is hopeless: so I said no more to him'.

Byron was familiar with Wordsworth's view that 'every Author, as far as he is great and at the same time *original*, has had the task of *creating* the taste by which he is to be enjoyed'. It was clear to Wordsworth that it was a task that Byron had shirked: hence the immediate and extraordinary popularity that he had enjoyed ever since the first edition of Cantos I and II of *Childe Harold* sold out in three days and Byron awoke to find himself famous. *Don Juan* circulated just as widely. As one reviewer observed, 'scarcely any poem of the present day has been more generally read'.[48] But the responses to *Don Juan*, and, still more gallingly, the refusal of either of the two great reviews to notice the poem, show that Byron, just as much as Wordsworth, found himself in the position of having to teach the reading public how his poem should be read. By 1825, George Darley could see that Byron's supreme talent, the gift that placed him in the same company as Shakespeare, was 'the faculty of passing from the solemn to the ludicrous, of dropping from the empyreal heights of fancy to the low concerns of reality – in one stroke of the wing', which was precisely the faculty that the poem's earliest reviewers had found so disconcerting. It seemed to Jeffrey that Byron was mocking his readers by immediately subjecting to ridicule the feelings that he had himself elicited. Like Francis Cohen, Jeffrey did not accept that anyone could be drenched and scorched at the same time. But for Byron our experience of the world is not whole but fractured. Our days are not bound each to each, they are discontinuous. Byron is flamboyantly inconsistent, given to self-contradiction, but that serves only to make his testimony more authoritative. Wordsworth and Coleridge, and even Byron's friend Shelley, are in the habit of speaking of 'the poet', but for Byron there is no such thing: there are only poets. Juan is introduced to the greatest living poets in the drawing rooms of London, all eighty of them. Wordsworth denied that Byron had the right to call himself a poet at all, but it was not a verdict that Byron reciprocated. Wordsworth and Coleridge and Southey may be 'shabby fellows' but they are 'poets still / And duly seated on the immortal hill' (Dedication, 6). Byron finds room for them in his poem for the same reason that his similes multiply, because the world we live in is a world defined by its differences. He and Wordsworth are poets of a very different kind, but it does not follow that the title of one of them to be a poet must be fraudulent. The poet who speaks to a various world, a world in which everything is more like itself than it is like anything else, needs must be aware of his own difference. He must accept that he will differ from his readers, just as those readers will differ from each other. That acceptance comes all the more easily for Byron because he is so happy to acknowledge that he is a man who often differs from himself. It is because *Don Juan* so wholeheartedly embraces difference that J. G. Lockhart, the most perceptive of all the poem's early readers, believed that Byron, alone amongst his contemporaries, offered an adequate picture of the age in which he lived: 'There is nobody but yourself who has any chance of conveying to posterity a true idea of the *spirit* of England in the days of his Majesty George IV.'[49]

CHAPTER 7

Mine Irregularity of Chime

In *Don Juan*, Byron is forever reminding his readers that they are reading a poem that rhymes. One of the major differences between Byron and his hero is that Juan 'did not rhyme' (XI, 53). 'Prose poets like blank-verse, I'm fond of rhyme', Byron confides (I, 201). He refers to rhymes and rhyming fifty-one times in the poem. He ends the second canto not just because Juan and Haidée have consummated their love but because he has completed '[t]wo hundred and odd stanzas': 'That being about the number I'll allow / Each canto of the twelve, or twenty-four' (II, 216). He keeps the reader in mind, too, of the particular stanza he has chosen. He has been obliged, he confesses, to add a syllable to a quotation from Horace. The adjustment would not have been necessary had he chosen to write his poem in 'the pink of old hexameters', but he is shackled to the ten syllable iambic line, and the extra syllable had to be 'thrust in to close the octave's chime' (VI, 18). His readers will be unused, he fears, to a poet who so frankly lays bare his own workings. The manner will strike them as 'exotic', and they are right in their suspicion that it belongs to a foreign literary tradition. Byron has been seduced by the poetry of the country in which he is writing: 'Pulci was sire of the half-serious rhyme' (IV, 6). Self-consciousness, it is true, is a common property in the poetry of the period. Wordsworth is fully aware that the devious route by which he came to be a poet has its fitting counterpart in 'the turnings intricate' of the *Prelude*'s blank verse, and Keats seems always, as he writes his poems, to be watching himself, a rapt witness of that 'warm scribe', his hand, as it moves across the paper. But neither of them is so repeatedly and so flamboyantly conscious of himself as writing a poem as Byron in *Don Juan*. Given this, one might expect Byron's poem to be the prize exhibit in Michael O'Neill's *Romanticism and the Self-Conscious Poem*, and O'Neill does find room for some acute remarks on *Don Juan*, but it interests him less than other poems by Byron, less than *Manfred* and *Childe Harold*, and the reason is not hard to seek. O'Neill's interest is focused on those moments when the story of the poem and the story in the poem converge. He is struck, for example, by the moment in the 'Immortality Ode' when Wordsworth voices his faith that even as they grow older our souls can 'see the children sport upon the shore, / And hear the mighty waters rolling evermore', and forges as he does so a line, an alexandrine, as rolling and as mighty as the ocean that it describes.[1] For O'Neill Byron is most thrillingly self-conscious in the third canto of *Childe Harold*, at the moment when he realises that the truth of his poetic credo is manifested in the rise and swell of the verse in which he has rehearsed it:

> 'Tis to create, and in creating live
> A being more intense, that we endow
> With form our fancy, gaining as we give
> The life we imagine, even as I do now.   (III, 46–9)

Self-consciousness in *Don Juan* works very differently. Life is one thing in *Don Juan* and poems quite another, and the moments of self-consciousness are those in which Byron is struck most forcibly by the disparity between them. When he has written his elegy for Haidée, he performs one of those sudden pirouettes so characteristic of the poem:

> But let me change this theme which grows too sad,
>   And lay this sheet of sorrows on the shelf;
> I don't much like describing people mad,
>   For fear of seeming rather touch'd myself –
> Besides I 've no more on this head to add;
>   And as my Muse is a capricious elf,
> We 'll put about, and try another tack
> With Juan, left half-kill'd some stanzas back.   (IV, 74)

Juan had fallen, bleeding from wounds to his arm and his head, and when Byron returns to him he reminds the reader of just how much time has passed since. There has been a delay of twenty-five stanzas to be precise. The narrative has been suspended, and the effect is to dramatise the difference between stanzas and 'sabre gashes' (IV, 49). It is much the same at the very end of the poem:

> Our Hero was, in Canto the Sixteenth,
>   Left in a tender moonlight situation.   (XVII, 12)

Juan had been abandoned, frozen, at the moment when his hand was pressed against the Duchess of Fitz-Fulke's warm breast, and the dark cowl that had disguised her had fallen back to reveal her 'full, voluptuous' body. Byron leaves Juan there while he considers the predicament of only children, the need to safeguard freedom of speech, the ill treatment accorded the 'loftiest minds' whose misfortune it was to have 'outrun their tardy ages', and his own regrettable but fascinating self-contradictions: 'Modest I am – yet with some slight assurance' (XVII, 11). All through *Don Juan* Byron is as aware as Laurence Sterne, who exerts a potent influence on the poem, that there is a gulf that can never be bridged separating the event from the act of narration. Lambro cocks his pistol: 'one instant more / Had stopp'd this Canto and Don Juan's breath' (IV, 42). The turn of phrase underlines the difference between breaking off a poem and breaking off a life. It makes that difference the more startling by seeming to ignore it.

In this, as in so much else, *Don Juan* lives by difference. In his moments of self-consciousness what tends to strike Byron is how far his poem and his story have diverged. All through the poem that divergence is played out not just in the poem's digressions but in its metrics and its rhymes. Reviewers objected to Byron's outrages against the formal conventions of verse almost as often as they protested against his outrages against moral conventions, and some thought of the two kinds of offence as related.[2] A reviewer in the *British Critic* relied on alliteration to make the connection: Byron's poem was 'a narrative of degrading debauchery in doggerel rhyme'.[3] A reviewer in the *European Magazine*, even if he did not dismiss the poem as doggerel, agreed that some of Byron's rhymes were 'unallowable'.[4] William Jerdan in the *Literary Gazette* was of the same opinion. He was in the habit, when he reviewed an instalment of *Don Juan*, of complaining that Byron's rhyming was defective and listing the rhymes that failed to meet his standards. In his review of Cantos VI, VII, and VIII he offers a representative sample from 'hundreds such rhymes', and lest his selection be thought mischievous he also offers in support of his case one entire stanza:[5]

> By Jove! he was a noble fellow, Johnson,
>   And though his name, than Ajax or Achilles,
> Sounds less harmonious, underneath the sun soon
>   We shall not see his likeness: he could kill his
> Man quite as quietly as blows the Monsoon
>   Her steady breath (which some months the same *still* is):
> Seldom he varied feature, hue, or muscle,
> And could be very busy without bustle.   (VIII, 39)

One knows what Jerdan means. Byron makes his rhymes only by dislocating the language. 'Which some months the same *still* is' has claims to be the clumsiest inversion in the whole poem, and 'underneath the sun soon' is not much better. The rhymes for Achilles are outré, particularly the second of them, although no more so than many others in the poem, and 'Monsoon' makes an approximate rhyme with 'Johnson' only by wrenching the accent. But in the course of the stanza Byron allows that Johnson's name is 'less harmonious' than Ajax or Achilles, and the concession might have given Jerdan pause for thought. Ajax and Achilles are easily accommodated in the noble hexameters of Homer's warrior epic, but *Don Juan* is an anti-heroic poem, and John Johnson, as the rhyming indicates, is not a comfortable fit for the role of military hero that Byron allots him. He may be a good soldier, but, unlike Ajax and Achilles, the battlefield is not his true home. It is not the place where he can be most himself. He has 'an English look', 'square / In make, of a complexion white and ruddy' (V, 11). He is Byron's version of John Bull. John Johnson may know how to comport himself in the ranks of the imperial Russian army, just as he knows how to behave when he finds himself in a slave market, but he is out of place in both, and the rhymes and the syntax of the stanza that Jerdan reprehends point that out. He has served with Suwarrow before, and contemplates death almost as nonchalantly as his general. He has learned to 'kill his / Man quite as quietly as blows the Monsoon / Her steady breath'. Byron recognises this as an accomplishment, but, like Johnson, he is an Englishman, and the equanimity with which Suwarrow contemplates death, the death of the men who serve under him as much as that of his enemies, does not come naturally to him. Byron signals as much by cobbling a stanza that no reader could possibly recite with a 'steady breath'.

The Russians set up batteries on an island which allows them to bombard the city, reducing to rubble private as well as public buildings, '[n]o matter what poor souls might be undone'. The object is to terrorise the city into surrender without the need for a costly assault. Jerdan objects to the couplet in which Byron dismisses any such hope as futile. It is no more than

> A phantasy which sometimes seizes warriors,
> Unless they are game as Bull-dogs and Fox-terriers.   (VII, 24)

'Warriors', in Jerdan's opinion, does not rhyme with 'terriers'. But the stanza works at once to recognise warrior courage and to put it in its place, which makes it entirely proper for Byron to choose a rhyme that brings his stanza to a close in a pointedly unheroic couplet. Warriors who do not succumb to fantasy have a certain stature, but it is a stature that puts them,

Byron's rhyme suggests, on a level with their pets. Jerdan points out a still more desperate rhyme in an earlier stanza which requires the incompetent military engineer, ironically described as 'this new Vauban', who was responsible for Ismail's inadequate defences, to rhyme with 'hang' and 'slang'. But this stanza, like the stanza on Johnson, features an apology, 'Prithee, excuse this engineering slang' (VII, 11). Modern warfare, of which Vauban, military engineer to Louis XIV, was one of the chief architects, can only be described in a vocabulary that, like the name Vauban, resists rhyme. Its poet has to sing of batteries of which one is 'case-mated', the other 'a barbette': it demands a vocabulary much more easily accommo-dated in Byron's prose source, Castelnau's history of Russia, than in the octaves of Byron's poem. Most poets would have been anxious to disguise the difficulty. Byron is just as anxious to point it out. 'I did not think a battle could be turned into anything so entertaining', Wellington told John Wilson Croker when he read *The Battles of Talavera*, Croker's celebration of one of Wellington's victories.[6] Byron has no ambition to match Croker's feat. The siege of Ismail resists being turned into an entertaining poem: it can be reduced to ottava rima stanzas only by a poet willing to adopt desperate measures, by a poet, for example, ready to allow 'warriors' to rhyme with 'terriers' and 'Vauban' to rhyme with 'hang' and 'slang'.

Unlike the siege of Troy, a modern battle is not fought by men whose names are 'harmonious' like Ajax and Achilles but by John Johnson and others whose names are still more discordant, still more resistant to any attempt to tune them into verse. Most of those who took part in the sacking of Ismail have Russian names, names '[e]nding in "ischskin", "ousckin", "iffskchy", "ouski"' names that may be 'fitted for the peror-ation / Of Londonderry' (VII, 16), Castlereagh, that is, whose speeches are so remarkable for their 'set trash of phrase' (Dedication, 13), but are far less easily fitted into Byron's ottava rima. Two millennia have passed since Homer wrote the *Iliad*, and Europe has 'armies still / And Southey lives to sing them very ill' (Dedication, 16). But Byron's, unlike Southey's, is a 'true Muse', and one mark of its truth is that his Muse refuses to conceal the grim realities of modern warfare by cloaking them in poetic fictions: 'Call them Mars / Bellona, what you will – they mean but wars' (VIII, 1). The imperfect rhyme with which that stanza ends, the rhyme of 'Mars' with 'wars', is one of the ways that Byron shows himself immune from the cult of military glory to which poets like Croker and Southey subscribe. The names of those who fought just wars, Leonidas and Washington, are musical. They are names that might inspire true poems: 'How sweetly on the ear such echoes sound!' (VIII, 5). But those who took the city of Ismail had no noble motive. The city was taken 'mere conquest to advance', and battles of that kind are 'nothing but a child of Murder's rattles' (VIII, 4). The taking of Ismail is cacophonous, 'sounds of horror chime / In like church bells, with sigh, howl, groan, yell, prayer' (VIII, 58), and its poet, if he is a true poet, must be willing to sound just as harshly on the ear as the battle that he is describing.

The war cantos, it might be thought, are a special case, but when Jerdan reviewed the last two cantos of the poem he found the rhyming no better. Norman Abbey is not, like Suwarrow's encampment, inhabited by those remarkable for their inharmonious names. 'There's music in all things, if men had ears', and Byron is alert to the music in the name of his principal heroine:

> The Lady Adeline Amundeville,
> A pretty name as one would wish to read,
> Must perch harmonious on my tuneful quill.   (XV, 5)

But in his review of the last two cantos, Jerdan continued to object to 'rhymes which hardly approximate in sound'.[7] As in his review of the war cantos some of Jerdan's complaints seem specious. What is the objection to rhyming 'urn' with 'stern' (XVI, 18)? But even Byron admits that his rhymes are loose. When the Duchess of Fitz-Fulke disguises herself as the ghostly friar, she paces '[w]ith awful footsteps regular as rhyme, / Or (as rhymes may be in these days) much more' (XVI, 113). But irregularity, Byron insists, has its uses. Women who have led irregular lives, for example, are able to pass on to their daughters 'their knowledge of the world, and sense / Of the sad consequence of going astray' (XII, 44), and the stanza enforces the point by itself going a little astray: 'sense' is supplied as a rhyme for 'once' and 'dunce'. Sometimes Jerdan objects not because the rhyme words are too different in sound but because they are too similar. Juan's social manner is unaffected. There is nothing of the coxcomb in him. He carries himself modestly:

> his regard
> Was such as rather seem'd to keep aloof,
> To shield himself, than put you on your guard.   (XV, 14)

The rhyme of 'regard' with 'guard' is just as unshowy as Juan, so muted that Jerdan thinks it not a rhyme at all. Or there is the stanza in which the architect proposes to 'restore' the Abbey. He had been invited down 'to survey these grey walls, which though so thick, / Might have from time to time acquired some slight defect', and 'after rummaging the Abbey through thick / And thin', he 'produced a plan whereby to erect / New buildings of correctest conformation, / And throw down old, which he called *restoration*' (XVI, 58). Rhyme in these stanzas dwindles into repetition – 'thick' rhymes with 'thick', just as in the earlier stanza 'gard' had rhymed with 'guard'. But rhymes like these have their own appropriateness when the society that Byron is describing makes his task so difficult by insisting that those who belong to it muffle all their differences. It is a society in which differences, eccentricities, have all been ironed out. 'There now are no Squire Westerns as of old', only 'gentlemen in stays, as stiff as stones' (XIII, 110), which is why the modern architect, who knows his customers, proposes 'improvements' that promise to eliminate everything that is quirky and distinctive in the architecture of Norman Abbey, and why Byron pre-empts him in the rhymes chosen to describe his project. No writer has succeeded in sketching the beau monde exactly as it is because 'in fact, there's little to describe' (XV, 20). It is a society that encourages 'a smooth monotony / Of character, in those at least who have got any'. Its denizens share 'a sameness',

> A dull and family likeness through all ages,
> Of no great promise to poetic pages.   (XIV, 15–6)

The lack of promise is borne out by rhymes too like one another, and borne out too by other rhymes that Jerdan also finds defective, rhymes so muted that they scarcely impress themselves on the ear at all. A stanza on the perils that attend the 'young unmarried man, with a good name / And fortune' ends:

> For talk six times with the same single lady,
> And you may get the wedding dresses ready.   (XII, 58–9)

The rhyme is too quiet to clinch the joke, as if, in the beau monde, even laughter is half smothered. Byron is fond of that rhyme. Juan assures Lady Adeline

> That still he'd wed with such or such a lady,
> If that they were not married all already.   (XV, 30)

He is flirting of course, but the rhyme makes even the flirtatiousness languid, as though Juan has begun to share the lassitude that, Byron believes, so thoroughly infects the upper circles of English society.

In the English cantos Byron's material is, he tells us, unpoetic, like the breakfast served at Norman Abbey, the 'tea and toast, / Of which most men partake, but no one sings' (XVII, 13). The rhymes signal how

such material resists incorporation into Byron's stanzas. Even here the
'toast' can only be accommodated if it is allowed to rhyme with 'cost'.
Of all the countries of Europe, Great Britain is 'the most difficult to
rhyme at' (XII, 24), a remark that is the more pointed because there are
so very few rhymes for 'Britain'. But loose rhymes are just as common
in the early cantos of the poem, long before Juan moves to England.
A stanza in the third canto pointing out that tragedies always end in
a death and comedies always end in a marriage, and that neither kind
of play has anything to say of what comes afterwards, ends in a couplet
that rhymes 'ready' with 'Lady' (III, 9), and so does a stanza describing
Juan's reluctance to wear the women's clothes that Baba offers him (V,
73), and the episodes on the Greek island and in the Sultan's palace in
Istanbul seem very different from the English cantos. But even they are
not exempt from the ennui that casts its pall at odd, often unexpected
moments all through the poem. Ennui may be a French word, but it is,
Byron insists, 'a growth of English root' (XIII, 101). Writing *Don Juan*
was Byron's defence against his own ennui, his attempt to stifle 'that
awful yawn which sleep can not abate', and he offers the poem to his
readers in the hope that it will render them the same service.[8] But the
ennui that the poem so energetically resists infects its every canto. 'My
poem's epic', Byron insists at the end of the first canto (I, 200), and
reading Southey has taught him one thing about the epic: that 'its
grand ingredient is *ennui*' (III, 97). Ennui is an affliction that can strike
at any time. It strikes even at one of the poem's most rapt moments,
when Juan wakes to find that Haidée is gazing on him:

> When Juan woke he found some good things ready,
>   A bath, a breakfast, and the finest eyes
> That ever made a youthful heart less steady,
>   Besides her maid's as pretty for their size;
> But I have spoken of all this already –
>   And repetition 's tiresome and unwise, –
> Well – Juan, after bathing in the sea,
> Came always back to coffee and Haidee.   (II, 171)

Needing a second rhyme for 'ready' Byron settles for 'already'.[9] The choice
exactly reflects the shadow that darkens just for a moment the sunny
atmosphere of the Greek island as it crosses Byron's mind how many
times he has made verses on the fine eyes of a beautiful young woman:
'But I have spoken of all this already – / And repetition's tiresome and
unwise.' Byron writes, he tells us, in the tradition of Pulci, but Pulci gives

us '[t]rue knights, chaste dames, huge giants, kings despotic', all but the last of which are now obsolete: 'I chose a modern subject as more meet' (IV, 6). In the fourth canto Juan is still blissfully occupied with Haidée on Lambro's island, '[o]ne of the wild and smaller Cyclades' (II, 127). There is nothing particularly modern about the episode, except that it is a canto that offers its reader material so perfectly designed to appeal to the jaded modern palate. 'Get very drunk', Byron advises his reader as the episode begins, and when you wake, call for your valet, and 'bid him quickly bring / Some hock and soda-water'. For a man with a hangover nothing, not even 'the blest sherbet, sublimed with snow', can vie with it (II, 180). In the Haidée episode Byron is content to act as the valet offering his world-weary reader the literary equivalent of that refreshing glass of hock and soda water.

Not many of the rhymes in *Don Juan* are so tired as the rhyme that pairs 'ready' with 'already'. 'Prose poets like blank verse, I'm fond of rhyme', Byron remarks (I, 201), and the whole of *Don Juan* is a testament to that fondness. But one of the things he likes about rhyme is its arbitrariness, how it imposes obligations that have to be fulfilled no matter how difficult the task may be.[10] Rhyming poets are given to fostering the illusion that the rhyme word is the natural choice, and if it should happen to rhyme it does so only by a happy accident. Samuel Rogers is a poet of that kind. The massy doors in the Sultan's palace could be opened easily by the black dwarfs who guard them because the doors have hinges 'smooth as Rogers' rhymes' (V, 89). Love poets, according to Byron, are particularly given to these feats of legerdemain. 'Amatory poets' like to 'pair their rhymes as Venus yokes her doves' (V, 1), hiding from the reader any sense of the constraints under which the poet operates, a feat the easier to accomplish because they are given to choosing rhymes so hackneyed that the reader scarcely notices them (Byron offers his own barbed tribute to such habits in his own stanza by rhyming 'doves' with 'loves'). He is probably thinking of Thomas Moore in particular. Moore was the exemplary amatory poet of the age, not the Moore who wrote *The Twopenny Post-Bag* or *The Fudge Family in Paris* but the Moore who translated Anacreon and wrote the *Irish Melodies*. Byron thought of *Don Juan* as the antidote to poetry of that kind. It was why, he believed, his poem was so disliked by its women readers: 'The truth is that *it is too true* – and the women hate every thing which strips off the tinsel of *Sentiment*.'[11] One of the ways that he strips the poem of sentiment is frankly to acknowledge the arbitrariness of rhyme. In *Beppo*, Byron pretends (or does he confess?) that when he is looking for a rhyme he sometimes has recourse to a rhyming dictionary: he is prepared to 'take for rhyme, to hook my rambling verse on, / The first that Walker's Lexicon unravels' (*Beppo*, 52). He begins *Don Juan* by surveying all the celebrated people that he might have chosen as the hero of his poem. Amongst the French he picks out 'Mirabeau', 'La Fayette', and 'Moreau', but at once admits that there are many others who have been '[e]xceedingly remarkable at times', 'but must remain unmentioned because they are 'not at all adapted to my rhymes' (I, 3). Murat was at least as great a general as Moreau, but not nearly so easy a rhyme. Fighting with the Russian army are 'several Englishmen of pith / Sixteen called Thomson, and nineteen named Smith', one of whom prompts an impressive feat of rhyming:

> But when I've added that the elder Jack Smith,
> Was born in Cumberland among the hills,
>   And that his father was an honest blacksmith,
> I've said all *I* know of a name that fills
>   Three lines of the dispatch in taking 'Schmacksmith.'
> A village of Moldavia's waste, wherein
> He fell, immortal in a bulletin.   (VII, 20)

The feat is a little less impressive for those who know, or guess, that Schmacksmith is a village unknown to cartographers, but the stanza exhausts Byron's inventiveness. The death of another of the Smiths prompts a comically meagre epitaph: 'Smith; / One of the valourous Smiths whom we shall miss / Out of those nineteen who late rhymed to "pith"' (VII, 25). Leigh Hunt, in one of his poems for *The Liberal*, claims that 'writing for the rhyme' is a capital crime in poetry.[12] If so, Byron is a habitual offender. All through *Don Juan* he happily exposes how what he has to say is at the mercy of his rhyme scheme. As he puts it in *Beppo*, 'just as the stanza like to make it, / It needs must be' (*Beppo*, 63). He enjoys setting himself a stern rhyming test and flunking it. He is, as Jane Stabler points out, keen to insist on the 'constraints' of rhyme', as in the epigraph from Fielding's *Amelia* he chooses for *Hints from Horace*: 'Rimes are difficult things, they are stubborn, things, Sir.'[13] When Julia becomes conscious of her feelings for Juan, she finds herself contemplating the possibility that her husband might die and she be left a widow:

> But just suppose that moment should betide,
>   I only say suppose it – *inter nos* –
> (This should be *entre nous*, for Julia thought
> In French, but then the rhyme would go for nought.)   (I, 84)

Is his confession supported or undermined by the oddity that Julia thinks in a foreign language? Is it an eccentricity that bestows on her an individual presence, or the desperate stratagem of a poet who cannot call to mind the expression *entre nosotros*, or has decided that, if he were to use it, the metre rather than the rhyme would go for nought? Byron finds himself in a similar plight when Juan trips over the petticoat 'white as milk' that Baba has given him to wear:

> Which – as we say – or as the Scotch say *whilk*,
> (The rhyme obliges me to this; sometimes
> Monarchs are less imperative than rhymes) –
>
> Whilk, which (or what you please), was owing to
> His garment's oddity, and his being awkward.   (V, 77–8)

Byron at this moment is just as awkward as his hero, but manages to carry the awkwardness off with a lordly effrontery that Juan cannot match. The demands of rhyme, like the demands made by monarchs, are arbitrary: they may even oblige us to deny what we know very well to be the case, as when the Sultan's concubines return in stately procession to their harem. They 'paced on most maiden-like and melancholy':

> Like water lilies floating down a rill
> Or rather lake – for *rills* do *not* run *slowly*.   (VI, 33)

In a stanza that sets out to distinguish the several varieties of 'love', Byron finds himself in a still worse plight:

> (I needs must rhyme with dove,
> That good old steam-boat which keeps verses moving
> 'Gainst Reason – Reason ne'er was hand-and-glove
> With rhyme, but always leant less to improving
> The sound than sense).   (IX, 74)

Rhyme is often out of sync with reason, but, then, so too is love, which is one reason, perhaps, why Byron thinks them so closely connected. 'Middle-aged ladies', unlike young women, 'know what's what'. The young

> Know little more of Love than what is sung
> In rhymes, or dreams (for Fancy will play tricks)
> In visions of those skies from whence Love sprung.   (X, 10)

But, the lines prompt us to ask, is love quite so easily separated from dreams and visions and poets' rhymes, and if not, might it be that the

young women have a better notion of it after all than women who have
lived long enough to know 'what's what'? It is at least a question worth
asking. Byron ticks off Walter Scott for the much quoted lines in *Lay of the
Last Minstrel*, in which he pays his own tribute to love:

> Love rules the court, the camp, the grove,
> And men below, and saints above,
> For love is heaven, and heaven is love.
>
> (*The Lay of the Last Minstrel*, III, ii)

Cash, Byron retorts, has a better claim to rule than love: 'Cash rules the
grove, and fells it too besides':

> And as for 'Heaven being Love', why not say honey
> Is wax? Heaven is not love, 'tis Matrimony.

Byron concedes that '[p]erhaps there may be something in "the
grove," / At least it rhymes to "Love"' (XII, 13–14). And so it does,
but it is an eye rhyme: that is, it is a rhyme that looks perfect but
sounds off, which neatly encapsulates Byron's thinking on the relationship between rhyme and love.

   Byron finds room for love poetry in *Don Juan* just as he finds room for
poetry of almost every other kind, but by and large he chooses not to rhyme
like the amatory poets, pairing his rhymes as Venus pairs her doves. He
presents himself instead as a master of comic rhyme. A reviewer in the
Monthly Magazine dismisses those offended by 'his lordship's heinous
outrages' against what they 'conceive to be legitimate rhyme'. How, he
asks, would such critics respond to Samuel Butler's *Hudibras* if it were
newly issued from the press?[14] Comic rhyming is founded on difference, on
incongruity. Comic rhymes do not connect: they mark points of disjunc-
ture, and in this they mirror Byron's stanza, the 'special characteristic' of
which, as Catherine Addison notices, is disjunction, the disjunction
between the first six lines and the concluding couplet.[15] When Moore
read the first canto of *Don Juan* in manuscript, he noted how, when he
introduced Donna Inez, Byron rhymed dimity 'very comically to
sublimity':[16]

> Her serious sayings darken'd to sublimity;
> In short, in all things she was fairly what I call
> A prodigy – her morning dress was dimity.   (I, 12)

'Sublimity' makes Donna Inez the peer of Germaine de Staël: 'dimity' puts
her in company with Harriet Smith, fingering the stuffs at Ford's while

Emma gazes impatiently through the doorway. The most famous comic rhyme in the whole poem works similarly: it pits not just husbands against wives, but the polysyllabic epithet 'intellectual' against the four monosyllabic words with which it rhymes:

> But – Oh! ye lords of ladies intellectual,
> Inform us truly, have they not hen-peck'd you all. (I, 22)

Byron was so taken with the rhyme that paired Cato with potato that he used it three times (once in the plural: see VII, 4; XIII, 92; and XV, 37). It is not always clear if he is thinking of Cato the Elder or his great-grandson, but in either case what strikes is the delightful incongruity of juxtaposing the stern Roman republican and the earthy Irish tuber. Byron particularly prizes rhymes that bring together the ancient and the modern or the native and the exotic. Lady Adeline serves her guests 'gibier' rather than game. Byron uses the French term, he claims, to make his 'rhymes run glibber'. A native dish such as bubble and squeak would 'spoil [his] liquid lay', a claim, of course, that contradicts itself because, even as he points out the impossibility, he manages to place bubble and squeak so winningly in his ottava rima stanza. Spare ribs are another dish that Byron fears may not be poetical enough to accommodate in verse, a fear that he at once puts to rest (or maybe justifies) by making a stanza in which 'spare rib here' rhymes with 'gibier' and 'glibber' (XV, 71). When Byron mentions Lope de Vega, the greater part of whose work Donna Inez knows by heart, 'Lopé' rhymes with 'prompter's copy' and 'shut up shop – he' (I, 11). He is particularly fond of rhyming across languages.[17] Numa Pompilius, a name out of Livy, is made to rhyme with 'bilious' (I, 35), and 'Aeneids, Iliads, and Odysseys' rhyme with 'pantaloons or boddices' (I, 41). Byron's travels had taken him as far as the Black Sea, but when he revisits the experience in *Don Juan*, he brings to bear on it a distinctively English vocabulary:

> There's not a sea the passenger e'er pukes in,
> Turns up more dangerous breakers than the Euxine. (V, 5)

Rhyme is one of the features of poetry that is lost in translation, which may be one reason that Byron is so fond of rhyming between languages. 'Praise' rhymes with 'Bouts rimés' (XVI, 50), and 'true is' with 'petits puits' (XV, 48) (although in both cases only if the French phrase is allowed, like the name of the poem's hero, an emphatically English pronunciation). But 'mi vien in mente' would rhyme well enough with

'five-and-twenty' even if spoken by an Italian (I, 62). Rhymes like these
are Byron's way of insisting that England is one nation in a world of
many nations. They are rhymes that rehearse a principle that Byron
had upheld from the very beginning of his career, when he chose as the
epigraph to the first canto of *Childe Harold* a quotation from Fougeret
de Monbron's *Le Cosmopolite*: 'L'univers est une espèce de livre, dont
on n'a lu que la première page quand on n'a vu que son pays.' But
rhyming in *Don Juan* is very different from the rhyming of *Childe
Harold*. Both poems are written in an exacting stanza, but in *Childe
Harold* Byron cultivates the impression that he can write Spenserian
stanzas effortlessly. He may grant himself an occasional licence, rhyming 'lost' with 'coast' (I, 25), or 'brook' with 'duke' (I, 33), but such
infractions are slight and rare. He anticipates the rhyming of *Don Juan*
only when the rhyme scheme forces him into a quaint medievalism, as
when the buildings and the citizens of Lisbon are described as
'unsightly to strange ee' (I, 17), or in the final stanza of the first
canto when he promises the reader, 'he that rhymeth now may scribble
moe' (I, 93). But that is the only line in the whole poem in which
Byron speaks of himself as a rhymer. In *Don Juan*, the reader is always
being reminded of it, as when the rhyme scheme obliges Byron to
borrow from the Scots the word 'whilk', prompting the confession that
'[t]he rhyme obliges me to this' (V, 77). John Johnson is, despite his
name, a father figure for Don Juan, the fount of a good deal of worldly
wisdom. The ups and downs of life, he advises, just have to be borne
with:

> Men are the sport of circumstances, when
> The circumstances seem the sport of men.   (V, 17)

It is a truth that he encapsulates in a couplet, and a truth that Byron acts out
all through a poem in which he represents himself so often as a poet who has
become the sport of his rhyme scheme, a poet in thrall to 'the wicked
necessity of rhyming',[18] who likes nothing better than, as Rachel
Brownstein puts it, to leave his reader 'wondering whether the poet is forcing
his stanza or the stanza its poet'.[19] Johnson offers the couplet to Juan as
a consolation when Juan is in 'a pickle', chained and offered for sale in the
Istanbul slave market. Byron too, tightly chained by his ottava rima stanza, is
forever finding himself in a pickle. When Raucocanti, the opera buffo,
describes how the whole troupe had been sold into slavery by their
'Machiavellian impresario', Byron seems to have set himself an impossible
rhyming challenge. He can meet it only because it is an Italian opera

company, which allows the buffo to complain that he and his colleagues had been left without 'a single scudo of salario', and licenses Byron to devise for him an Italian oath, 'Corpo di Caio Mario!', even if it is an oath with which no Italian would be familiar (IV, 82).[20]

Poets like Rogers work hard to make their rhymes seem inevitable, but in *Don Juan* Byron reverses the procedure. He glories in the arbitrariness of his rhymes. *Don Juan* is a wayward poem, a poem so capricious in its movements that its readers, at the mercy of a poet who never knows 'the word which will come next' (IX, 41), often lose all sense of where they are going. But neither the poet nor his readers are ever allowed to forget the vehicle they are travelling in, even if sometimes, as in the case of the kibitka, that 'cursed sort of carriage without springs' in which Juan and Leila make their journey to St Petersburg (IX, 30), it is the jolts that serve to remind them. The poem's waywardness is throughout countered by the regularity of 'the octave's chime' (VI, 18). Rhyme is the only constant that Byron recognises in *Don Juan*,[21] but he chooses rhymes that never try to conceal from the reader the knowledge that rhyme is an arbitrary principle. The order that rhyme gives to the poem is no less arbitrary than the European order devised by Castlereagh and Metternich at the Congress of Vienna, where they had busied themselves '[c]obbling at manacles for all mankind' (Dedication, XIV). Byron does not think of the world as naturally ordered, still less as under the benign supervision of a divine providence. It is the fate of this world, as of all the worlds that preceded it and all those that will follow it, to be 'hurled / First out of and then back again to Chaos' (IX, 37). Chaos is its natural state, and Byron's rhymes reveal as much even as they impose on the poem its one, fragile, sometimes desperately contrived principle of organisation.

William Jerdan does not limit his strictures to Byron's rhyming. He has a habit of choosing certain stanzas, the opening stanzas of Canto VII for example, and reprinting them as prose. It is his way of lending support to the claim that *Don Juan* is not written in 'metred lines', but in Byron's 'own unmusical rhythm'.[22] In the stanzas that begin Canto VII, Byron seems to admit as much himself. His poem is '[a] non-descript and ever varying rhyme'. That is what makes it like the 'Love' and 'Glory' that Byron invokes in the first stanza of the canto. They gleam with a light that is 'transcendant' but fleeting, a light not to be relied on. 'Chill, and chained to cold earth', we lift up our eyes in search of 'either lovely light':

> A thousand and a thousand colours they
> Assume, then leave us on our freezing way.   (VII, 1)

Byron's rhythms in *Don Juan* are apt, even when they are at their most entrancing, quite suddenly to lapse, and when they lapse the charm is broken and the poem's readers feel abandoned, left upon their freezing way. It is in the very next stanza that Byron celebrates his poem as

> A non-descript and ever varying rhyme,
> A versified Aurora Borealis,
> Which flashes o'er a waste and icy clime.

And then, all at once, the celebration is cut short, interrupted by a line that seems, in comparison with the lines that precede it, uncertain in its movement, tremulous – 'When we know what all are, we must bewail us' – before the stanza ends flamboyantly, with a flourish:

> But, ne'ertheless, I hope it is no crime
> To laugh at *all* things – for I wish to know
> *What* after *all*, are *all* things – but a *Show*?   (VII, 2)

Appearances, it seems, are all that we have, except that appearances never quite offer a secure shelter from the truth that they disguise, the emptiness at the heart of things. Metre in *Don Juan* is 'a *Show*'. It imposes on the verse a fragile order, like the order imposed by rhyme, an order maintained in the lines I have just quoted only by Byron's italics. But it was the third stanza of the canto that must have persuaded Jerdan to pick out this passage for special reprehension, because it is in the third stanza that Byron rounds on his critics, amongst them, Jerdan may have suspected, himself:

> They accuse me – *Me* – the present writer of
> The present poem – of – I know not what, –
> A tendency to under-rate and scoff
> At human power and virtue, and all that:
> And this they say in language rather rough.
> Good God! I wonder what they would be at!
> I say no more than has been said in Dante's
> Verse, and by Solomon and by Cervantes.   (VII, 3)

Byron responds roughly here to the rough language of his critics: 'rough' in the stanza rhymes harshly with 'of' and 'scoff'. In the first two lines, indignation all but breaks free of metrical constraints. Byron may claim for his practice the authority of Dante, but he allows, as Dante would never have done, the phrase 'Dante's / Verse' to straddle the line break. Byron is confronting his detractors, and one of the ways that he does so is to allow his iambic pentameter lines to be contaminated by the irregular rhythms of their critical prose, the kind of prose with which the reviewers had belaboured him and his poem.

By the time he embarks on the seventh canto, Byron, whatever captious critics like Jerdan might say, had given ample proof of his extraordinary facility in meeting the demands that his chosen stanza imposed on him. By and large he wears the form as gracefully as Juan carries off the women's clothes that Baba supplies him with, but, and in this he is again like his hero, Byron makes no attempt to conceal that the fit is sometimes awkward:

> But tugging on his petticoat he tripp'd,
>   Which – as we say – or as the Scotch say *whilk*,
> (The rhyme obliges me to this; sometimes
> Monarchs are less imperative than rhymes) –   (V, 77)

Juan trips, 'Whilk, which (or what you please), was owing to / His garment's novelty, and his being awkward' (V, 78). Byron recognises that his 'way of writing will appear exotic' to his readers (IV, 6), just as exotic as it feels to Juan to be wearing a petticoat, and he sometimes allows himself as well as his hero to trip, to trip up in his metre or in his rhyme. Metre, he knows, casts a spell over the reader, and Byron claims to be an adept: he has or at least he had, he claims, an ear. It was an ear that had once served him 'prettily' (XII, 75). But he is a metrical wizard just as fascinated by moments when 'the spell is broke', moments when his readers are jerked out of their trance, like the dreamer startled into wakefulness '[b]y the watchman, or some such reality, / Or by one's early valet's cursed knock' (II, 152). The first of those two lines is an iambic pentameter but a pentameter most easily read as if it were a snatch of prose. In *Don Juan*, the metrical flow is often interrupted by prose rhythms. When Juan rejects Gulbeyaz's advances, Byron, as is his wont, offers a choice of similes to describe her condition:

> A tigress robb'd of young, a lioness,
>   Or any interesting beast of prey,
> Are similes at hand for the distress
>   Of ladies who cannot have their own way.   (V, 132)

This is Byron making poetry by rote, and he admits as much: the epithet for the beast of prey, 'interesting', confides in his readers. It offers them a knowing wink. But the fourth line of the stanza is more cunning. It distresses the ear by resisting the metre, as if the poet can no more have his own way than the ladies. The line proves almost as intractable to the reader's metrical demands as Juan proves to be when Gulbeyaz propositions him. It is a common effect in the poem. Women who have a reputation, women who have been 'in their youth a little gay', are better guides when it comes to affairs of the heart than 'the harsh Prude':

> I think you'll find from many a family picture,
>   That daughters of such mothers as may know
> The world by experience rather than by lecture,
>   Turn out much better.   (XII, 45)

The difference between knowing by experience and knowing by lecture is made palpable when Byron points it out in a line so very hard to read as an iambic pentameter. His assaults on the reader's ears are sometimes more violent, as when he contrasts English with 'Continental oaths', oaths in comparison with which the English '"Damme's" quite ethereal'. He offers no example of the kind of continental oath he has in mind, fearing it might 'have a sound affronting in't', but offers in its stead a line that affronts the ear more violently perhaps than any line in the poem: 'Spirit would name, and therefore even I won't anent' (XI, 43). The metrical effects are commonly gentler. Catherine the Great, '[t]hough somewhat large, exuberant, and truculent', has 'as fine a figure / As those who like things rosy, ripe, and succulent, / Would wish to look on' (IX, 62), a judgement supported by lines that wear so gracefully their two extra syllables. 'The heroic lay is tuneless now', the turncoat bard laments on Lambro's island (III, 715). In its place Byron offers his own unheroic lay, which is not tuneless, but is nevertheless a lay perfectly willing to accommodate tunelessness, if only to acknowledge that its ultimate loyalty is not to the tune but to the truth.

H. N. Coleridge remembers S. T. Coleridge, who was his uncle and his father-in-law, inveighing against the metrical laxity of modern poets: 'How lamentably the *art* of versification is neglected by most of the poets of the present day! – by Lord Byron, as it strikes me, in particular, among those of eminence for other qualities.' But Coleridge made an exception of the third canto of *Don Juan*. He thought it 'the best, that is the most individual thing', in all he knew of Byron's work, and he picked out one stanza in particular for commendation:[23]

> A band of children, round a snow-white ram,
>   There wreathe his venerable horns with flowers
> While peaceful as if still an unwean'd lamb,
>   The patriarch of the flock all gently cowers
> His sober head, majestically tame,
>   Or eats from out the palm, or playful lowers
> His brow, as is in act to butt, and then
> Yielding to their small hands, draws back again.   (III, 32)

From the stanza's first line, so calmly grand in its movement, Byron elimin-
ates all the 'irregularity of chime' (XV, 20) so evident elsewhere in the poem.
His metrical exuberance is majestically tamed, gentled down to a point at
which it meets with Coleridge's approval. But the island episode is a special
case. Juan is washed up on the beach and loses consciousness. When he
emerges from his trance and opens his eyes, Haidée is bending over him. His
eyes are 'swimming', and it takes time before he is able 'slowly' to resolve
what he sees into a 'lovely female face of seventeen' (II, 112–13). The Haidée
he sees for the first time is like a woman he has dreamed of come magically to
life, and all through the episode she retains that character. Julia and
Catherine, Lady Adeline Amundeville and 'her frolic Grace – Fitz-Fulke',
all remain separate from Juan, independent of him, but, when he and
Haidée consummate their love, 'heart, and soul, and sense, in concert
move' (II, 186). It is not just that body and spirit are perfectly in tune, the
point is that there is no telling the heart or the soul of one of them from the
heart and the soul of the other. They are as one, a condition that is only
possible, perhaps, because they have no language in common. It is because
'their speech / Was broken words' that they come to feel that they have no
need of any material means of communication: 'they *thought* a language
there' (II, 189). The illusion cannot survive Lambro's return, and even before
then the lovers have a premonition of what awaits them. They are gazing at
the sunset when 'a sudden tremor came, / And swept as 'twere, across their
heart's delight, / Like the wind o'er a harp-string'. The two of them feel that
tremor as if they were a single person, but it makes them recognise for the
first time their difference from each other:

> And thus some boding flash'd through either frame,
> And call'd from Juan's breast a faint low sigh,
> While one new tear arose in Haidée's eye.   (IV, 21)

In that 'sudden tremor' the lovers imagine themselves separated from
each other. He sighs, but she cries. Two stanzas later, when one of
them, Haidée, speaks her fear, she reveals how that sudden tremor has
affected her. Her voice quite suddenly loses all its confidence: 'If it
should be so, – but – it cannot be – .' That line can be read so that it
makes metrical sense, and it can be read so that it makes emotional
sense, but I do not think it can be read in a way that makes both kinds
of sense at the same time.[24]

Most poets foster the illusion that, by some happy accident, their formal
obligations exactly coincide with their duty to speak of the world as it is.
The word that rhymes, they make us believe, is the only word that could so

precisely express what they wanted to say. In the same way they foster the impression that each sentiment has its proper rhythm which, as if by magic, always turns out to be a rhythm adapted to the movement of the iambic pentameter line, if that should be the metre they happen to have chosen. Fostering that illusion is what Coleridge calls the art of versification, and, as Coleridge noted with approval, it is an illusion that Byron sustains almost all the way through the episode in which Juan and Haidée fall in love on Lambro's island. All through this episode rhyme and metre move in concert, and they do so in sympathy with Juan and Haidée, with the two lovers whose 'heart, and soul, and sense, in concert move'. As the outcome of their love story reveals, it proves in the end to be an illusion that they have only one heart and one soul between them, but it is a precious illusion, an illusion that Byron all through the third canto seems happy to foster. It is after all one of the abiding human dreams. But Byron knows very well that in all ordinary human experience heart, and soul, and sense do not move in concert. Much more often they jar against one another, and the poet who recognises that must be prepared to abandon what Coleridge thinks of as the art of versification for the irregularity of chime that is more in tune with the world as we experience it.

In *Don Juan* Byron takes up the stanza he had used in *Beppo*, and would use again in *The Vision of Judgement*. By then it had become a stanza that he had made entirely his own, so much his own that W. H. Auden, when he came to write his *Letter to Lord Byron*, judged that it would be unbecoming in him to appropriate it: he made the tactful decision to write his tribute to Byron in rhyme royal instead. But however comfortable with the stanza Byron became, it always remained for him a kind of fancy dress. He was adopting a way of writing that his readers, he knew, would find 'exotic'. He wrote his ottava rima poems while he was living in Italy, where the stanza had its origin, but, for all that he settled into a comfortably domestic relationship with Teresa Guiccioli, it was a country in which Byron never felt quite at home: he never became a naturalised Italian. He regarded his role as Teresa's cavalier servente with dry amusement, aware that he was playing a part. 'I am drilling very hard to learn how to double a Shawl', he told Richard Hoppner, 'and should succeed to admiration – if I did not always double it the wrong side out'.[25] He wore his role as cavalier servente a little like the Albanian dress in which he had posed for Thomas Phillips so dashingly, and he puts on the ottava rima stanza in much the same way. Byron sustains that stanza all the way through the sixteen cantos of the poem, and he does so without ever allowing his 'kind readers' to forget their first impression. From first to last his way of writing feels exotic. In

C/f

englishness?

140

that respect Byron's stanza works a little like the hexameter line that Arthur Hugh Clough, who is more in debt to Byron than any other of the major Victorian poets,[26] uses in his most important poems. In each case the reader wonders at the poet's astonishing fluency, but wonders the more because neither poet allows us quite to forget that he is writing in a foreign poetic language.

Juan's passage through the poem, as I pointed out in Chapter 6, is charted by his switches of costume, but all his costumes, however various they may be, have one thing in common. They are all of them fancy dresses of one kind or another, from the trousers of flesh-coloured silk that Juan dons at Baba's request when he joins the harem to the military costume that he assumes at Catherine's court – at St Petersburg he is a Cupid in uniform, his wings 'subdued to epaulettes' (IX, 45) – and the dandy's uniform he takes up in England where only the distraction of meeting a ghost can explain his negligence in allowing himself to appear in a neckcloth tied '[a]lmost an hair's breadth too much on one side' (XVI, 29). The dress he wears at Haidée's feast is, of course, just as fancy, the 'shawl of black and gold', matched with a white baracan 'so transparent / The sparkling gems beneath you might behold' (III, 77). It is just that on the island the reader is allowed to imagine for a short while a world in which there is no difference between art and nature, or between fancy dress and our natural dress. We are invited to contemplate Juan and Haidée as though they were creatures of flesh and blood who, despite that, make up between them a perfect sculptural group, 'a group that's quite antique, / Half naked, loving, natural, and Greek' (II, 194). Whatever costume Juan adopts, he wears it well. He is a supremely adaptable young man. He can make himself at home in any society in which he finds himself, even the all-female society of the harem. He shares with Lady Adeline and with Byron, his creator, the 'vivacious versatility' that the French call 'mobility', the faculty of 'being strongly acted on by what is nearest' (XVI, 97). It is, Byron assures us in a note, 'a most painful and unhappy attribute', though neither Juan nor Lady Adeline seems to find it so. Those gifted with mobility can never safely be identified with the character they are for the moment assuming. They remain somehow always separate from themselves. Ottava rima is the garb that Byron chooses to assume in *Don Juan*, and like all the costumes that the poem's hero assumes, it remains, however freely Byron moves in it, a variety of fancy dress. Byron wields the stanza more flexibly than any poet had before him, more flexibly even than any of its Italian masters, and yet the stanza still remains somehow separate from him, something that from time to time he finds he has to tussle with, as when he misquotes Horace in a desperate ploy to bring a stanza to its end, contriving a line which, he confesses, 'cannot well be worse, / And was thrust in to close the octave's chime' (VI, 18).

The obvious contrast is with Wordsworth. Wordsworth rarely gives the impression that he remains separate from whatever verse form he happens to be using, more rarely still when he is writing in his favourite blank verse. The 'turnings intricate of verse' that reveal Wordsworth's world to the reader seem inseparable from the turnings of Wordsworth's mind as he contemplates that world. The blank verse becomes itself the most powerful exemplification of his faith that the world and the mind are exquisitely fitted one to the other. But Byron is the poet of a world in which the mind and the world do not fit one another at all. Little Leila's ignorance leaves her 'ill fitted . . . to jostle / With this o'erwhelming world', but, as Byron at once admits, we all share her plight: it is a world in which 'all must err', a world that can only be jostled with (X, 52). From its very outset the poem is propelled by Byron's failure to find any hero 'in the present age / Fit for [his] poem' (I, 5). For Byron the fit between the mind and the world is at best 'awkward'. When Julia first wakens to her feelings for Juan, her heart is 'in an awkward state' (I, 75). At the end of the fifth canto Byron had left Juan and Gulbeyaz in '[a] kind of state more awkward than uncommon' (VI, 7). Awkwardness is a state very far from uncommon in *Don Juan*: Byron uses the word twenty-three times in the poem. When Juan puts on the women's clothes that Baba offers him, he trips over the petticoat,

> Whilk, which (or what you please), was owing to
> His garment's novelty, and his being awkward.   (V, 78)

The predicament in which Juan finds himself is excuse enough for his clumsiness, but feeling awkward is, the poem suggests, the experience that best characterises the human condition. It is the common lot of all of us to find ourselves, as Julia finds herself when she begins to yearn for Juan, 'in an awkward state'. General Suwarrow takes it upon himself to put 'the awkward squad' through their drill (VII, 52). It is a squad of which we might all claim membership. One of the ways Byron reminds us of that is that his poem never for long lets the reader forget the awkwardness of having to keep metre and find rhymes. Juan is awkward when he trips, and so is Byron when he reports it, obliged by the necessities of rhyme to use the word 'whilk', a Scots word so palpably out of place in the Istanbul palace. Byron's metrics and his rhyming in *Don Juan* are fabulously resourceful, but Byron's are the conjuring tricks of a poet always finding himself in seemingly impossible predicaments from which he can extricate himself only by demonstrating Houdini-like skills as an escapologist. They are the special skills demanded of what Byron calls '*that there* sort of writing',[27] but that there sort of writing is the kind of writing best equipped to describe the world as Byron understands it, a world that is for all of us at best an awkward fit, which is one more reason why he could go on to claim in that letter to Douglas Kinnaird: 'As to "Don Juan" . . . is it not *life*, is it not *the thing*?'

CHAPTER 8

This Is a Liberal Age

Don Juan expresses the spirit of its age, and Byron defines that spirit clearly enough. 'This is a liberal age' (IV, 7), which must have been why, when he joined with Leigh Hunt and Shelley in launching a literary magazine, the title he chose for it was *The Liberal*.[1] But it is far from clear what Byron meant when he described his age as liberal. As D. M. Craig points out, 'even by the end of the eighteen-twenties . . . it remained unclear precisely what a "liberal" was'.[2] In the editorial that Leigh Hunt wrote to introduce the new magazine he made a virtue of that lack of clarity. 'We wish', he wrote, 'the title of our work to be taken in its largest acceptation, old as well as new'.[3] Hunt accepts that it was a word with at least two meanings, but the old and the new senses of the word were not so easily reconciled as he so airily pretends. The eighteenth-century sense of the word remained current. For Samuel Johnson it was a word connected with a person's social standing. A liberal was not mean, not low in birth, and, by an easy extension, not low in mind. To act liberally was to act in a manner becoming a gentleman. Liberality was a virtue (it was no longer a word that connoted, as it once had, licentiousness), but it was for Johnson a virtue peculiar to the rich. It denoted munificence, generosity. The new sense of the word was very different. In its French and Spanish and Italian inflections it was the word that defined the politics of those who opposed the European settlement worked out at the Congress of Vienna in the wake of Napoleon's defeat. The *Literary Chronicle* quoted approvingly the definition of a liberal offered by a foreign diplomat in his *Essay on Liberalism*: a liberal was 'a person having, or professing to have, political principles averse to most of the existing governments of Europe, under the pretence that they are not sufficiently popular'.[4] In Byron's draft preface to *Don Juan* the poem's narrator, 'our friend the story-teller', is a 'Spanish gentleman' who is 'perhaps one of the Liberals'. He belongs, that is, to the Spanish party of opposition, a party that was nationalistic, anti-monarchical, and anti-clerical (although Byron's Spanish gentleman is in

186

affable conversation with 'the curate of the hamlet'). In Italy Byron was affiliated to the Carbonari, the secret society of Italian revolutionaries, and in his letters he is in the habit of referring to the Carbonari simply as 'the Liberals'.[5] Liberalism in this new sense was foreign, scarcely more English than jacobinism, an ideology with which it was closely associated at least by conservative commentators. It was the creed, according to *Blackwood's*, of 'the Statesmen of Cockaigne' (that is, of Leigh Hunt and Hazlitt), and of the unholy alliance of 'Benthamites and Byronites' that dominated the London Greek committee. It was the label under which all 'those Englishmen who mingled contempt of their own country with their adoration of foreign ones' banded together.[6] The English and foreign senses of the word were, then, very different, so different that their meanings might at times be 'the very reverse of each other'. That is the view of one contributor to *Blackwood's*, who goes on to offer his own solution to the problem. The difficulty would be overcome, he suggests, if, when the word was used in its new sense, 'the French spelling and pronunciation had been retained'.[7]

When Byron describes his as a liberal age it seems reasonable to ask in which sense, old or new, English or foreign, he is using the word. But it may be that Byron thinks of his age as liberal precisely because the word can accommodate meanings 'sometimes the very reverse of each other'. If 'liberal' means one thing in Italy and another in Great Britain, then it is a word well adapted to describe a Europe ever more clearly characterised by the differences between its nations, and particularly well adapted to a poem that takes those differences as its primary material.[8] *Don Juan* is a poem attentive throughout to the differences between Britain and Europe, of which Britain is a part and from which it is so deeply divided. It is written in an Italian stanza, and in an Italian manner, but Byron insists on his Englishness even in moments when he breaks into Italian. '*Cosi Viaggino i Ricchi*' (This is the way the rich travel), he remarks when he describes how Lord This and Lady That race out of London as soon as the season ends to take up residence in their country seats, and at once apologises for the expression in an aside '(Excuse a foreign slipslop now and then, / If but to show I've travell'd)' (XIII, 47). Slipslop is so very English a word for a foreign tag. *Don Juan* is full of foreign words, but, as Peter Graham notes, Byron has a tendency when he uses a foreign word to insist on an emphatically English pronunciation, a habit of which the most prominent but by no means the only example is the name of the poem's hero, Juan.[9]

Liberal was certainly a partisan word. Peacock thought it a fatal mistake to have chosen it as the title of a magazine. 'A literary periodical', he felt, 'should have a neutral name'. A periodical might be 'on one side or the other', but it should not advertise its partisanship in its title.[10] When Keats imagined how he might make a living from his pen, he accepted that he would have to write for whoever would pay him, but he would write only, he insisted, 'on the liberal side of the question'.[11] To call oneself a liberal was to take sides: it was to identify oneself, as Byron did, as 'a friend to and a Voter for reform'. But the friends of reform, as Byron very well knew, were not at all a homogeneous group. There were people like Lord George Gordon, John Wilkes, Sir Francis Burdett, Horne Tooke, and Byron's close friend John Cam Hobhouse, who were all 'men of education and courteous deportment',[12] and there were those like William Cobbett and Henry Hunt, 'Orator' Hunt, who had given the principal speech at the Manchester demonstration, who were in Byron's view 'low designing dirty levellers who would pioneer their way to a democratical tyranny'. 'Why', he told Hobhouse, 'our classical education alone – should teach us to trample on such unredeemed dirt as the *dis*honest bluntness – the ignorant brutality, the unblushing baseness of these two miscreants', and he bolstered his point by quoting a line from *Don Juan*, '"Arcades Ambo" blackguards both'.[13] He was confident that his loathing of Hunt and Cobbett did nothing to undermine his liberal credentials: 'I think I have neither been an illiberal man nor an unsteady man upon politics', he told Hobhouse.[14]

Liberalism might be defined very differently. Leigh Hunt's nephew, for example, writing in the *Literary Examiner*, insisted that those who excoriated *Don Juan* only pretended to be scandalised by Byron's licentiousness. Their real objection was to his politics. They were outraged by the spectacle of a 'liberal Lord', who 'has burst the enthralment of rank and station' and 'declared for the Many against the Few'[15] (Leigh Hunt had flinched from publishing *The Mask of Anarchy* when Shelley offered it to him in the immediate aftermath of Peterloo, but the poem seems to have stuck in his nephew's mind). For Henry Leigh Hunt the mark of a liberal was that he had escaped enthralment to rank. Hazlitt agreed, but he doubted that Byron had done any such thing. For Hazlitt, Byron remained in thrall to his sense of his own aristocracy, which was why in his essay on Byron in *The Spirit of the Age* he describes Byron's liberalism as 'preposterous', and Byron often writes in a way that seems to support Hazlitt's point of view.[16] A liberal man was still for Byron, as he had been for Samuel Johnson, gentlemanly. A liberal was a man who had benefited from the classical education that he and Hobhouse shared, a liberal education as it was already beginning to be known, that is, an education not designed to fit them for any particular profession but the education proper to a gentleman.

Hazlitt builds his case for the preposterousness of Byron's liberalism on Byron's prose, on the manner that Byron adopts when referring to people like William Roberts, editor of the *British Review*, and the poet William Lisle Bowles. In Byron's letter 'To the Editor of the *British Review*', he subjected William Roberts to 'the sort of *quizzing* he might use to a person who came to hire himself as a valet to him at *Long's*' (the New Bond Street hotel), and in his dispute with the Reverend William Lisle Bowles on the merits of Pope, he clapped his fellow poet on the back 'with a coarse facetious familiarity, as if he were his chaplain whom he had invited to dine with him, or was about to present to a benefice'. *Don Juan* would have done nothing to change his mind. Hazlitt would have been alert to the pride underlying the ruefulness when Byron recalls Erneis and Radulphus, ancestors of his who came over with the conqueror, and, as the Domesday Book records, were well rewarded for their loyalty:

> eight-and-forty manors
> (If that my memory doth not greatly err)
> Were their reward for following Billy's banners.   (X, 36)

In *Don Juan*, it would have seemed to Hazlitt, Byron introduced himself to his reader much in the way that John Johnson introduces himself to Juan in the Istanbul slave market. He singles Juan out from the 'motley crew / Of Georgians, Russians, Nubians, and what not' because in the whole market '[t]he only gentlemen seem I and you' (V, 13). *Don Juan*, unlike *The Prelude*, is liberally sprinkled with the Latin tags that marked those who used them as the products of England's public schools and its ancient universities. 'Tantaene', Byron exclaims, trusting that the single word will be all that his reader needs to supply Virgil's line (XII, 33).[17] And there are Greek tags too. But in this, as in much else, Byron's poem has a double character. It is a poem written by a gentleman and addressed to a readership of his peers, and it is at the same time a poem which, in part by the accident of its pricing, 'was read by more people in its first twenty years than any previous work of English literature',[18] read by both men and women,[19] and by readers of all ranks, on sale at John Murray's at 50 Albemarle Street, and sold by William Benbow alongside the pornography and cheap reprints of Tom Paine and *Queen Mab* that formed the stock of the bookshop that Benbow chose to call, significantly enough, The Byron's Head.[20] That was why it seemed to reviewers so significant when, after the first five cantos of the poem had been published by John Murray, Byron entrusted all the later cantos to John Hunt. John Hunt told Benjamin Haydon that no one who followed his profession could ever aspire to the status of a gentleman.[21] John Murray by contrast, who made of his drawing room in Albemarle Street a literary salon in which authors and aristocrats might mingle (it was the scene of the first meeting between Byron and Walter Scott), was widely recognised as the first gentleman publisher. When Murray refused a manuscript that John Cam Hobhouse had offered him, Hobhouse responded politely. He regretted that Murray's misgivings were to 'deprive [him] of the only liberal publisher in London'.[22] The epithet alluded to the generosity of the terms Murray offered his writers, but complimented him too on his social standing. He was London's liberal publisher even though, as Hobhouse very well knew, he was a Tory. John Hunt was a liberal of a very different stripe. His liberalism was ratified not by his gentlemanly demeanour but by the two terms of imprisonment he had served in Coldbath Fields. There was scorn in John Hunt's refusal of the gentle-manly status that John Murray craved. *Don Juan* was clearly a liberal poem, but when Byron changed publishers, it led his critics to suspect that it might be a liberal poem of a very different character than they had supposed.

It might be, as the review in the *Literary Examiner* urged, that those who objected to *Don Juan* were responding to its liberal politics, but it was still far from clear what a liberal politics might be. The conspiracy theorist who warned in *Blackwood's* against the dangers of the 'Liberal System' was in no doubt that those who called themselves liberals were extremists. Whether they were 'Benthamites' or 'Byronites', liberals were believers in 'jacobin liberty' rather than the 'constitutional liberty' that British citizens enjoyed. But in 1819, *Blackwood's* had printed the first of a series of letters from 'Metrodorus', a contributor who describes himself as a 'liberal Whig', and what Metrodorus means by that is that he is a Whig remarkable for his moderation, a Whig open-minded enough to see both sides of a question. In his first contribution to the magazine he displays his open-mindedness by offering a tempered defence of *Don Juan* against the charges of immorality that the *Blackwood's* reviewer had levelled against the first two cantos of the poem.[23] Leigh Hunt was so conscious of this other sense of the word that in the inaugural issue of the new magazine he felt the need to fend it off. He delivers a smart rebuff to the 'old club-house Gentleman, in a buff waistcoat and red face' who is under the impression that a liberal is a man who recognises that 'there are good hearty fellows in all parties, and that the great business is to balance them properly'.[24] Hazlitt thought Byron's liberalism preposterously inconsistent, but even Hazlitt recognised that there was another kind of liberalism that was all but defined by its inconsistency. The *New Times,* edited by his brother-in-law, John Stoddart, he suggested, was a newspaper that promulgated so extreme a doctrine of passive obedience that its columns might serve a useful purpose in firming up the views of 'the liberal or wavering'.[25] The Byron who allowed the Carbonari to store their weapons in his apartments in the Palazzo Guiccioli in Ravenna was one kind of liberal, but the Byron who refused to follow the example of his friend Hobhouse and part company with the Whigs, the Byron who was proud to 'retain [his] "buff and blue"' (Dedication, 17), had more in common with the red-faced old clubhouse gentleman summoned up by Leigh Hunt. Byron after all had friends even amongst the Tories, which was why he was so dismayed when Arthur Thistlewood and the other Cato Street conspirators plotted to blow up the Tory Cabinet as they dined at Lord Harrowby's: 'And if they had killed poor Harrowby – in whose house I have been five hundred times – at dinners and parties – his wife is one of "the Exquisites" – and t'other fellows – what end would it have answered?'[26] *Don Juan* is written by a poet who has come to the conclusion that 'Revolution / Alone can save the Earth from Hell's pollution': (VIII, 51) '"God save the king!" and kings! / For if *he* don't, I doubt if *men* will longer' (VIII, 50). And it is also written by a constitutional monarchist who has Juan, his hero, come to England in the hope of witnessing

> That noble sight, when really free the nation,
> A king in constitutional possession
>   Of such a throne as is the proudest station,
> Though despots know it not – till the progression
>   Of freedom shall complete their education.
> 'Tis not mere splendour makes the show unjust
> To eye or heart – it is the people's trust.   (XII, 84)

In Canto XII, Byron did identify himself as a 'republican', but only to cancel the description.[27] Metrodorus, the liberal Whig who corresponded with *Blackwood's,* quarrelled with Hobhouse's description of people such as himself. Hobhouse had described them as

> Vile neutrals, who in caution's middle steering
> Are neither fish, nor flesh, nor good red herring.[28]

Hobhouse, according to another *Blackwood's* writer, was the leader of the 'Byronites', who were, together with the Benthamites and the Statesmen of Cockaigne, the chief proponents in Britain of the 'Liberal System'. But by the time that Hobhouse wrote the couplet that Metrodorus deprecated, he had good reason to suspect that Byron himself had parted company with the Byronites and taken his stand alongside the vile neutrals who were the particular objects of Hobhouse's ire.

Hobhouse had been defeated in 1819 when he stood for Westminster in the by-election following Sir Samuel Romilly's suicide. Henry Hunt, Cobbett, and Major John Cartwright made sure of that. They were determined to challenge the aristocratic Sir Francis Burdett's claim to the radical leadership and to defeat Hobhouse, his preferred candidate, even if it only resulted in the election of George Lamb, Lady Caroline's brother-in-law, who was an orthodox Whig. Hobhouse responded by cultivating the men responsible for his defeat. He published an inflammatory pamphlet that asked, 'What prevents the people from walking down to the House, and pulling out the members by the ears, locking up their doors, and flinging the keys into the Thames?' In consequence, as he must surely have foreseen, he was confined for a period in Newgate. He attended the dinner that the London radicals gave for Henry Hunt after the Manchester massacre, and he became one of Queen Caroline's closest advisers in her dispute with her husband, the new King. The tactic worked. In the 1820 general election, Hobhouse stood for Westminster again and was triumphant. Byron viewed Hobhouse's doings from afar, from Italy, and delivered on them his own mocking, occasionally spiteful commentary. Even Castlereagh, he told Augusta Leigh, was to be preferred to Henry Hunt, because 'a Gentleman scoundrel is always preferable to a vulgar one',[29] and yet Hobhouse had taken it into his head to attend the dinner given in Hunt's honour. Byron tested Hobhouse's patience to breaking point when he sent Murray a squib that Murray, as Byron should have guessed he would, arranged to be published in the *Morning Post* during Hobhouse's election campaign. It was presented as the comment of 'a Noble Lord of the highest poetical fame' on his 'quondam friend':

> Who are now the people's men,
>   My boy Hobbie O?
> There's I and Burdett – Gentlemen
>   And blackguard Hunt and Cobby O.   (9–12)

Hobhouse was understandably wounded.

In the years during which Byron wrote *Don Juan* the word liberal had many senses. It might be a word that defined a characteristically English way of thinking or a way of thinking exclusively foreign. It might be a word that betokened one's rank or it might give a name to the principled refusal to distinguish between people of different ranks. It might denote a political position defined by its extremism or by its moderation. When 'Candid' described it in *Blackwood's* as a word that was sometimes used with 'a meaning opposite to its usual and natural acceptation', many, perhaps a majority, of those who used the word would have agreed with him, but there would have been no such agreement as to which of the word's meanings was the 'usual and natural' one. Byron's peculiarity in *Don Juan* is that his liberalism accommodates all of the positions that I have outlined, occupies them even, or perhaps especially, when those positions are antithetical. On most matters after all he holds '[o]pinions two', even when the two opinions seem to be '[t]win opposites' (XV, 87). 'Opinions', he told John Murray, 'are made to be changed – or how is truth to be got at? we don't arrive at it by standing on one leg'.[30] He is a contradictory man, a man who cannot help contradicting 'every body / Even my veracious self', as he admits before immediately contradicting the admission (XV, 88). Byron was a liberal, perhaps, because liberal was the only available description of his views flexible enough to accommodate their variousness. He is a liberal precisely because it is a word that so often carries 'a meaning opposite to its usual and natural acceptation'.

Byron introduces *Don Juan* by identifying Robert Southey, the poet laureate, as his twin opposite, but Southey, as he well knows, is at once his antithesis and his counterpart, his 'dark shadow'.[31] In Canto III, 'The Isles of Greece', the most famous lyric in the whole poem is sung by both of them. The lyric offers the briefest, most trenchant illustration of Jerome McGann's thought that in *Don Juan* 'hypocrisy and the true voice of feeling cannot be separated (even if they can be distinguished)'.[32] It is a lyric in which Byron's and Southey's voices join, but not in harmony. They join in discord. Byron introduces his lyric by a portrait of its author, a poet who had once been an 'eastern antijacobin' but has since learned that it pays better to sing 'the Sultan and the Pacha' (III, 79):

> He lied with such a fervour of intention –
> There was no doubt he earn'd his laureate pension.   (III, 80)

This poet, the 'sad trimmer' (III, 82), is evidently offered as a caricature of Southey, but it is a caricature of a peculiar kind, a caricature always on the point of morphing into a selfie. He is a poet who had 'travell'd 'mongst the Arabs, Turks, and Franks' and had 'pick'd up several odds and ends / Of free thoughts in his travels'. He boasts of 'having lived with people of all ranks' (III, 83–4), prides himself on being '[i]n company a very pleasant fellow', and knows what it means to win '[t]he glorious meed of popular applause' (III, 82), in all which respects he seems rather more like Byron than Southey.[33] Byron describes a married couple as a 'moral centaur' (V, 158), and the author of 'The Isles of Greece' is another such centaur, a hybrid in which warring elements are joined, not man and wife on this occasion but Byron and his arch-antagonist Robert Southey. Southey is the poet whose pen is for hire, Byron the poet who speaks his mind no matter the consequence:

> The mountains look on Marathon –
> And Marathon looks on the sea;
> And musing there an hour alone,
> I dream'd that Greece might still be free;
> For standing on the Persian's grave,
> I could not deem myself a slave.   (13–18)

If this stanza is the work of the sad trimmer, it must be understood as tailoring a sentiment carefully designed to meet the tastes of the Greek audience. In another country the Southeyan poet would have offered something very different:

> In France, for instance, he would write a chanson;
> In England, a six canto quarto tale.   (III, 86)

But readers of *Don Juan* were from the first much more likely to read the stanza as Byron's recollection of the afternoon of 24 January 1810, when he and Hobhouse rode over the plain where the battle of Marathon had been fought, passing by without noticing it the mound that marked the grave of the Athenian warriors who had fallen there, and to understand it as Byron's noblest articulation of the cause for which, three years later, he was to die. But there remain other possibilities. Byron allows that the sad trimmer might have recovered just this once, even if only for the duration of his song, the idealism of his youth. He might have grasped the opportunity, 'being in a lone isle, among friends', to make amends for a long career of tergiversation:

> And singing as he sung in his warm youth,
> Agree to a short armistice with truth.   (III, 83)

And in any case the turncoat poet is not quite so different from the Byronic poet as might at first glance seem. Both kinds of poet are, after all, like Lady Adeline Amundeville, remarkable for their 'mobility': they are both apt to be 'strongly acted on by what is nearest' (XVI, 97). The Southeyan poet is taunted for his versatility, for his facility in all kinds of poetry '[f]rom the high lyric down to the low rational', but it seems an odd charge when brought by the author of *Don Juan*, whose muse seems even readier than Southey's to make 'increment of any thing' (III, 85). Byron most often represents himself in *Don Juan* as unfazed by the hostile reception of his poem, the antithesis of a poet such as Southey, so fawningly willing to truckle to the demands of his audience, but 'The Isles of Greece' was popular from its first publication in 1821. Byron was surely well aware that he was offering his readers, so many of whom had been disconcerted by the first two cantos of the new poem, the kind of 'high lyric' at which he was known to excel, and a lyric that expressed sentiments with which a large majority of his readers (the *Blackwood's* contributor so alert to the dangers of the 'liberal system' excepted) would be happy to concur. 'The Isles of Greece' is a liberal poem in what Leigh Hunt calls the modern sense: it sides with the Greeks in their demand to become a free nation, but it is a liberal poem too because it allows so many shades of meaning to play across its surface, which is a characteristic that it shares with the word liberal itself. 'Liberal' was a self-contradictory word, a word rather like Byron's lyric 'The Isles of Greece', the song sung in unison by Byron and by Southey, and that was just another reason why it was the proper word to describe Byron's age, the self-contradictory spirit of which he believed *Don Juan* so completely to express.

But liberal was not just a self-contradictory word. It was also a fissiparous word, a word that might describe a kind of education, the classical education that Byron thought of as distinguishing him and Hobhouse from the likes of Henry Hunt and Cobbett, or a kind of economics (in a review of Ricardo's *Political Economy* the *Edinburgh Review* refers to a free market as 'a liberal commercial system'[34]). Byron's Lambro for one is a firm believer in liberal economics, an enthusiastic practitioner of free trade. It might identify a person as a freethinker (Hobhouse points out that the 'calumnies about Atheism' brought against Byron have also been brought against 'every distinguished liberal writer that ever lived'[35]). It very often denominated a person's politics but might equally well be a word deployed to describe those politics as moderate or a word used to categorise them as extreme. It might name an association with a political party, or it might denote a freedom from any party affiliation. Byron offered it as proof that he was not an illiberal man that he still sported the Whig colours, that he retained his 'buff and blue' (Dedication `17)), but when he claimed that 'being of no party' he was likely to 'offend all parties' (IX, 26), he was equally intent on striking a liberal pose. The term might attach itself to a transnational ideology or to an ideology that celebrated national difference.[36] In large part the word retains even today that miscellaneous character. Even the most recent attempts to define liberalism tend to go about it by identifying a fissure within the term.[37] Commentators on *The Liberal*, the short-lived magazine with the title chosen by Byron, often ask themselves whether the magazine had a 'coherent political philosophy' or whether it is better characterised by its 'messy miscellaneousness'.[38] It might rather be the case that it is the magazine's miscellaneousness that makes it true to the title Byron chose for it.

Liberalism in the early decades of the nineteenth century and since is best understood as an umbrella term. It might carry an ethical or a political sense, but more often than not those two senses converge and jostle against one another. 'It always struck [Hazlitt] as a singular proof of good taste, good sense, and liberal thinking, in an old friend who had Paine's Rights of Man and Burke's Reflections on the French Revolution, bound up in one volume, and who said, that, both together, they made a very good book.'[39] Walter Scott's politics, as Hazlitt knew very well, were at the opposite extreme to his own, and yet he offers as evidence of Scott's 'liberal' mind that he was in the habit of choosing the epigraphs to his chapters from poets 'of all factions in poetry and literature'. He may choose a stanza of Coleridge or Wordsworth, but he was just as likely to select a stanza from Byron.[40] In both cases, the word seems to suggest an open-mindedness, a freedom from narrow partisanship, and yet, as the references to the political differences that separate Burke from Paine and Wordsworth from Byron suggest, it was a word that summoned up party differences even when it was being used to discount them.

'This is a liberal age', Byron remarks. It seems on the face of it an unlikely claim to have made in 1819. In Britain the Tories seemed to be permanently entrenched in power. When Byron asks, 'Where' are 'my friends, the Whigs?' he answers, 'Exactly where they were' (XI, 79). All over Europe, in France, in Spain, in Italy, and even in Greece, the forces of liberalism seemed to be in retreat. But for Byron what marks his age as liberal is that it is an age better characterised by the differences between people rather than by what they have in common. For Malcolm Kelsall, who finds Byron's liberalism just as preposterous as Hazlitt, the impossibility of defining what Byron meant when he described the age as liberal only serves to expose his political impotence. The many and often self-contradictory senses of the word are evidence for Kelsall only of 'the fragmentation of the language of opposition' in the face of the more powerful conservative language of those who re-drew the map of Europe at the Congress of Vienna.[41] But I would prefer to argue that the language of liberalism in the nineteenth century was powerful precisely because it was fragmented. *Don Juan* is 'an epic as much in the spirit of our day as the Iliad was in Homer's', and the spirit of the day was remarkable for its divisions. *Don Juan* is the epic poem of its age because it takes difference as its principal topic: the difference between high literature and low, between Britain and the countries of the Mediterranean, between men and women, between the mind and the body, between the public and the private, and between love and marriage. It was Byron's daughter Ada who worked with Charles Babbage to develop his difference engine, but *Don Juan* is a difference engine too, although a difference engine of a very different kind.

Byron identified his age as liberal in 1819, towards the end of the second decade of what was to prove, although the Tories were in government for half of it, a liberal century. It was a liberal century in part because liberalism is the only term plastic enough to accommodate the variety of political postures that the century assumed, but it was not just that. Some of the century's most distinctively liberal measures, the Great Reform Bill for example, were passed into law by Liberal governments. It was Lord Melbourne's government that was responsible for passing into law the Custody of Infants Act in 1839, and the Married Women's Property Act of 1882 was the work of another Liberal government led by Gladstone. But Catholic emancipation was secured in 1829 by a government headed by Byron's bête noir the Duke of Wellington. The Corn Laws were repealed in 1846 by Robert Peel, another Conservative prime minister and Byron's schoolfellow at Harrow (they were 'both at the top of [their] remove' and were 'on good terms', although it was Peel's brother who was Byron's 'intimate friend'[42]), and it was another Conservative, the arch Byronist Benjamin Disraeli, who secured the passage of the 1867 Reform Act that at last enfranchised the urban working class. Still more to the point, it had been yet another Tory, the foreign secretary George Canning, almost a universal genius according to Byron, and the cabinet minister who gave the speech to his Liverpool constituents with which I began, who did more than any other British politician to secure Greek independence, the liberal cause for which Byron died.[43]

It was not that party antagonisms had lapsed. The political and personal relations of Disraeli and Gladstone, for example, were famously vituperative. It was rather the case that Britain had become ungovernable except by those prepared to regulate their actions in accord with loose, usually unstated liberal principles. Canning had criticised the crowd that met in

Manchester in August 1819 to demonstrate in favour of parliamentary reform as 'an aggregation of individuals', a coming together of those who had 'no permanent relation to one another, no common tie'. As the century wore on, it became ever clearer that Canning's description applied not just to the Manchester demonstrators but to the population of Great Britain as a whole, and such a population could be governed only by those willing to accommodate its differences. In 1823, J. S. Boone offered his own blithe understanding of liberalism: 'We imagine liberality to consist in exercising a perfect freedom of thought and opinion ourselves, and *in allowing an equal freedom to other men*.'[44] He offers the definition in correction of a note to the fourth canto of *Childe Harold* in which the claim is made that we have 'outlived the old meaning of "liberality," which is now another word for treason in one country, and for infatuation in all'. Boone believes that he is disagreeing with Byron. In fact, the note had been written by Hobhouse some time before, it should be noted, he had taken the decision himself to become a liberal in the modern sense and make common cause with men like Henry Hunt. Boone seems more or less in accord with the Byron of *Don Juan*, although Byron, we can at least hope, might have thought to add that freedom is never perfect and rarely equal. 'This is a liberal age, and thoughts are free' (IV, 7), Byron writes. A population made up of heterogeneous individuals, a population that only ever amounted to an aggregation, could not be governed unless its thoughts were allowed to be free, unless difference of opinion, at least up to a point, was tolerated, although tolerated, it may well be, in some more than others, which is why throughout the century British governments of whatever stripe were all in a loose sense liberal.

In 1826, just three years after the final cantos of *Don Juan* were published, Disraeli's Vivian Grey, as I pointed out in Chapter 1, was already claiming that the 'reign of Poesy is over'. Grey has ambitions to write an epic, 'but', he insists, 'it shall be in prose'. Six years later, in *Contarini Fleming*, Disraeli continued to insist that 'the age of versification has passed'.[45] By the time that Victoria came to the throne the epic ambitions that so many of the Romantic poets shared had passed to the novelists.[46] It was the novelists, Disraeli amongst them, who were the true heirs of *Don Juan*, and the Victorian novel, in the loose sense in which I am using the term, is a liberal literary form. It was a form that evolved to represent a society that was an aggregation rather than a community, by which I mean a society best described by attending to the differences between its members. The influence of *Don Juan* is most obvious in the fiction of the 1820s and 1830s when the market was dominated by two kinds of novel, the Newgate novel and the fashionable or silver fork novel. The two kinds seem antithetical, except that both had their origin in *Don Juan*. The germ of the Newgate novel (an early example, *Paul Clifford* (1830), was written by Disraeli's fellow Byronist Edward Bulwer) can be traced to Juan's encounter with Tom the highwayman in Canto XI, and the fashionable novel, as I pointed out in Chapter 1, still more evidently has its origins in the English cantos of Byron's poem. *Beppo*, according to Catherine Gore, the most successful fashionable novelist of all, may take its place on the shelves, whereas *Don Juan* must be 'hidden behind an edition of Chesterfield's works'.[47] But although its presence may be hidden, *Don Juan* is never far from the minds of the fashionable novelists. In Thomas Lister's *Granby*, Caroline Jermyn has 'a *naïveté*, a sort of intellectual verdure, which to use a hackneyed expression, was perfectly "refreshing"'.[48] It was Byron who had alerted Lister to the cliché:

> And one good action in the midst of crimes
> Is 'quite refreshing,' in the affected phrase
> Of these ambrosial, Pharisaic times.   (VIII, 90)

The character in Lord Normanby's *Matilda* who is interrupted in the composition of verses bidding farewell to his native land when his 'patriotic sickness yielded to one of a less sentimental description'[49] very obviously mimics Byron's Juan, his noble adieu to Donna Julia and to Spain interrupted when he grows 'inarticulate with retching' (II, 20). Byron laments the passing of the dandies, 'Where's Brummel? Dished. Where's Long Pole Wellesley? Diddled' (XI, 78), and the line lingered in Disraeli's mind when he was writing *The Young Duke*: 'Lord Hounslow was done, and Lord Bagshot was diddled.' *The Young Duke*, still more than the other fashionable novels, is an echo chamber for *Don Juan*. 'Where are the Lady Carolines and Franceses?' asks Byron (XI, 80), and Disraeli too invokes 'Ye Lady Carolines and Franceses', only adding 'ye Lady Barbaras and ye Lady Blanches'. 'It was a night', writes Disraeli, 'soft as the rhyme that sighs from Rogers' shell'. He is remembering the hinges of the palace doors in *Don Juan* that turn 'as smooth as Rogers' rhymes' (V, 89). 'To stand amid the cold ashes of your desolate hearth, with all your Penates shivered at your feet' is a circumstance, Disraeli remarks, that would 'tell in a novel'. But he thinks so only because it had already told in a poem. Juan's father, abandoned by his mother, finds himself '[s]tanding alone beside his desolate hearth / Where all his household gods lay shiver'd round him' (I, 36).[50] It is entirely appropriate, as I pointed out in Chapter 1, that Byron should make an appearance as a leading character in one of the last and most successful of the fashionable novels, Catherine Gore's *Cecil: or, the Adventures of a Coxcomb* (1841).

Don Juan leaves its mark on later Victorian novels too.[51] Lady Glencora, the leading character in Trollope's Palliser novels, is a direct descendant of Lady Adeline Amundeville. Lord Henry leaves Lady Adeline to attend to his despatches (he is a Privy Councillor), and 'as he went out, calmly kissed her, / Less like a young wife than an aged sister' (XIV, 69). Charlotte Brontë, like all her siblings, was an enthusiastic Byronist, and she surely remembered Lord Henry's kiss when St John Rivers, at the urging of his sisters, first kisses Jane Eyre, and she recognises at once that the kiss he bestows on her is no different from the kiss with which he salutes his sisters.[52] Byron's country girl in her close cap and scarlet cloak might not have been remembered so sharply, but she prefigures any number of young women in nineteenth-century novels, from George Eliot's Hetty Sorrel in *Adam Bede* and Hawthorne's Hester Prynne to Hardy's Fanny Robin in *Far from the Madding Crowd*. But my point is not just that the project Byron sets himself in *Don Juan*, the plan to write a poem as much in the spirit of a liberal age as the *Iliad* is in Homer's, is a project taken up after Byron's death by the novelists rather than the poets. I want to suggest that in important ways the Victorian novelists failed to match Byron's achievement. In *Don Juan*, I want to claim, Byron contrived an epic more in tune with the liberal age that it addressed than any of the novelists who succeeded him quite managed.

Victorian novels arrive at a resolution. A will is discovered, a hidden ancestry comes to light, the young couple whose love has long been thwarted meet at the altar. Byron, too, imagined *Don Juan* coming to a conclusion, the poem's hero turning Methodist at the last, or guillotined in the French Revolution like Anarcharsis Clootz, but long before the poem was interrupted by the death of its author it was clear that he was never going to finish it, if only because he would never have been able to bring himself to let it go.[53] Byron understood very well the urge that the Victorian novelists satisfy for fictions to reach a conclusion. He knows that

> All tragedies are finish'd by a death,
> All comedies are ended by a marriage.   (III, 9)

But it is not an urge that he surrenders to himself. He feels no need to tie up his loose ends. He is happy to leave them loose, and that is just one sign of his willingness not to offer his readers a fiction from which a clear pattern emerges that will console them for the inchoate messiness of their lives.

The closed endings favoured by Victorian novelists were needed to transform the aggregation of individuals that consumed their fictions into a community of like-minded readers, which was a kind of community that in the nineteenth century could only ever be realised through fiction. Thackeray never had a good word to say about Byron. Byron might have been a great poet, he once suggested, if only he had 'taken his meals properly, and allowed himself to grow fat': 'If that man had respected his dinner, he would never have written *Don Juan*.'[54] But it is Thackeray in *Vanity Fair* who of all the Victorian novelists comes closest to replicating Byron's achievement. Like *Don Juan*, *Vanity Fair* has a showman narrator, and Thackeray finds himself just as much as Byron in want of a hero: *Vanity Fair*, as its subtitle announces, is a novel without one, although in compensation Thackeray, like Byron, offers his readers more than one heroine. Thackeray is like Byron, too, in cultivating an aggressive relationship with his readers, and in refusing to truckle to their sentimental tastes. But Byron imagines *Don Juan* being read by a greater variety of readers than Thackeray accommodates. The 'prudish readers' (I, 209) are prominent amongst them, but Byron is aware that he has other, very different readers, some of them 'atrocious' (XIV, 97). He has readers like Douglas Kinnaird, for example, who upbraids him for being too hard on Catherine the Great ('why blame her for liking fucking?').[55] He has readers whose great object is to find in their reading relief from the 'longueurs' of their lives (III, 97). He has impercipient readers, readers whose special gift it is to close ''gainst the light their orbs of vision' (VI, 88), readers who do not have the wherewithal to 'constitute a reader' (XIII, 73), and he has other, quite different readers, readers in whom he is happy to place his trust: 'A lively reader's fancy does the rest' (VI, 98). There is the 'gentle reader', shocked by 'vulgar oaths' (VIII, 1), and there are the readers who gloat over reports of crim. con. cases in the newspapers (XII, 65). There are, it is true, 'common readers' (VII, 33), a phrase that may conjure up a reading community but in *Don Juan* is just as likely to refer to readers that Byron thinks of as beneath him (Byron knows that he has readers 'of every degree' (XII, 20)). He differs from the Victorian novelists who came after him in refusing to make any attempt to dragoon all these readers into a community of the like-minded, into 'a multitude', as Dickens put it, 'moved by one sympathy'.[56] He allows his readers to be different from one another, and still more importantly he allows them, too, to be different from himself.[57]

In George Eliot's *Middlemarch*, Fred Vincy takes the view that 'all choice of words is slang'. Slang is language that 'marks a class', and because no one, in Fred's view, can claim independence of the class system, it

follows that everyone speaks slang. Rosamond, Fred's sister, believes that
there is a difference between slang and 'correct English', but Fred replies
that 'correct' English is just 'the slang of prigs who write history and
essays'.[58] Byron sometimes imagines, like Rosamond, that there is such
a thing as correct English – it is the kind of English that Castlereagh cannot
speak – but far more often he sides with Fred. There is no common
language, only a variety of slangs, a variety, that is, of ways of speaking
and writing that mark the class or the profession of their speakers. There
are the 'phrases of refinement', words such as 'empressement', that English
people of a certain class 'borrow / From our next neighbours' land', and
there is the native 'Billingsgate' language preferred by their social inferiors
(XI, 42). There is naval slang, there is 'engineering slang' (VII, 11), there is
the 'flash' slang of Tom the highwayman, and the slang of the fox-hunting
men, who are impressed by Juan's performance in the field – he 'never
craned' (XIV, 33). But *Middlemarch* works only because George Eliot when
she speaks in her own person writes an English free from Fred Vincy's
strictures. She writes an English that takes all her readers by the hand and
guides them through the novel. Byron makes no such claim. His English,
he knows, is just as much a slang as every other kind of English. It marks his
class – he fears becoming 'one of many "wooden spoons" / Of verse (the
name with which we Cantabs please / To dub the last of honours in
degrees)' (III, 110) – and it marks his profession. Fred Vincy suspects that
his sister will not be able to tell apart 'bits of slang and poetry', and Byron is
inclined to agree with Fred that poetry is just another kind of slang, one
subspecies of which he must take the blame for having introduced himself.
The names of 'oriental plants' that are found in such abundance in modern
poems, the 'orange bowers, and jasmine, and so forth', have become so
popular only because 'one poet travell'd 'mongst the Turks' (V, 42). Byron
makes no claim to write a common language, a language that all his readers
will recognise as their own. The only claim that he makes is to be fluent in
a wider variety of the slangs that constitute English in the early nineteenth
century than most of his readers.[59]

There is, for Byron, no King's English in comparison with which all
other kinds of language are illegitimate. It is one of the cornerstones of his
liberalism. He had once been recognised as the 'grand Napoleon of the
realms of rhyme', but he no longer wants to exercise absolute Napoleonic
authority over all poetry, or even over the readers of his own poem (XI, 55).
He holds in 'plain, sworn, outright detestation . . .every despotism in every
nation', even the despotism that he had once himself been ceded. He
claims, too, however much we may doubt it, that he is as free from class

allegiance as he is impartial between nations. He wishes all 'men to be free /
As much from mobs as kings – from you as me'. He looks with equal
suspicion on Cobbett and on Castlereagh. He is a man who 'neither wishes
to be bound nor bind' (IX, 24–6). It is not the poem's finest moment. The
claims that Byron makes on his own behalf seem a little too self-
congratulatory. He is always more winning when his self-regard is more
rueful. But that should not bar us from recognising him as making a claim
in these stanzas central to his project for the whole poem.

Don Juan has the most dominant narrator of any major poem in all of
English literature. In comparison, the narrator of *The Prelude* seems diffi-
dent. But Byron, like Sterne before him (Byron said of *Don Juan* 'I mean it
for a poetical T Shandy'[60]), presents himself to his readers as dominant by
virtue of his oddness, of his eccentricity. He is, it may be, loveably eccentric,
but he remains all the same a character so swaddled in his eccentricity that his
difference from his readers is always preserved. Byron finds in *Don Juan*
a poem of a kind that allows him as much scope as he could wish to cultivate
his own outré individuality, but because he is at once dominant and eccentric he can be dominant without ever running the risk of becoming
dominating.[61] Byron's earlier poems are remarkable for the hold they exert
over the reader. The poems themselves, as Clara Tuite points out, exercise
the same erotic sway over their readers that their heroes exercise over the
poems' other characters. Tuite locates that dark glamour even in a late
poem such as *Cain*.[62] When Adah finds in Lucifer a 'fastening attraction'
that '[f]ixes [her] fluttering eyes on his' (I, i, 410–11), she gives potent
expression not just to the sway Lucifer exercises over her but to the hold
that Byron maintained over his readers, readers of both sexes, but women
readers, it may be, even more than men. In *Don Juan*, he lets it all go. He
gives up his claim to erotic power – 'But now at forty years my hair is grey /
I wonder what it will be like at forty?)' (I, 213). He gives up his claim even to
narrative power ('I can't oblige you, reader, to read on' (XII, 87)). It was one
reason, perhaps, why he imagined that its women readers in particular did
not take to the poem. But the decision is an index of how seriously he has
taken the resolution neither to be bound nor bind.

At the centre of most epic poems is a scene of instruction. Virgil instructs
Dante before Virgil's role is taken up by Beatrice, and Milton's Raphael
instructs Adam on how he should regulate his post-lapsarian life. In scenes
like these, epic poets betray their own ambition to instruct their readers.
When Byron introduces a scene of instruction in *Don Juan*, it is very
different, erotic rather than educational: ''Tis pleasing to be school'd in
a strange tongue / By female lips and eyes' (II, 164). Byron is careful in *Don*

Juan not to put his readers to school. He claims no prophetic powers.[63] Keats thought himself a Shakespearean rather than a Wordsworthian poet, but he was more in thrall to the 'wordsworthian or egotistical sublime' than he was prepared to admit. Endymion, he told Benjamin Haydon, 'being mortal, is led on, like Buonaparte, by circumstance; whereas the Apollo in Hyperion being a fore-seeing God will shape his actions like one'.[64] He is contrasting the heroes of his two long poems, but the contrast he draws is as much between the immature poet who wrote *Endymion* and the grown-up poet of *Hyperion* as it is between the poems' heroes. Or it might be better to suggest that Keats, like Wordsworth, scarcely makes a distinction between hero and poet, between Endymion and Apollo and himself. Byron by contrast is emphatic in his refusal to act as the 'fore-seeing God' of *Don Juan*. Juan might, for all he knows, end up guillotined or a Methodist. 'I never know the word which will come next' (IX, 41), he confesses. He has, he claims, much the same relation to his own poem as his reader: he has at any rate no more notion than the reader as to how things are going to turn out.

The plot of his own poem is one of a host of things that Byron confesses in the course of *Don Juan* that he does not know. Julia plans to preside over Juan's amatory education, and teach him 'I really don't know what, nor Julia either' (I, 81). On the critical day, the sixth of June, Julia and Juan meet in as pretty a bower as can be imagined:

> I know not well
> How this same interview had taken place,
> And even if I knew I should not tell.   (I, 105)

Julia squeezes Juan's hand; 'I cannot know what Juan thought of this' (I, 112). Juan's hand slips around Julia's waist:

> And then – God knows what next – I can't go on;
> I'm almost sorry that I e'er begun.   (I, 115)

His poem, Byron promises, will be filled 'with many things that no one knows' (I, 204), and it is filled too with all the things that Byron does not know: how he came to have 'a deal of judgement', for example, '[t]hough heaven knows how it ever found a lodgement' (I, 215). All this is from the first canto, but Byron continues to remark on all the things he does not know throughout the poem. The direction of the harem is entrusted to a woman whose title is 'the Mother of the Maids', 'Whether she was a "mother," I know not, / Or whether they were maids' (VI, 30). He cannot tell whether the lamp in Juan's chamber at Newstead Abbey stood '[u]pon his table or his toilet' (XVI, 16). He cannot be quite sure what paragraph of the newspaper

Juan reads before undressing: it was 'I think about Horne Tooke' (XVI, 27). And he leaves unresolved the issue of what happened between Juan and the Duchess of Fitz-Fulke: 'I leave the thing a problem, like all things' (XVII, 13). He is not even sure whether or not his poem is any good. He has thought it better to choose 'a modern subject', but how he has treated it he does not know (IV, 7). Byron never had the chance to read Wordsworth's great poem on the growth of a poet's mind, but it was not a poem that he could have written himself. He could, he claims, give his 'whole soul up to mind', except that he has no notion what either word might mean:

> Though what *is* soul or mind, their birth or growth,
> Is more than I know – the deuce take them both! (VI, 22)

He cannot answer Hamlet's question, whether to be or not to be, because he would first 'have to know that which *is being*' (IX, 14). It is 'very puzzling', Byron acknowledges,

> on the brink
> Of what is called Eternity, to stare,
> And know no more of what is here than there. (X, 21)

But that is the brink on which Byron takes his stand all the way through *Don Juan*.

Byron offers his own nescience in place of the epic poet's authority; that is, he bases his claim to authority on his knowledge of how little he knows: 'For me I know nought; nothing I deny, / Admit, reject, contemn' (XIV, 3). He has after all the very best authority for doing so:

> Socrates said, our only knowledge was
> 'To know that nothing could be known.' (VII, 5)

But Byron manages to regard even Socrates's scepticism sceptically. What, after all, does it achieve: it 'levels to an ass' every wise man, including Socrates himself, and for that matter Byron too. But, whatever his misgivings, throughout *Don Juan* Byron repeatedly places himself in the sceptical tradition:

> 'Que scais-je?' was the motto of Montaigne,
>   As also of the first Academicians:
> That all is dubious which man may attain,
>   Was one of their most favourite positions.
> There's no such thing as certainty, that's plain
>   As any of Mortality's Conditions;
> So little do we know what we're about in
> This world, I doubt if doubt itself be doubting. (IX, 17)

And he confirms in the very next stanza that the only reason he is not quite comfortable in classing himself amongst the sceptics is that he has his doubts about them.[65] It might be pleasant 'to float / Like Pyrrho on a sea of speculation', but he doubts whether the sceptical Pyrrho has borne in mind the danger that 'carrying sail' might 'capsize the boat': 'Your wise men don't know much of navigation.' Thomas Browne doubted whether there were impossibilities enough in religion for an active faith. Byron reverses that position. He doubts whether sceptics, even Pyrrho, the founder of the sceptical tradition, are sceptical enough: 'Oh, Doubt! – if thou be'st Doubt, for which some take thee, / But which I doubt extremely' (XI, 2). *Don Juan* is the epic poem of doubt, which makes it especially pleasant to note that one of the most prominent verbal tics in this poem so given to doubting is the use of the phrase 'no doubt'. Byron uses it on no less than fifty-seven occasions, to which should be added the eighteen occurrences of the expression 'doubtless'.

Byron's doubts converge on the question of a future life, the question that he confronts most poignantly in the fifth canto when he watches as the military commandant, shot just outside his house, dies of his wounds. But it is an issue that Byron returns to from first to last. In this poem that has no ending, Byron is especially interested in ends. 'End' is a word, as he points out in the first canto, with two meanings. Our end is at once our purpose in life ('Few mortals know what end they would be at'), and it is what brings our life to a close ('we die, you know – and then –' (I, 113)). The stanza ends wistfully, but when the thought is taken up in the following stanza, the wistfulness has become tart: 'What then? – I do not know, no more do you – / And so good night' (I, 134). But it is a question that cannot be dismissed so easily. Byron returns to it over and over again:

> What are we? and whence came we? what shall be
> Our ultimate existence? what's our present?
> Are questions answerless, and yet incessant.   (VI, 63)

Asking such questions is a waste of time:

> our days are too brief for affording
> Space to dispute what *no one* ever could
> Decide, and *every body one day* will
> Know very clearly or at least lie still.   (XI, 4)

But even though there may be no possibility of finding an answer, these are the questions that he cannot stop asking.

Thanks in large part to *Cain*, Byron had gained a reputation as a 'reviler of religion',[66] but *Don Juan* is not an irreligious poem. The questions it asks are the questions that only religions can answer.[67] If Byron had to choose between philosophy and religion, he would certainly choose the latter. The problem is that there are just too many religions to choose from: 'Religion? Yes; but which of all her sects? / Some millions must be wrong, that's pretty clear' (XV, 89–90). The Muslims defending Ismail fight

> As though there were one Heaven and none besides –
> Whereas, if all be true we hear of Heaven
> And Hell, there must at least be six or seven. (VIII, 114)

Unlike Muslims Zoroastrians recognise 'two Principles', but even Zoroastrianism 'leaves behind / As many doubts as any other doctrine' (XIII, 41). Liberalism was sometimes associated with free thought, but in *Don Juan* it reveals itself most commonly as a willingness to recognise all religions and an unwillingness to espouse any of them.[68] Byron neither believes nor disbelieves: he doubts. It was the position he maintained all through his long conversations in Greece with James Kennedy, the earnestly pious staff surgeon who attempted in the last weeks of Byron's life to win him for Christ.[69] But in *Don Juan* Byron's scepticism serves a larger purpose. The epic poem expressed the spirit of the age, and its religious spirit in particular. Dante's *Divine Comedy* is the epic of Thomist Christianity, and *Paradise Lost* is the Protestant epic. But Byron's liberal epic must be sceptical not because his was an age of scepticism (although for some, Byron amongst them, it was) but because the liberal poet 'neither wishes to be bound nor bind' (IX, 26). Only a sceptical epic, only an epic prepared to allow the big questions ('What are we? and whence came we? what shall be / Our ultimate existence?') to remain 'answerless', can express the spirit of a liberal age, because only the sceptical epic can satisfy Byron's wish that men should be free not just '[a]s much from mobs as kings' but as much 'from you as me'. None of the Victorian novelists is as ready as Byron to renounce an ambition to act as the reader's guide, to act as Virgil to the reader's Dante, which is why no Victorian novel, not even *Vanity Fair*, threatens Byron's claim to have fashioned in *Don Juan* the true epic poem of a liberal age.

All through *Don Juan* Byron offers a flamboyant display of his difference, of all that separates him from a readership that did not have ancestors who were presented with eight and forty manners as a reward for following King Billy's banners, that did not inherit in their youth a medieval abbey, that had never travelled 'mongst the Turks, that would not dream of attempting to swim the Hellespont, and that had never persuaded a young wife that her duty both to man and God required her to leave the marital home never to return.[70] Byron had long been irritated by readers' tendency to confuse him with his heroes and to think of Childe Harold or the Corsair as if they were Byronic self-portraits, but there was no confusing him with the hero of *Don Juan*. For one thing, Juan 'shone in the best part of dialogue', by which Byron means that he had the gift of keeping quiet: 'there never was a better hearer' (XIV, 37). Byron on the other hand, as the whole poem bears witness, is a man who counts 'chat' amongst his favourite things, as much a favourite with him as 'lobster-salad, and champagne' (I, 137). Byron underlines his differences from his hero just as he flaunts his differences from his readers.[71] But even as he does so he grants his readers their right to be different from him, and he grants too their differences from each other. To recognise and to accept difference is for Byron the defining characteristic of a liberal cast of mind. He is not, of course, recommending that he and his readers join together in the exercise of a bland tolerance. He likes an honest hater just as much as Samuel Johnson, and punctuates his poem with violent outbursts against Castlereagh and Henry Brougham and Samuel Romilly and Robert Southey. But even though he marks these men as the objects of his detest-ation, he does not deny them their right to differ from him. Southey, Wordsworth, and Coleridge strike him as 'shabby fellows', but they are 'poets still / And duly seated on the immortal hill' (Dedication, 6), and it is that willingness to allow the Lake Poets, however much he dislikes them, their place on the hill that suggests how Byron's variety of liberalism, his preposterous liberalism as Hazlitt describes it, offers something that even his readers in the twenty-first century might profitably attend to. As they read through *Don Juan*, those readers will rather often come across sentiments, attitudes, turns of phrase that they will quite properly find abhorrent. The doors to Gulbeyaz's chambers are guarded by pigmies whose 'wond'rous hideousness' is summed up in their skin colour, an 'extraneous mixture' neither 'black, nor white, nor gray' (V, 88). When Byron asks who rules the world, he answers, 'Jew Rothschild, and his fellow Christian Baring' (XII, 5). There are the widows of forty who wonder, as the Russian troops pillage Ismail, '[w]herefore the ravishing did not begin!' (VIII, 132). There is the casually dismissive reference to Coleridge's and Southey's marriages: they '[e]spoused two partners (milliners of Bath)' (III, 93). A competition to select the most offensive line in the poem would prompt a rather lively debate. My own vote might go to a line in the thirteenth canto, 'And Mrs. Rabbi, the rich banker's squaw' (XIII, 79). Many of the poem's first readers too found it offensive, although the passages that offended them were not always the same as those that will offend a modern reader. They were more outraged than modern readers are likely to be by the parody of the commandments ('Thou shalt believe in Milton, Dryden, Pope' (I, 205)) and by a rough humour that struck them as heartless ('They grieved for those who perish'd with the cutter, / And also for the biscuits casks and butter' (II, 61)). *Don Juan* tested then as it tests now the limits of its readers' tolerance. It is a large poem that demands, as Bernard Beatty puts it, 'an answering largeness in its readers and critics'.[72] The poem must be liberally understood if it is to be enjoyed, but it also and rather wonderfully exemplifies the kind of liberal understanding that it demands, and in that the poem has as much, perhaps, to teach its readers now as it had to teach the very different readers who first encountered the poem 200 years ago.

Notes

Introduction

1. Thomas Medwin, *Conversations of Lord Byron: Noted During a Residence with His Lordship at Pisa, in the Years 1821 and 1822* (London: Henry Colburn, 1825), 200.
2. On Peterloo, see John Gardner, *Poetry and Popular Protest: Peterloo, Cato Street, and the Queen Caroline Controversy* (Basingstoke: Palgrave Macmillan, 2011).
3. Canning's speech is reproduced in full in 'The Warder', *BEM*, 7 (April 1820), 11–21.
4. Peter Manning describes Byron's mode in *Don Juan* as 'aggregative'. See Peter J. Manning, 'Byron's Imperceptiveness to the English Word', in *Longman Critical Readers: Byron*, ed. Jane Stabler (London: Longman, 1998), 180–93, p. 188.
5. Benjamin Disraeli, *Coningsby*, Book III, chapter 5. *Coningsby* was published in 1844 but Disraeli is describing Manchester as it was in 1835, just fifteen years after Canning's speech.
6. See William St Clair, *The Reading Nation in the Romantic Period* (Cambridge: Cambridge University Press, 2004).
7. The magazines of the period, *Blackwood's* amongst them, succeeded, as David Stewart has pointed out, by offering their readers 'a distinctly modern kind of miscellaneousness, addressed to an audience that was as miscellaneous as the writing it consumed'. See David Stewart, *Romantic Magazines and Metropolitan Literary Culture* (Basingstoke: Palgrave Macmillan, 2011), 51.
8. Jerome J. McGann, *Don Juan in Context* (London: John Murray, 1976),114.
9. *BLJ*, 6, 208.
10. See Angela Esterhammer, *Print and Performance in the 1820s: Improvisation, Speculation, Identity* (Cambridge: Cambridge University Press, 2020), 209. Esterhammer suggests that the writing of the 1820s aspired to be 'profoundly ephemeral'.
11. McGann, *Don Juan in Context*, 19–21.

12. *London Magazine*, 3 (January 1821), 56.
13. Timothy Webb traces in Byron's relations with his publisher John Murray, his chief adviser William Gifford, and the friends who read his poems in manuscript a 'struggle between liberty and constraint', which is 'replicated and intensified in *Don Juan*, where it is enacted when Byron, as he does so often, calls attention to his predicament in having to meet the formal obligations demanded by the exacting stanza that he has chosen'. See Timothy Webb, 'Free Quills and Poetic Licences: Byron and the Politics of Publication', in *Liberty and Poetic Licence: New Essays on Byron*, ed. Bernard Beatty, Tony Howe, and Charles E. Robinson (Liverpool: Liverpool University Press, 2008), 219–32.
14. [Benjamin Disraeli], *Vivian Grey*, 2 vols. (London: Henry Colburn, 1826), 2, 178.

1 My Poem's Epic

1. Jerome J. McGann, *Don Juan in Context* (London: John Murray, 1976), xii. On the continuing debate as to the epic status of *Don Juan*, see Nicholas Halmi, 'The Very Model of a Modern Epic Poem', *European Romantic Review*, 21 (2010), 589–600.
2. *BLJ*, 6, 105.
3. *BLJ*, 6, 232.
4. *Samuel Taylor Coleridge: Selected Letters*, ed. H. J. Jackson (Oxford: Clarendon Press, 1987), 58.
5. *BLJ*, 6, 105. Murray's letter to Byron of 19 March 1819 had reported Ugo Foscolo's regrets 'that a Man of your genius will not occupy some Six or Eight years in the Composition of a Work & Subject worthy of you – and this you have promised to Gifford long ago & to Hobhouse & Kinnaird –since'. *The Letters of John Murray to Lord Byron*, ed. Andrew Nicholson (Liverpool: Liverpool University Press, 2007), 267.
6. Thomas Medwin, *Conversations of Lord Byron: Noted During a Residence with His Lordship at Pisa, in the Years 1821 and 1822* (London: Henry Colburn, 1825), 200.
7. Medwin, *Conversations of Lord Byron*, 278.
8. *Letters of Percy Bysshe Shelley*, ed. Frederick L. Jones (Oxford: Clarendon Press, 1964), 2, 357–8.
9. Medwin, *Conversations of Lord Byron*, 340.
10. *Literary Examiner*, 1 (5 July 1823), 9.
11. *Monthly Magazine*, 48 (August 1819), 56.
12. *British Critic*, 12 (August 1819), 197.
13. *British Review*, 18 (December 1821), 246.

14. *Literary Gazette*, 346 (6 September 1823), 562.
15. *BLJ*, XI, 117.
16. *Quarterly Review*, 27 (July 1822), 477.
17. Edward Lytton Bulwer, *England and the English*, 2 vols. (London: Richard Bentley, 1833), 2, 69, 73.
18. John Nichol, *Byron* (London: Macmillan, 1880), 208.
19. *A Selection from the Works of Lord Byron*, ed. and prefaced by Algernon Charles Swinburne (London: Edward Moxon, 1866), x. On Byron and Swinburne, see Richard Cronin, 'A. C. Swinburne and Byron's Bad Ear', in *Byron Among the English Poets: Literary Tradition and Poetic Legacy*, ed. Clare Bucknell and Matthew Ward (Cambridge: Cambridge University Press, 2021), 287–302.
20. When Swinburne speaks of 'the broad backs of the sea' he is, I suspect, misquoting James Russell Lowell, whose Columbus rides 'The broad backs of the waves which jostle and crowd / To fling themselves upon that unknown shore' (*Columbus*, 6–7), but it is Swinburne's phrase that Andrew Lang recycles.
21. W. MacNeile Dixon, *English Epic and Heroic Poetry* (London: J.M. Dent, 1912), 312; Herbert F. Tucker, *Epic: Britain's Heroic Muse 1790–1910* (Oxford: Oxford University Press, 2008), 231.
22. *The New Oxford Book of Light Verse*, ed. Kingsley Amis (Oxford: Oxford University Press, 1978), v.
23. *The Oxford Book of Light Verse*, ed. W. H. Auden (Oxford: Oxford University Press, 1938), xvii.
24. See, for example, John Lauber, 'Don Juan as Anti-Epic', *Studies in English Literature, 1500–1900*, 8 (1968), 607–19. Lauber concludes, 'Far from being a modern epic, or an adaptation of the epic to the nineteenth century, *Don Juan* systematically parodies or attacks the major conventions of epic poetry as set forth by neoclassic criticism.' Drummond Bone's view is more poised. '*Don Juan*', he writes, 'continually invokes and evokes the epic genre in order to distance itself from it', and yet he still classifies the poem 'as a human (as opposed to a divine) epic'. See Drummond Bone, *Byron* (Tavistock: Northcote House, 2000), 60.
25. 'Epic satire' is the generic description preferred by Elizabeth French Boyd, *Byron's Don Juan* (London: Routledge and Kegan Paul, 1945), 31–44, and Frederick L. Beaty, *Byron the Satirist* (DeKalb: Illinois University Press, 1985), 138–46.
26. *BLJ*, 6, 208.
27. Quoted by Tucker, *Epic*, 17 (footnote).
28. Beaty, *Byron the Satirist*, 138.

29. On Byron's interest in history, see Carl Pomarè, *Byron and the Discourses of History* (Farnham: Ashgate, 2013).
30. Hugh Blair, *A Critical Dissertation on the Poems of Ossian*, 2nd ed. (London: T. Becket and P.A. De Hondt, 1765), 4. On the transition from formal to cultural definitions of epic, see Herbert Tucker, 'The Very Idea: Epic in the Head', in *Epic*, 1–48.
31. It is in large part Tucker's answer: *Don Juan* is the epic of a period when 'no poem of culturally comprehensive ambition could afford not to be, in substantial part, mock-epic'.
32. A point made long ago by Claude Fuess, *Lord Byron as a Satirist in Verse* (New York: Columbia University Press, 1912), 160 (note).
33. Some of these instances are identified by George M. Ridenour, *The Style of Don Juan* (New Haven: Yale University Press, 1960), 136.
34. On this, see Roger B. Salomon, 'Mock-Heroes and Mock-Heroic Narrative: Byron's *Don Juan* in the Context of Cervantes', *Studies in the Literary Imagination*, 9.1 (1976), 69–87.
35. *BLJ*, 10, 68, 98.
36. [George Darley], 'Juaniana', *London Magazine*, 1 (January 1825), 82–95, p.82.
37. *London Magazine*, 3 (January 1821), 50–61, p. 57. On the disgrace of Byron's association with the Hunts, see [Henry Southern], 'Personal Character of Lord Byron', 10 (October 1824), 337–47.
38. *New Monthly Magazine*, 12 (August 1819), 75–8.
39. 'Letters of Timothy Tickler, Esq. to Eminent Literary Characters, No. VII', *BEM*, 14 (July 1823), 80–92, p. 88; 'ODoherty on Don Juan Cantos IX. X. XI', *BEM*, 14 (September 1823), 282–93, p. 282.
40. '"Luctus" on the Death of Sir Daniel Donnelly', *BEM*, 7 (May 1820), 186–205, p. 186.
41. *BLJ*, 9, 103; 'Noctes Ambrosianae, No. 1', *BEM*, 11 (March 1822), 369–89, p. 376.
42. 'Noctes Ambrosianae, No. 4', *BEM*, 12 (July 1822), 100–14. The affinity between the 'Noctes' and *Don Juan* is pointed out by their most recent editor. See *Noctes Ambrosianae, 1822–3*, ed. Mark Parker, vols. 3 and 4 of *Blackwood's Magazine, 1817–25: Selections from Maga's Infancy*, gen. ed. Nicholas Mason (London: Pickering and Chatto, 2006), viii.
43. 'Remarks on Don Juan', *BEM*, 5 (August 1819), 512–18, p. 512.
44. 'ODoherty on Don Juan Cantos IX.X. XI', 283.
45. 'Noctes Ambrosianae, No. 4', 106.
46. 'Notices to Correspondents', *BEM*, 2 (March 1818). The verses, probably written by Lockhart, were prefixed to the March number, and preface the second volume of the magazine. Thomas Chalmers, a celebrated minister of the Church of Scotland, was controversial because of his interest

in social reform. The neighbour was Archibald Constable, Blackwood's rival as a publisher, and, as the proprietor of the *Edinburgh Review*, a principal target of *Blackwood's*.

47. On imitations of Byron's ottava rima poems in *Blackwood's* and other magazines, see Richard Cronin, *Paper Pellets: British Literary Culture after Waterloo* (Oxford: Oxford University Press, 2010), 177–84.

48. [John G. Lockhart], *John Bull's Letter to Lord Byron*, ed. Alan Lang Strout (Norman: University of Oklahoma Press, 1947), 90–1. It was Strout who first definitively identified Lockhart as the author of the pamphlet.

49. See *BEM*, 3 (July 1818), 402–7; 3 (August 1818), 530; 4 (February 1819), 563–7; 4 (March 1819), 729–34.

50. *BEM*, 6 (January 1820), 390.

51. See Lee Erickson, *The Economy of Literary Form* (Baltimore: Johns Hopkins University Press, 1996), 71–103.

52. Bulwer, *England and the English*, 2, 51–67.

53. 'The Periodical Press', Howe, XVI, 231.

54. 'Detached Thoughts on Books and Reading', *London Magazine*, 6 (July 1822), 33–6, p. 33.

55. 'Remarks on Don Juan', 518.

56. [Lockhart], *John Bull's Letter to Lord Byron*, 95–6.

57. 'Odoherty on Cantos IX, X, and XI', *BEM*, 14 (September 1823), 282–93, p. 284.

58. Letitia Landon, *Romance and Reality*, ed Cynthia Lawford, vol. 2 of *Silver Fork Novels, 1826–1841*, gen. ed. Harriet Devine Jump (London: Pickering and Chatto, 2005), 95.

59. *The Journal of Sir Walter Scott*, ed. David Douglas, 2 vols. (Cambridge: Cambridge University Press, 1980), 1, 164.

60. Thomas Henry Lister, *Granby*, ed. Clare Bainbridge, vol. 1 of *Silver Fork Novels, 1826–1841*, gen. ed. Harriet Devine Jump (London: Pickering and Chatto, 2005), 323.

61. Benjamin Disraeli, *The Young Duke*, 3 vols. (London: Henry Colburn, 1831), 2, 46. Fashionable novels, most of which were published by Henry Colburn, were expensively priced, usually at a guinea for the three volumes, but the circulating libraries made them widely available.

62. Bulwer, *England and the English*, 2, 108.

63. Edward Copeland makes a strong case for Jane Austen as the chief precursor of the fashionable novelists. See Edward Copeland, *The Silver Fork Novel: Fashionable Fiction in the Age of Reform* (Cambridge: Cambridge University Press, 2012), 37–64. But April Kendra suggests that fashionable novelists are of two kinds: dandy novelists and fashionable novelists, the former being male and the latter female. See April Kendra, 'Gendering the Silver Fork: Catherine

Gore and the Society Novel', *Women's Writing*, 11.1 (London: Pickering and Chatto, 2005), 25–39. Byron is the progenitor of the dandy novel, and Jane Austen of the society novel. The dandy novel, although male, might be written by a woman, as, for example, Catherine Gore's *Cecil: Or, the Adventures of a Coxcomb*.

64. [Benjamin Disraeli], *Vivian Grey*, 2 vols. (London: Henry Colburn, 1826), 2, 178.

65. Disraeli completed his prose epic in the 1840s in his trilogy of novels, *Coningsby*, *Sybil*, and *Tancred*. In 1836, he did publish his own attempt at a verse epic, *The Revolutionary Epic*, but, as he had predicted, the attempt is disastrous. The poem remained unfinished.

66. [Disraeli], *Vivian Grey*, 2, 162.

67. Disraeli, *The Young Duke*, 2, 7.

68. Lord Normanby, *Matilda: A Tale of the Day* (London: Henry Colburn, 1825), 33.

69. Bulwer, *England and the English*, 2, 108.

70. Catherine Gore, *Women as They Are, or the Manners of the Day*, 3 vols. (London: Henry Colburn and Richard Bentley, 1830), 2, 235.

71. Gore, *Cecil*, 88.

72. Bulwer, *England and the English*, 2, 109.

73. Angela Esterhammer, *Print and Performance in the 1820s: Improvisation, Speculation, Identity* (Cambridge: Cambridge University Press, 1820), 209.

74. The relationship between *Don Juan* and pantomime has been often remarked. See especially Frederick L. Beaty, 'Harlequin Don Juan', *Journal of English and Germanic Philology*, 67.3 (1968), 395–405; Peter W. Graham, 'All Things – But a Show?', in *Don Juan and Regency England* (Charlottesville: University Press of Virginia, 1990), 62–88.

75. The meeting is described by Fiona MacCarthy, *Byron: Life and Legend* (New York: Farrar, Straus and Giroux, 2002), 184–5.

76. As Brian Nellist puts it, Byron exerts an authority that is only manifest 'in the process of reading his work': it is not available for interpretation or even description. See 'Lyric Presence in Byron: From the *Tales* to *Don Juan*', in *Byron and the Limits of Fiction*, ed. Bernard Beatty and Vincent Newey (Liverpool: Liverpool University Press, 1988), 39–77, p. 39.

77. In *Print and Performance in the 1820s* Angela Esterhammer offers the 'conjunction' of a medium such as theatrical performance defined by its ephemerality and the medium of print publication, which ordinarily aspires to permanence, as the defining characteristic of the cultural moment of the 1820s. She maps that conjunction in the magazine writing of the 1820s, in the performances of Tommaso Sgricci and the other improvisatori, in the comic improvisations of Charles Matthews on the English stage, in the magazines,

which, as she notes, were at the centre of 1820s culture, and elsewhere. As one would expect, Esterhammer includes *Don Juan* in her account, but without making the claim that Byron's poem ought to be recognised as the epic poem of the cultural moment that Esterhammer explores so searchingly.

2 I Want a Hero

1. Howe, XI, 77.
2. *BLJ*, 5, 243; Samuel Smiles, *A Publisher and His Friends: Memoir and Correspondence of the Late John Murray*, 2 vols. (London: John Murray, 1891),1, 391. The bust was owned by Hobhouse, who had paid for it.
3. *BLJ*, 8, 237.
4. Harriet Lee, *Canterbury Tales* (London: G. and J. Robinson, 1801), 4, 227.
5. *The Deformed Transformed*, Part I, scene i, 261–4.
6. *Marino Faliero*, Act III, scene i, 87–92.
7. *BLJ*, 3, 75; 5, 227.
8. Edward J. Trelawny, *Recollections of the Last Days of Shelley and Byron* (London: Edward Moxon, 1858), 213.
9. Quoted by Jerome McGann, *CPW*, 5, 769.
10. *British Critic*, 20 (August 1823), 178.
11. Marchand, 3, 963.
12. *British Critic*, 16 (September 1821), 252.
13. Jerome J. McGann, *Don Juan in Context* (London: John Murray, 1976), 19–21.
14. See Anna Camilleri, 'Byron's Cunning Poetics', *Essays in Criticism*, 66.2 (2016), 221–41.
15. In the English cantos, as Stabler puts it, 'Byron multiplies the possibilities of a female hero by three'. See Jane Stabler, *Byron, Poetics and History* (Cambridge: Cambridge University Press, 2002), 196. Franklin remarks that *Don Juan* 'consists predominantly of a gallery of female portraits', and that the focus on the Byronic hero has prevented a recognition that 'none appears in his masterpiece'. See Caroline Franklin, *Byron's Heroines* (Oxford: Clarendon Press, 1992), 99.
16. *BLJ*, 6, 237.
17. Jerome Christensen, *Lord Byron's Strength: Romantic Writing and Commercial Society* (Baltimore and London: Johns Hopkins University Press, 1993), 306.
18. Byron inspected the monuments to Marceau and Hoche in 1816, on his way to Switzerland. See *BLJ*, 5, 77.
19. *BLJ*, 8, 78.
20. Anthony Howe, *Byron and the Forms of Thought* (Liverpool: Liverpool University Press, 2013), 159.

21. 'On This Day I Complete My Thirty-Sixth Year', 37–8.
22. Byron sent Murray to be inserted as a note to the first canto of *Don Juan* a furious rebuttal of Hazlitt's charge that he had 'lauded Buonaparte to the skies in the hour of his success', and turned against him after his downfall. He had been consistent, he insists, in recognising 'the incredible antitheses of [Napoleon's] character' throughout (*CPW*, 5, 682–3).
23. Napoleon's troops gave him the nickname after the battle of Lodi in 1796, when he had insisted on sighting himself the cannons that secured the French victory.
24. See his letter to Douglas Kinnaird of 24 September 1822, *BLJ*, 11, 215.
25. *CPW*, 5, 735.
26. *BLJ*, 8, 38 and 9, 216.
27. Howe, IV, 214.
28. Leigh Hunt quotes Wordsworth's line in his report of the Peterloo massacre as the work of 'a pathetic court poet'. See 'Disturbances at Manchester', *The Examiner*, 608 (22 August 1819), 529–31, p. 532. Shelley parodies it in *Peter Bell the Third*. One of Peter's 'odes to the Devil' asks that 'Carnage and Slaughter, / Thy niece and thy daughter ... / Glut thee with living and dead' (636–40). Hazlitt adduces it repeatedly. See Howe, IV, 214; V, 348; VII, 96, 142; IX, 39; XII, 374.
29. In 1820, Byron wrote to Murray instructing him to send 'no *more modern* poesy', 'neither Mrs. Hewoman's – nor any female or male Tadpole of Poet Turdsworth's'. *BLJ*, 7, 158.
30. Byron sometimes imagined even greater numbers. In August 1820, he remarked to John Murray, 'I believe that (except Milman perhaps) I am still the youngest of the fifteen hundred first of living poets – as Wm Turdsworth is the oldest' (*BLJ*, 7, 168) and in his dedication of *Marino Faliero* to Goethe he computed that of '*ten thousand living English authors*' 'nineteen hundred and eighty seven' were poets, 'all alive at this moment'.
31. *European Magazine*, 76 (July 1819), 53. On *Don Juan* and pantomime, see Frederick L. Beaty, 'Harlequin Don Juan', *Journal of English and Germanic Philology*, 67 (July 1968), 395–405. There was no English production of Mozart's *Don Giovanni* until 1817, although it is possible that Byron saw the opera in Venice.
32. *The Examiner*, 471 (5 January 1817), 7.
33. Jerome McGann, 'The *Biographia Literaria* and the Contentions of English Romanticism', in *Coleridge's Biographia Literaria: Text and Meaning*, ed. Frederick Burwick (Columbus: Ohio State University Press, 1989), 233–54, pp. 247–53. The suggestion had been made earlier by Elizabeth French Boyd, *Byron's Don Juan* (London: Routledge and Kegan Paul, 1945), 36.
34. *BLJ*, 5, 267. In 1816, at Byron's behest John Murray had published *Christabel, Kubla Khan* and *The Pains of Sleep* as a pamphlet. McGann's suggestion is

supported in the Dedication of *Don Juan* when Byron extends his description of Coleridge to include Wordsworth and Southey: 'You're shabby fellows' (Dedication, 6).

35. *BLJ*, 6, 190.
36. Michael G. Cooke defines the mode that Byron employs, particularly in the Ismail cantos of *Don Juan*, as 'counter-heroic humanism'. See Michael G. Cooke, *The Blind Man Traces the Circle* (Princeton: Princeton University Press, 1969), 175.

3 Especially upon a Printed Page

1. *The Diary of Virginia Woolf*, 5 vols. ed. Ann Olivier Boyd (London: Hogarth Press, 1977), 1, 180–1.
2. Kingsley Amis, *I Like It Here*, chapter 3 (Penguin, 1968).
3. Reported in an article in *Urania or the Astrologer's Chronicle, and Mystical Magazine* in 1825, reproduced in Mona Wilson, *The Life of William Blake*, 2nd edition, ed. Geoffrey Keynes (Oxford: Oxford University Press, 1971), 380–1.
4. Samuel Taylor Coleridge, *The Complete Poems*, ed. William Keach (London: Penguin, 1997), 249–50.
5. Leigh Hunt, *Lord Byron and Some of His Contemporaries* (London: Henry Colburn, 1825), 37–8.
6. In the 1832 edition and in many later editions, this stanza is printed as a headpiece to the poem. See *CPW*, 5, 88, 687. McGann notes that there is no evidence that Byron had intended that it should serve as a headpiece, and that in the manuscript original the stanza is cancelled.
7. *Eclectic Review*, 5 (June 1816), 565.
8. Howe, V, 149.
9. *BLJ*, 3, 206.
10. *BLJ*, 3, 206.
11. *BLJ*, 3, 100.
12. [John G. Lockhart], *John Bull's Letter to Lord Byron*, ed. Alan Lang Strout (Norman: University of Oklahoma Press, 1947), 103.
13. As reported by Thomas Moore. The copy of the poem annotated by Byron was in John Murray's possession.
14. *'Don John', or Don Juan Unmasked* (London: William Hone, 1819), 37.
15. John Thelwall quoted these lines to demonstrate that Byron, for all that he 'withholds his name from the title page, stamps the broad seal of his acknowledgement' on the poem. See *The Champion*, 1 (August 1819), 490. Byron had advertised his feat in his poem 'Written after swimming from Sestos to Abydos May 9 1810', published with the first two cantos of *Childe Harold* in 1812.

16. *'Don John'*, or *Don Juan Unmasked*, 30.
17. See the preface to *Joan of Arc* in *The Poetical Works of Robert Southey* (London: Longman, Green, 1876), 2.
18. Samuel Taylor Coleridge to Joseph Cottle, 28 May 1798, in *Collected Letters of Samuel Taylor Coleridge*, ed. Earl Leslie Griggs, 6 vols. (Oxford: Clarendon Press, 1956–71), 1, 412.
19. The legal position was unclear. Jerome Christensen summarises it in *Lord Byron's Strength: Romantic Writing and Commercial Society* (Baltimore: Johns Hopkins University Press, 1993), 237–42. But Murray decided not to risk bringing the matter to court.
20. C. C. Cotton, *Remarks Critical and Moral on the Talents of Lord Byron and the Tendencies of Don Juan* (London, 1819), 17.
21. *Don Juan* (London: Hodgson, 1822), vi.
22. From a paper on a number of copyright infringement cases, *Quarterly Review*, 27 (1822), 123–38, p. 128.
23. On this see Jane Stabler, *Byron, Poetics and History* (Cambridge: Cambridge University Press, 2002), 101.
24. *'Don John'*, or *Don Juan Unmasked*, 6.
25. 'Letters of Timothy Tickler, Esq. to Eminent Literary Characters, No. VII', *BEM*, 14 (July 1823), 80–92, pp.88–9. The reviewer for *British Critic* also suspects that Leigh Hunt had been allowed to 'perpetrate' an interpolation in the text of the poem. See *British Critic*, 20 (August 1823), 180.
26. Hunt offered each batch of cantos in more expensive formats too, designed to appeal to wealthier readers.
27. *Literary Gazette*, 339 (23 July 1823), 451; 346 (6 September 1823), 562.
28. 'Remarks on Don Juan', *BEM*, 5 (August 1819), 512–18, p. 512; 'Don Juan', *British Critic*, 12 (August 1819), 195–205, p.197.
29. William Blake, 'A Memorable Fancy', in *The Marriage of Heaven and Hell*.
30. 'A Suppressed Passage' printed at the end of Hone's, *Don Juan, Canto III*. See Peter Cochran's edition of the poem, https://petercochran.files.wordpress.com/2009/03/canto-iii.pdf, p. 252.
31. *BLJ*, 10, 158.
32. John G. Lockhart, *Some Passages in the Life of Mr Adam Blair, Minister of the Gospel at Cross-Meikle* (Edinburgh: Edinburgh University Press, 1963), 160.
33. *Knight's Quarterly Magazine*, 1 (June–October 1823), 28.
34. William M. Thackeray, 'De Juventute', in *Roundabout Papers, The Works of William Makepeace Thackeray*, 22 vols. (London: Smith, Elder, 1869), 20, 85.
35. Will Self, 'Grubby Business', *Times Literary Supplement*, 6110 (8 May 2020), 17.
36. *The Works of Thomas DeQuincey*, ed. Grevel Lindop, 21 vols. (London: Chatto and Pickering, 2000–1), 11, 257–8.

37. Quoted by Edgar Johnson, *Walter Scott: The Great Unknown*, 2 vols. (London: Hamish Hamilton, 1970), 1,214.
38. *BLJ*, 5, 265.
39. After he and Moore had become friends, Byron acknowledged that, since he felt it opportune to 'find fault' with Moore's verse, he had fixed on 'the trite charge of immorality'. See *BLJ*, 2, 160.
40. For Pulci's influence on Byron, see Lindsay Waters, 'The "Desultory Rhyme" of *Don Juan*: Byron, Pulci, and the Improvisatory Style', *ELH*, 45.3 (1978), 429–42.
41. In the preface to his *A Vision of Judgement* (1821).
42. A point made in a quite different context by Gavin Hopps, '"Eden's Door": The Porous Worlds of *Don Juan* and *Childe Harold's Pilgrimage*', *Byron Journal*, 37.2 (2009), 109–20.
43. On Byron's liking for quotation, see Stabler, *Byron, Poetics and History*, 65–72.
44. Jane Austen, *Mansfield Park*, chapter 34.
45. Howe, V, 144.
46. The intermingling of low journalism and high literature in *Don Juan* is explored by Stabler, *Byron, Poetic and History*, 136–71.
47. On advertising and *Don Juan*, see Hadley J. Mozer, '"I Want a Hero": Advertising for an Epic Hero in *Don Juan*', *Studies in Romanticism*, 44.2 (2005), 239–60.
48. *The Prose Works of William Wordsworth*, ed. W. J. B. Owen and Jane Worthington Smyser, 3 vols. (Oxford: Clarendon Press, 1974), 1, 481.
49. This is one reason why *Don Juan* exercised, as I point out in Chapter 1, so potent an influence on the fashionable or silver fork novel.
50. Thomas Henry Lister, *Granby*, 6 vols. ed. Clare Bainbridge, vol. 1 of *Silver Fork Novels, 1826–1841*, gen. ed. Harriet Devine Jump, (London: Pickering and Chatto, 2005) 42.
51. Howe, XVII, 209 (note).
52. Howe, V, 150.
53. *British Review*, 14 (August 1819), 266–8. Byron's response, 'Letter to the Editor of My Grandmother's Review', was published in the first issue of *The Liberal*, 1 (October 1822), 41–50.
54. *Eclectic Review*, 12 (August 1819), 149.
55. *Edinburgh Review*, 36 (February 1822), 413–52.

4 The Gate of Life and Death

1. Susan J. Wolfson, '"Their She Condition": Cross-Dressing and the Politics of Gender in *Don Juan*', *ELH*, 54 (Autumn 1987), 585–617. Jonathan Gross goes further, arguing that the heterosexual shenanigans of Byron's hero are reported by a gay narrator. He bases his case on the narrator's sensitivity to

Juan's physical beauty, his unwillingness to specify quite what knowledge it was that he picked up in college (I, 52–3), and, a little more oddly, he also adduces the narrator's hostility to marriage and his misogyny. But the case has not persuaded many, and Gross accepts in any case that the gay narrator disappears from the poem after Canto V. See '"One Half What I Should Say": Byron's Gay Narrator in *Don Juan*', in *Byron: The Erotic Liberal* (Lanham, Boulder: Rowman and Littlefield, 2001), 129–52.

2. As Peter Graham remarks, 'Juan's expression of his feminine side is precisely what stresses his essential masculinity'. See *Don Juan and Regency England* (Charlottesville: University Press of Virginia, 1990), 84.

3. See F. H. Amphlett Micklewright, 'On the Bishop of Clogher's Case', *Notes and Queries*, 214 (November 1969), 421–30. It is uncertain whether Byron's references to Castlereagh's suicide are barbed by the suspicion that Castlereagh, as he admitted to George IV, had been accused of 'the same crime as the Bishop of Clogher'. On this possibility, see Clara Tuite, *Lord Byron and Scandalous Celebrity* (Cambridge: Cambridge University Press, 2015), 122–8. Byron refers again just as unsympathetically to Clogher's disgrace in a stanza that he did not find a place for in Canto XI. See *CPW*, 5, 494.

4. Louis Crompton, *Byron and Greek Love: Homophobia in 19th-Century England* (Berkeley: University of California Press, 1985), 241.

5. *BLJ*, 5, 93.

6. *BLJ*, 6, 66.

7. *BLJ*, 6, 92.

8. *BLJ*, 5, 162–3.

9. *BLJ*, 6, 40.

10. *BLJ*, 6, 55.

11. *BLJ*, 6, 180.

12. Crompton, *Byron and Greek Love*, 127–9.

13. *BLJ*, 1, 110.

14. *BLJ*, 2, 116.

15. Gary Dyer argues for the subliminal presence in *Don Juan* of '*the mysterious*' codes that Byron used when referring to same-sex encounters, but he accepts, despite this, that in *Don Juan* Byron is 'addressing the public at large, rather than a small, sympathetic circle of associates'. See Gary Dyer, 'Thieves, Boxers, Sodomites, Poets: Being Flash to Byron's Don Juan', *PMLA*, 116.3 (May 2001), 562–78, p. 572.

16. On the Queen Caroline scandal, see John Gardner, *Poetry and Popular Protest: Peterloo, Cato Street, and the Queen Caroline Controversy* (Basingstoke: Palgrave Macmillan, 2011).

17. *BLJ*, 11, 197.

18. See *De Rerum Natura*, I, 1–2.
19. *British Review*, 18 (December 1821), 261.
20. *BLJ*, 5, 78. Byron is recalling Davies's unhappy encounter with a woman at Brighthelmstone, when, it seems, he had 'encountered ossified barriers to "the forefended place"' (*BLJ*, 5, 74).
21. *BLJ*, 5, 215.
22. See *BLJ*, 5, 216, 231, 234.
23. 'cunnus taeterrima belli / causa', Horace, *Satires*, Book I, poem iii, 107–8.
24. *The Letters of John Keats*, ed. Hyder Edward Rollins, 2 vols. (Cambridge: Cambridge University Press, 1958), 1, 200.
25. *BLJ*, 6, 5.
26. *BLJ*, 5, 168.
27. See David Woodhouse, 'Hazlitt and Byron: Hereditary Prejudices and Liberal Sympathies', *The Hazlitt Review*, 12 (2019), 37–60, p. 52.
28. *BLJ*, 6, 232.
29. *CMP*, 128.
30. Peter Cochran's online edition of Byron's correspondence. See https://peter cochran.files.wordpress.com/2009/02/15-genoa-1822-182312.pdf.
31. John Clare, a keen student of Byron, seems to have understood the centrality of the two monosyllables to Byron's poem. See Simon Kovesi, 'Masculinity, Misogyny and the Marketplace: Clare's Don Juan A Poem', in *John Clare: New Approaches*, ed. John Goodridge and Simon Kovesi (Peterborough: The John Clare Society, 2000), 187–201.
32. *CMP*, 128.
33. *Boswell's Life of Johnson*, ed. George Birkbeck Norman Hill and L. F. Powell, 6 vols. (Oxford: Oxford University Press, 1934), 4, 221.
34. Jane Stabler, *Byron, Poetics and History* (Cambridge: Cambridge University Press, 2002), 154.
35. *Byron's Bulldog*, 275.
36. *BLJ*, 11, 181.
37. *BLJ*, 5, 9.
38. *Literary Gazette*, 1823.
39. *BLJ*, 11, 175–6.
40. *Byron's Bulldog*, 301–2.
41. *BLJ*, 2, 95.
42. *BLJ*, 8, 51.
43. Matthew Bevis suggests that the 'tangled unpredictable relations between body and mind' might be the principal subject in *Don Juan*. See Matthew Bevis, 'Byron's Feet', in *Meter Matters: Verse Cultures of the Long Nineteenth Century*, ed. Jason David Hall (Athens: Ohio University Press, 2011), 78–104, p. 91.

44. Even in a passage in which Byron decries Lucretius's epicureanism he describes *De rerum natura as* 'the first of Latin poems', *CMP*, 144. It was a taste that he shared with Lady Oxford, who was 'an adept in the text of the original (which I like too)' (*BLJ*, 3, 210). Clara Tuite convincingly suggests that Byron's 'libertine materialism' is 'underpinned' by Lucretius. See Tuite, *Lord Byron and Scandalous Celebrity*, 185–7.

45. *BLJ*, 2, 89.

46. *BLJ*, 3, 48.

47. Byron had made the same observation in 1813, in a letter to Lady Melbourne describing his relations with Lady Frances Wedderburn Webster, who had consented to an 'indulgence of attachment in some sort of etherial process in which the soul is principally concerned'. Byron commented, 'one generally *ends* & *begins* with Platonism – & as my proselyte is only twenty – there is time enough to materialize'. By six o'clock that evening as he reported to Lady Melbourne *'Platonism'* was 'in some peril' (*BLJ*, 3, 135–6).

48. *CMP*, 136.

49. *BLJ*, 7, 171. The letter is in Italian.

50. *CMP*, 129. Byron is objecting specifically to William Lisle Bowles's *Invariable Principles of Poetry*.

51. *The Letters of John Murray to Lord Byron*, ed. Andrew Nicholson (Liverpool: Liverpool University Press, 2007), 322; *BLJ*, 7, 139.

52. It is, as Stephen Cheeke points out, one of those 'moments in Byron's writing where the notion that sexual love might overcome all difference is allowed brief room'. See Stephen Cheeke, *Byron and Place* (Houndsmills: Palgrave Macmillan, 2003), 128.

53. As Peter Manning puts it, 'The less Juan and Haidée can talk, the more intensely they share'. See Peter Manning, '"Don Juan" and Byron's Imperceptiveness to the English Word', *Studies in Romanticism*, 18.2 (1979), 207–33, p. 209.

54. Anne Barton suggests that their love remains 'fundamentally extra social' in large part because it is never incorporated into language. See Anne Barton, '*Don Juan* Reconsidered: The Haidée Episode', *Byron Journal*, 15 (1987), 11–20, p.18.

5 Allusions Private and Inglorious

1. *Byron's Bulldog*, 256–60. Kinnaird's and Frere's opinions are reported by Hobhouse. Hobhouse's concern that Byron risked being accused of blasphemy was borne out. The *European Magazine*, for example, deplored these stanzas as an 'unpardonable and profane parody'. *European Magazine*, 76 (July 1819), 54.

2. See Clara Tuite, *Lord Byron and Scandalous Celebrity* (Cambridge: Cambridge University Press, 2015), 171–2.

3. See, for example, *BLJ*, 4, 48.

4. *The Journal of Thomas Moore*, ed. Wilfred S. Dowden, 6 vols. (Newark: University of Delaware Press, 1983), 1, 141–2. As Byron noted in the journal that he kept when he retreated to Switzerland after his separation from his wife, 'I hate short women – for more reasons than one.' See *BLJ*, 5, 103.

5. *Edinburgh Monthly Review*, 2 (October 1819), 483.

6. 'Remarks on Don Juan', *BEM*, 5 (August 1819), 512–18.

7. McGann reproduces the page. See *CPW*, 5, facing 17.

8. McGann has 'hint allusions', but Jane Stabler points out that the manuscript clearly reads 'hunt', and 'hunt' makes better sense.

9. *BLJ*, 6, 96. Byron substituted for it another quotation from Horace, 'Difficile est proprie communia dicere', a line that he translates in *Hints from Horace*, "'Tis no slight task to write on common things'.

10. Peter Manning is surely right to insist that 'a reader who excludes on principle Byron's tantalising play with the demarcations between biographical revelation and fiction sacrifices the essential quality of the poem'. See Peter J. Manning, *Byron and His Fictions* (Detroit: Wayne State University Press, 1978), 177.

11. *BLJ*, 4, 258.

12. *BLJ*, 6, 69.

13. Byron was given an annuity of £10,000 in Lady Noel's will provided that he adopted the name Noel, which he did. The will also stipulated that Byron's portrait was not to be shown to his daughter, Ada, until she was 21.

14. George Eliot, *Middlemarch*, 'Finale'.

15. Marguerite Gardiner, Countess of Blessington, *Conversations of Lord Byron with the Countess of Blessington* (London: Henry Colburn, 1834), 42.

16. *Edinburgh Monthly Review*, 2 (October 1819), 486.

17. A spectacular instance is the case brought against Edmund Kean by Alderman Cox for the seduction of his wife. The following day a full transcript of the trial was published in *The Times*. The incident is discussed by Richard Cronin, *Paper Pellets: British Literary Culture after Waterloo* (Oxford: Oxford University Press, 2010), 66–71.

18. As Peter Graham points out, Byron's was a 'very public private life'. See *Don Juan and Regency England* (Charlottesville: University Press of Virginia, 1990), 187.

19. See *CPW*, 5, 295.

20. The three 'Epigrams on Lord Castlereagh' that Byron published in the first issue of *The Liberal* also brought together public disapproval and private animus, outraging readers of the magazine just as he had outraged readers of the third instalment of *Don Juan*. See *The Liberal*, 1 (October 1822), 164.

21. *BLJ*, 6, 90. Byron explains Romilly's offence, as he understood it, in 'Some Observations upon an Article in *Blackwood's Edinburgh Magazine*', where he writes that he had been 'much hurt by Romilly's conduct (he having a general retainer for me had acted as adviser to the adversary – alledging on being reminded of his retainer, that he had forgotten it as his Clerk had so many)'. *CMP*, 97.

22. *Poems on His Domestic Circumstances by Lord Byron*, ed. William Hone (London: William Hone, 1816), 5–6.

23. The deleted stanzas are reproduced by McGann, *CPW*, 5, 85–8.

24. *BLJ*, 8, 187.

25. *BLJ*, 3, 189.

26. On Byron's admiration for Johnson, see Tony Howe, 'Uncircumscribing Poetry: Byron, Johnson, and the Bowles Controversy', in *Liberty and Poetic Licence: News Essays on Byron*, ed. Bernard Beatty, Tony Howe, and Charles E. Robinson (Liverpool: Liverpool University Press, 2008), 206–18.

27. *BLJ*, 3, 214. On the relationship between the two men, see Peter Cochran, *Byron and Bob: Lord Byron's Relationship with Robert Southey* (Newcastle: Cambridge Scholars, 2010).

28. *BLJ*, 3, 122.

29. *BLJ*, 6, 76.

30. 'Sardanapalus, a Tragedy', *Edinburgh Review*, 36 (February 1822), 413–52, p.452.

31. On *The Beacon* and *The Sentinel*, see Cronin, *Paper Pellets*, 13–21.

32. *Edinburgh Review*, 36 (February 1822), 446.

33. Jeffrey had, until 1822, refused for similar reasons to review *Don Juan*, and even in this issue the comments on *Don Juan* are tucked into his review of the volume in which Byron published *Sardanapalus*, *The Two Foscari*, and *Cain*.

34. *BEM*, 11 (May 1822), 601–18.

35. *BEM*, 10 (October 1821), 312.

36. *BLJ*, 6, 126, 257. The story was Byron's contribution to the competition to write a ghost story begun in the Villa Diodati in the summer of 1816 that inspired Mary Shelley's *Frankenstein* and Polidori's *The Vampyre*. Byron made his suggestion after Murray had become co-proprietor of *Blackwood's* in August 1818. Murray sold his share a year later, concerned by the magazine's growing notoriety. Byron responded to the 'Remarks on Don Juan' in 'Some Observations upon an Article in *Blackwood's Edinburgh Magazine*', an essay that he chose, in the end, not to publish.

37. *BLJ*, 8, 145.

38. *BEM*, 8 (March 1821), 674–5.

39. *BLJ*, 8, 38.

40. 'Some Observations Upon an Article in *Blackwood's Edinburgh Magazine*', in *CMP*, 88–119, p. 93.
41. The proof page is reproduced by Mc Gann, *CPW*, 5, facing 17.
42. *BEM*, 8 (November 1820), 78–105. William Maginn proved his right to be admitted to the *Blackwood's* stable of writers by submitting to the magazine, while he was still resident in Ireland, an equally brilliant sequel to Wilson's paper, 'Another Tete-a-Tete with the Public', *BEM*, 8 (February 1821), 529–35.
43. *London Magazine*, 4 (October 1821), 368; 2 (September 1820), 299.
44. 'Remarks on Don Juan', 514.
45. The full note was omitted from the first edition.
46. *BLJ*, 2, 255.
47. *BEM*, 2 (October 1817), 4; 13 (January 1823), 86.
48. In *John Bull*, 131 (16 June 1823), 189; 132 (23 June 1823), 197–8. *John Bull* published a letter from Hazlitt to Sarah Walker as proof of his authorship, and recommended that Hazlitt, if he felt aggrieved at the publication of a private letter, should recall that it was he who had first 'given publicity to the affair altogether'.
49. Bryan Procter (Barry Cornwall), *An Autobiographical Fragment and Biographical Notes* (London: Bell, 1877), 180–1.
50. Jonathan Gross, 'Hazlitt's Worshipping Practice in *Liber Amoris*', *SEL*, 35 (1995), 707–21.
51. William Jerdan in the *Literary Gazette* doubted, or claimed to, that Byron had written Cantos XV and XVI of *Don Juan*, preferring to believe that they were the work of 'some worthy brother of the school of Rimini and the new Pygmalion' (that is, of Leigh Hunt and Hazlitt), *Literary Gazette*, 376 (3 April 1824), 212. After the publication of *Liber Amoris* Hazlitt was dubbed by *Blackwood's* 'the new Pygmalion'.
52. Hazlitt claims in 'Arguing in a Circle', one of the papers that he contributed to *The Liberal*, that in England public opinion has a power to which even the King is subject. See Howe, XIX, 267–78, p. 268.
53. The duel is discussed by Cronin, *Paper Pellets*, 1–6.
54. From the lines from *The Recluse* quoted by Worsdworth in his preface to *The Excursion*, 29–41.
55. *Conversations with Goethe, from the German of Eckermann*, trans. Margaret Fuller (Boston: Hilliard, Gray, 1839), 303.
56. *BLJ*, 6, 96.
57. Jane Stabler points out that Byron was undecided whether to close one stanza (IV, 32) with the rhyme 'she thought' or 'me thought'.
58. *BLJ*, 8, 196.
59. *BLJ*, 7, 245–52.

60. Gardiner, *Conversations of Lord Byron with the Countess of Blessington*, 83.
61. Benjamin Disraeli, *Contarini Fleming: A Psychological Romance*, Part 1, chapter 13.

6 Taking Another Tack

1. Byron's first person, Clara Tuite suggests, 'confounds the convention of narrative objectivity that founds the epic genre', but it also supplies the epic genre with the inflection that fits it for the modern world. Post-classical epic, as is borne out by *Paradise Lost*, let alone *The Divine Comedy* and, to cite a still more extreme example, the epic in its Wordsworthian incarnation, is far less resistant to the first person. See Clara Tuite, *Lord Byron and Scandalous Celebrity* (Cambridge: Cambridge University Press, 2015), 179.
2. *BEM*, 3 (June 1818), 325.
3. *Edinburgh Review*, 29 (February 1818), 304.
4. *Edinburgh Review*, 36 (February 1822), 449–50.
5. *British Review*, 18 (December 1821), 256.
6. *Literary Chronicle*, 3 (11August 1821), 496.
7. *The Examiner*, issue 618 (31 October 1819), 700.
8. *London Magazine*, n. s. 1(January 1825), 82.
9. *London Magazine*, 3 (January 1821), 56.
10. 'Beppo', *British Review*, 11 (May 1818), 327–33, p. 330.
11. 'Notices to Correspondents', *BEM*, 2 (March 1818). The verses, probably written by Lockhart, were prefixed to the March number and preface the second volume of the magazine.
12. *BEM*, 21 (March 1827), 345.
13. 'Noctes Ambrosianae, No. 4', *BEM*, 12 (July 1822), 100–14.
14. 'Noctes Ambrosianae, No. 4', 106.
15. *BEM*, 9 (July 1821), 426.
16. On the import of Byron's insistence that his models in *Don Juan* are Italian, see Maria Schoina, 'Revisiting Byron's Italian Style', *Byron Journal*, 36.1 (2008), 19–27.
17. 'Chaucer and Don Juan', *BEM*, 10 (October 1821), 295–8.
18. This is from Lockhart's first and most savage published response to *Don Juan*, 'Remarks on Don Juan', *BEM*, 5 (August 1819), 512–18.
19. *The Examiner*, issue 618 (31 October 1819).
20. 'Don Juan', *Literary Speculum*, 1 (November 1821), 1–5. As Jane Stabler remarks, it became more common after Byron's death to 'unify division under the sign of biography'. See Jane Stabler, *Byron, Poetics and History* (Cambridge: Cambridge University Press, 2002), 41.

21. 'Lord Byron's Corsair', *British Critic*, 1 (March 1814), 277–96, p. 288.
22. Charles Dickens, *Oliver Twist*, chapter 17.
23. Charles Dickens, 'A Visit to Newgate', in *Sketches by Boz*.
24. It may be that Dickens recognized as much. 'The Boarding House, Chapter One' in *Sketches by Boz* introduces as one of the boarders Mr Septimus Hicks, whose conversation is liberally sprinkled with quotations from *Don Juan*, the only poem that he has ever read. Dickens's friend, the artist Leonardo Cattermole, made a sketch of the young Dickens in Cattermole's studio, sitting in Byron's chair. See Michael Slater, *Charles Dickens* (New Haven: Yale University Press, 2009), Plate 35.
25. *The Letters of John Murray to Lord Byron*, ed. Andrew Nicholson (Liverpool: Liverpool University Press, 2007), 279.
26. *BLJ*, 6, 207.
27. *Literary Speculum*, 1 (November 1821), 4.
28. Nicholson, *The Letters of John Murray to Lord Byron*, 72.
29. William St Clair, *The Reading Nation in the Romantic Period* (Cambridge: Cambridge University Press, 2004), 661.
30. Leigh Hunt, *Foliage; or Poems Original and Translated* (London: C. and J. Ollier, 1818), 14.
31. On the relationship between *Don Juan* and *The Excursion*, see Jane Stabler, 'Byron and "The Excursion"', *Wordsworth Circle*, 45.2 (2014), 137–47.
32. *BLJ*, 6, 77.
33. See Helen Groth, 'Kaleidoscopic Vision and Literary Invention in an "Age of Things": David Brewster, *Don Juan*, and "A Lady's Kaleidoscope"', *ELH*, 74.1 (2007), 217–37.
34. It is a thought that filters Cuvier through Thomas Love Peacock. In *Melincourt*, Mr Forester, an admirer of Lord Monboddo, believes modern man to be a shrunken descendant of his heroically sized ancestors.
35. *Sartor Resartus*, chapters 5,9.
36. For a positive reading of the association between poetry and bubbles, see Sarah Tindal Kareem, 'Enlightenment Bubbles, Romantic Worlds', *Eighteenth Century*, 56.1 (2015), 85–104.
37. A favourite thought. Compare IX, 13; XIII, 65; and XVI, 118.
38. *BEM*, 5 (August 1819), 515.
39. On the importance of 'system' in the period, see Clifford Siskin, *System: The Shaping of Modern Knowledge* (Cambridge, MA: MIT Press, 2016). On Byron's hostility towards systems, see Anthony Howe, *Byron and the Forms of Thought* (Liverpool: Liverpool University Press, 2013), 29–37.
40. *BLJ*, 6, 46.

41. Jerome J. McGann, *Don Juan in Context* (London: John Murray, 1976), 95. Jane Stabler suggests that it was a habit that Byron owed to Charles Churchill. See Stabler, *Byron, Poetics and History*, 55.
42. On simile in Romantic poetry, see Richard Cronin, 'Words of Love: The Erotics of Romantic Writing', *Coleridge Bulletin*, 41 (Summer 2013), 1–12.
43. *Shelley's Poetry and Prose*, ed. Donald H. Reiman and Neil Fraistat (New York and London: W. W. Norton, 2002), 503–4. The most elegant account of Shelley's philosophy of love and its incorporation into the texture of his poetry is William A. Ulmer's in *Shelleyan Eros: The Rhetoric of Romantic Love* (Princeton: Princeton University Press, 1990).
44. Elizabeth Bowen, *The Little Girls*, chapter 1.
45. 'Childe Harold's Pilgrimage: Canto IV', *Quarterly Review*, 19 (April 1818), 215–32, 520. The borrowing was pointed out by W. A. Stephenson, *Notes and Queries*, n. s. 22 (September 1975), 394.
46. *BLJ*, 6, 84.
47. Compare Byron's habit of offering alternative readings in the manuscripts of *Don Juan* he submitted to his publisher, and inviting John Murray or John Hunt or their readers to choose which reading they preferred.
48. *Monthly Magazine*, 56 (September 1823), 112.
49. [J. G. Lockhart], *John Bull's Letter to Lord Byron*, ed. Alan Lang Strout (Norman: University of Oklahoma Press, 1947), 95–6.

7 Mine Irregularity of Chime

1. Michael O'Neill, 'A Being More Intense: Byron', in *Romanticism and the Self-Conscious Poem* (Oxford: Clarendon Press, 1997), 93–116. Of all nineteenth-century poets Byron has most to say about rhyming, which might lead one to expect that he would also feature prominently in Peter McDonald's fine study, but McDonald treats Byron's case briefly and unsympathetically. He is most interested in poets such as Wordsworth, Keats, and Tennyson, who think through their rhymes, not in a poet such as Byron who is so ready to admit that rhyming may get in the way of his thinking. For Byron, McDonald remarks disapprovingly, 'rhyme is only rhyme (and reason only reason), and in neither case is there any need for meditative brooding'. His objection is not so much, one suspects, to the absence of brooding as to a poet so apt to recognize that rhyme and reason are very often at cross purposes. See *Sound Intentions: The Workings of Rhyme in Nineteenth-Century Poetry* (Oxford: Oxford University Press, 2012), 22–5.
2. The poem's early readers, the editors of a collection of essays on Byron remark, 'tended to associate its poetic licences of rhyme and diction with the poem's

ostentatiously sustained study of a variety of extra-marital sexual relations in differing social worlds'. See 'Introduction', in *Liberty and Poetic Licence: New Essays on Byron*, ed. Bernard Beatty, Tony Howe, and Charles E. Robinson (Liverpool: Liverpool University Press, 2008), 3.

3. *British Critic*, 12 (August 1819), 197.
4. *European Magazine*, 80 (August 1821), 181.
5. *Literary Gazette*, 339 (19 July 1823), 451–3.
6. *The Croker Papers: The Correspondence and Diaries of the Late Right Honourable John Wilson Croker*, ed. Louis J. Jennings, 3 vols. (London: John Murray, 1884), 1, 25.
7. *Literary Gazette*, 376 (3 April 1824), 212–13.
8. On boredom in the poem, see Daniel Gabelman, 'Bubbles, Butterflies and Bores: Play and Boredom in *Don Juan*', *Byron Journal*, 38.2 (2010), 145–56.
9. Compare Leigh Hunt's 'Rhymes to the Eye by a Deaf Gentleman', a squib that appeared in the third number of *The Liberal*, in which the deaf gentleman supports his opinion that '"pot" and "pot" rhyme very well together' by citing Pope who had rhymed 'way' with 'away'. *The Liberal*, 2 (January 1823), 186.
10. As Jim Cocola notes, Byron is given to emphasizing 'the very artifice of the rhyming function'. See Jim Cocola, 'Renunciations of Rhyme in Byron's "Don Juan"', *Studies in English Literature, 1500–1900*, 49.4 (Autumn 2009), 841–62, p. 844.
11. *BLJ*, 7, 202.
12. Leigh Hunt, '*The Choice*', *The Liberal*, 4 (July 1823), 266.
13. Jane Stabler, *Byron, Poetics and History* (Cambridge: Cambridge University Press, 2002), 78.
14. *Monthly Magazine*, 56 (December 1823), 417.
15. Catherine Addison, 'Heritage and Innovation in Byron's Narrative Stanzas', *Byron Journal*, 32 (2004), 9–20, p. 15.
16. *The Journal of Thomas Moore*, ed. Wilfred S. Dowden, 6 vols. (Newark: University of Delaware Press, 1983), 1, 141–2.
17. On this habit, see 'Byron the Polyglot' in Cocola, 'Renunciations of Rhyme in Byron's "Don Juan"', 848–51.
18. *Don Juan: A Variorum Edition*, ed. Truman Guy Steffan and Willis W. Pratt, 4 vols. (Austin: University of Texas Press, 1957), 3, 348 (note).
19. See Rachel Mayer Brownstein, 'Byron's *Don Juan*: Some Reasons for the Rhymes', *Modern Language Quarterly*, 28.2 (1967), 177–91, p.180.
20. It seems to have been an oath that Byron invented himself some years earlier, when he remarked to Hobhouse on the temerity of James Wedderburn Webster who had chosen to publish his letters to the Duke of Wellington: 'Corpo de Caio Mario! what will the world come to?' (*BLJ*, 2, 50).

21. Not entirely constant. The second line of XV, 66, for example, '"A l'Espagnole," "timballe," and "Salpicon"–', is unrhymed. As McGann suggests, Byron seems to have had second thoughts and decided to rhyme on 'Espagnole', but neglected to re-write the line.

22. 'Don Juan', *Literary Gazette*, 339 (19 July 1823), 451–3, p. 453.

23. *The Table Talk and Omniana of Samuel Taylor Coleridge*, ed. Humphrey Milford (London: Oxford University Press, 1917), 58 and note. Carl Woodring notes in his edition of the *Table Talk* for the Bollingen Coleridge that the passage does not appear in the manuscript.

24. Matthew Bevis astutely remarks Byron's penchant for suspending a line between rival possibilities of voicing it, just as he hovers between the French and the English pronunciation of Wellington's name, alerting the reader to the way in which 'Fame / Sounds the heroic syllables both ways' (IX, 1). See Matthew Bevis, 'Byron's Feet', in *Meter Matters: Verse Cultures of the Long Nineteenth Century*, ed. Jason David Hall (Athens: Ohio University Press, 2011), 78–104, pp. 86–7.

25. *BLJ*, 7, 28.

26. On Byron and Clough, see Richard Cronin, 'Byron, Clough, and the Grounding of Victorian Poetry', *Romanticism*, 14 (April 2008), 13–24.

27. *BLJ*, 6, 232.

8 This Is a Liberal Age

1. Leigh Hunt, *Lord Byron and Some of His Contemporaries*, 2 vols. (London: Henry Colburn, 1828), 1, 80.

2. David M. Craig, 'The Origins of "Liberalism" in Britain: The Case of *The Liberal*', *Historical Research*, 85 (August 2012), 469–87.

3. *The Liberal*, 1 (October 1822), viii.

4. *Literary Chronicle*, 34 (23 August 1823), 529–30.

5. See, for example, *BLJ*, 7, 235, 250, 251; 8, 16, 17, 18, 39, 117, 126, 155.

6. 'The Liberal System', *BEM*, 16 (October 1824), 442–55.

7. 'The Candid', *BEM*, 13 (January 1823), 108–24, p. 110. Byron's uses of the word have been studied by Jonathan Gross, who has located the forty-seven appearances of the word in the correspondence as well as its ten appearances in the poetry. Gross suggests that Byron begins by using the word in its English sense but after 1818 the foreign sense predominates. In Gross's terms, the change illustrates 'his movement from an aristocratic to a revolutionary brand of realism'. But Gross acknowledges too that 'liberalism' is a term that does not 'admit of an easy definition today any more than it did in Byron's day'. See Jonathan Gross, *The Erotic Liberal* (Lanham: Rowman and Littlefield, 2001), 5–6, 185.

8. On the interplay in *Don Juan* between nationalism and cosmopolitanism, see Kirsten Daly, 'Worlds Beyond England: *Don Juan* and the Legacy of Enlightenment Cosmopolitanism', *Romanticism*, 4.2 (1998), 189–201.

9. See Peter Graham, *Don Juan and Regency England* (Charlottesville: University Press of Virginia, 1990), 11–14; Charles Donelan, 'Learning to Say Juan', in *Romanticism and Male Fantasy in Byron's Don Juan* (Houndsmills: Macmillan, 2000), 31–67.

10. *Halliford Edition of the Works of Thomas Love Peacock*, ed. H. F. B. Brett-Smith and C. E. Jones, 10 vols. (London: Constable, 1934), 8, 126.

11. *The Letters of John Keats*, ed. Hyder Edward Rollins, 2 vols. (Cambridge: Cambridge University Press, 1958), 2, 176.

12. *BLJ*, 7, 44–5.

13. Compare *Don Juan*, IV, 93.

14. *BLJ*, 7, 81.

15. The review of *Don Juan*, cantos VI, VII, and VIII, *Literary Examiner*, 1 (5 July 1823), 6–12, pp. 7–8.

16. Howe, XI, 77.

17. 'Tantaene animis caelestibus irae?', 'Can such fierce resentment dwell in heavenly breasts?', *Aeneid*, I, 11.

18. William St Clair, *The Reading Nation in the Romantic Period* (Cambridge: Cambridge University Press, 2004), 333.

19. Byron's own fears that *Don Juan* was disliked and especially unpopular with women were soon allayed. In April 1823, he wrote to Douglas Kinnaird, 'I have just seen a young man who was Clerk to Galignani at Paris – he tells me that of all my works Juan is by far the most popular and sells best – especially with the women – who send by hundreds slily – for copies'. *BLJ*, 10, 145.

20. On Byron and The Byron's Head, see Clara Tuite, *Lord Byron and Scandalous Celebrity* (Cambridge: Cambridge University Press, 2015), 203–16.

21. See Timothy Webb's entry on John Hunt in the *Oxford Dictionary of National Biography*.

22. Hobhouse to Murray, 22 May 1816. See https://petercochran.files.wordpress .com/2009/02/07-switzerland-18166.pdf, p. 12.

23. 'Remarks on Some of Our Late Numbers; by a Liberal Whig', *BEM*, 6 (December 1819), 288–90. See also 'Second Letter from a Liberal Whig', *BEM*, 6 (February 1820), 492–4; 'Letters of a Liberal Whig, No III', *BEM*, 7 (April 1820), 21–4.

24. 'Preface', *The Liberal*, 1 (October 1822), iii–xii, p. ix.

25. Howe, XVI, 226.

26. *BLJ*, 7, 62.

27. See *CPW*, 5, 523.

28. See 'Letters of a Liberal Whig, No III', 21–4, p. 24.

29. *BLJ*, 6, 229.
30. *BLJ*, 5, 221.
31. The phrase is Jerome McGann's, *The Beauty of Inflections: Literary Investigations in Historical Method and Theory* (Oxford: Clarendon Press, 1985), 274. Peter Graham suggests that it may have been Southey who, in his *Letters from England*, gave Byron the cue to represent English society as seen through the eyes of a young Spaniard. See *Don Juan and Regency England*, 39–61. Byron's arch antagonists tend also to be his familiars, even Castlereagh, as Jerome Christensen points out in *Lord Byron's Strength: Romantic Writing and Commercial Society* (Baltimore: Johns Hopkins University Press, 1993), 216–18.
32. As McGann goes on to point out, in 'The Isles of Greece', 'the faces of Southey and Byron, those arch-antagonists, are superimposed on each other'. Jerome J. McGann, *Towards a Literature of Knowledge* (Oxford: Clarendon Press, 1989).
33. Again a point made by Peter Graham. See *Don Juan and Regency England*, 137.
34. 'Principles of Political Economy and Taxation', *Edinburgh Review*, 30 (June 1818), 59–87, p. 83.
35. *Byron's Bulldog*, 259.
36. Diego Saglia describes early nineteenth-century liberalism as 'a dialectical structure that moved between different voices', which seems accurate, except that one wants to say of the structure of liberalism as Milton says of death, if structure it can be called that structure hath none. See '"Freedom's Charter'd Air": The Voices of Liberalism in Felicia Heman's *The Vespers of Palermo*', *Nineteenth-Century Literature*, 58 (2003), 326–67, p. 339.
37. Peter Thorslev, for example, speaks of the dichotomy in liberalism 'that still dogs us' between liberals who champion individual freedom and liberals who believe that the freedom of the masses can only be secured by actions of the state. See Peter L. Thorslev, Jr, 'Post-Waterloo Liberalism: The Second Generation', *Studies in Romanticism*, 28 (Fall 1989), 437–61, p. 446.
38. See, for example, Daisy Hay, 'Liberals, *Liberales* and *The Liberal*: A Reassessment', *European Romantic Review*, 19.4 (2008), 307–20, p. 307.
39. Howe, XVII, 65.
40. Howe, XIX, 93.
41. Malcolm Kelsall, *Byron's Politics* (Brighton: Harvester, 1987), 150–1.
42. *BLJ*, 9, 43.
43. In a note to his preface to Cantos VI, VII, and VIII of *Don Juan*, Byron contrasts Canning and Castlereagh as foreign secretaries: 'Canning is a genius, almost a universal one, an orator, a wit, a poet, a statesman; and no man of talent can long pursue the path of his predecessor Lord C. If ever man saves his country Canning *can*, but *will* he? I, for one, hope so' (*CPW*, 5, 719).

44. J. S. Boone, *The Council of Ten*, 2 vols. (London: Longman, 1823), 2, 150.

45. [Benjamin Disraeli], *Vivian Grey* (London: Henry Colburn, 1826), 2, 178; Benjamin Disraeli, *Contarini Fleming: A Psychological Romance*, Part 4, chapter 3.

46. Victorian poets retained epic ambitions as Herbert Tucker has shown, but the difference in stature between Dickens, Thackeray, and George Eliot, and the Victorian poets such as John Fitchett, author of *Alfred: A Poem*, an epic that ran to forty-eight books, underlines my point. See Herbert F. Tucker, *Epic: Britain's Heroic Muse 1790–1810* (Oxford: Oxford University Press, 2008).

47. Catherine Gore, *Cecil: Or, the Adventures of a Coxcomb*, ed. Marie Mulvey Roberts, vol. 6 of *Silver Fork Novels, 1826–1841*, gen. ed. Harriet Devine Jump (London: Pickering an Chatto, 2005), 249.

48. Thomas Henry Lister, *Granby*, ed. Clare Bainbridge, vol. 1 of *Silver Fork Novels, 1826–1841*, gen. ed. Harriet Devine Jump, 77.

49. Lord Normanby, *Matilda: A Tale of the Day*, 2 vols. (London: Henry Colburn, 1825), 1, 126.

50. Benjamin Disraeli, *The Young Duke*, 3 vols. (London: Henry Colburn, 1831), 1, 164; 2, 139; 1, 276; 3, 104.

51. The mark left by *Don Juan* on the Victorian novel is discussed by Richard Lansdown, 'The Novelized Poem and the Poeticized Novel: Byron's "Don Juan" and Victorian Fiction', *Critical Review*, 39 (1999), 119–41.

52. Charlotte Brontë, *Jane Eyre*, vol. 3, chapter 34.

53. As Peter Manning argues, in *Don Juan* the 'condition of unfinishedness' is always implicit. See Peter J. Manning, 'Byron's Imperceptiveness to the English Word', in *Longman Critical Readers: Byron*, ed. Jane Stabler (London: Longman, 1998), 180–93, p. 181. Paul Elledge, discussing scenes of valediction in the poem in an article that focuses on the death of Tom the highwayman, points out that valediction in *Don Juan* always remains incomplete, an indication, it may be, of Byron's reluctance to bid farewell to his own poem. See Paul Elledge, 'Never Say(ing) Goodbye: Mediated Valediction in Byron's "Don Juan" XI', *Byron Journal*, 20 (1992), 17–26. See also Paul Elledge, 'Parting Shots: Byron Ending *Don Juan* I', *Studies in Romanticism*, 27.4 (1988), 563–77.

54. [William M. Thackeray], 'Memorials of Gormandising', *Fraser's Magazine*, 23 (June 1841), 710–25, pp. 712–13.

55. See Peter Cochran's edition of Byron's correspondence, https://petercochran .files.wordpress.com/2009/02/15-genoa-1822-182312.pdf.

56. The 'Preliminary Word' prefixed to the first number of *Household Words*.

57. As Peter Manning puts it, the poem works by 'returning each reader to the complex of private and public experiences which make up his particular life'.

See Peter J. Manning, '"Don Juan" and Byron's Imperceptiveness to the English Word', *Studies in Romanticism*, 18.2 (1979), 207–33, p. 232. Byron responds to his readers in the poem itself. He is, as Jerome NcGann points out, 'seriously interested' in what even the most foolish and unsympathetic of them, such as William Roberts, have to say. See Jerome McGann, *Byron and Romanticism*, ed. James Soderholm (Cambridge: Cambridge University Press, 2002), 128. Jane Stabler, in her exemplary account of Byron's digressive poetics, recognises that one of the primary effects of the digressive method is to empower the reader: 'the digressions keep the reader aware of alternative routes', so that each reader makes his own way through the poem. See Jane Stabler, *Byron, Poetics and History* (Cambridge: Cambridge University Press, 2002), 11. David Stewart has given a fascinating account of one episode that registers particularly well the power of *Don Juan* to divide its readership, the bitter controversy that rent the Literary and Philosophical Society of Newcastle when one of its members suggested that the society purchase a copy of *Don Juan* for its reading room. See David Stewart, 'The End of Conversation: Byron's *Don Juan* at the Newcastle Lit & Phil', *Review of English Studies*, n. s. 66 (April 2015), 322–41.

58. George Eliot, *Middlemarch*, chapter 11.
59. On this, see Richard Cronin, 'Words and the Word: The Diction of *Don Juan*', in *Romanticism and Religion from William Cowper to Wallace Stevens*, ed. Gavin Hopps and Jane Stabler (Aldershot: Ashgate, 2006), 137–54.
60. *BLJ*, 10, 150.
61. For Malcolm Kelsall, Byron's insistence that he speaks for no one but himself signals his political impotence, his failure to incorporate his political objectives in any collective action that had the power to carry them into effect. If the dream that Greece might yet be free is indulged only by the isolated individual Greece's liberation will scarcely be attainable. See Malcolm Kelsall, 'There Is No Alternative: *Don Juan*', in *Byron's Politics*, 146–93. But if Byron's liberal vision is founded on the possibility of a nation made up of autonomous individuals, the claim to speak only for himself becomes central to the kind of liberalism he is proposing.
62. See Clara Tuite, 'Lord Byron's Preposterous Liberalism', *Occasion*, 11 (2018), 1–17, pp. 8–9.
63. As always, Byron being what he is, there are exceptions, as when he vows to 'teach, if possible, the stones / To rise against earth's tyrants', and calls upon his 'children's children' to bear witness that he had shown '*what things were before the world was free!*' (VIII, 135).
64. Rollins, *The Letters of John Keats*, 1, 207.
65. On Byron's scepticism, see Terence Allan Hoagwood, *Byron's Dialectic: Skepticism and the Critique of Culture* (Lewisburg: Bucknell University

Press, 1993); Anthony Howe, *Byron and the Forms of Thought* (Liverpool: Liverpool University Press, 2013), 15–42. I agree with Howe rather than Hoagwood that Byron's scepticism is better understood as a function of his interest in poetic form than as a coherent philosophical belief.

66. 'The Liberal System', *BEM*, 16 (October 1824), 442–55, p. 444.
67. On this, see Gavin Hopps, 'Byron and the Post-Secular: Quia Impossibile', *Byron Journal*, 43.2 (2015), 91–108.
68. In this it resembles *The Liberal*, the Pisan journal given its title by Byron, one of the principal values of which, Jane Stabler argues, was freedom of worship. See Jane Stabler, 'Religious Liberty in the "Liberal," 1822–23', *BRANCH: Britain, Representation and Nineteenth-Century History*, ed. Dino Franco Felluga, extension of Romanticism and Victorianism on the Net (20 August 2020).
69. See James Kennedy, *Conversations on Religion with Lord Byron, and Others* (London: John Murray, 1830).
70. W. H. Auden insists that Byron, unlike Wordsworth, 'was not really odd': 'his experiences were those of the ordinary man'. But Seamus Perry is surely right to class this 'among the more bizarre accounts of Byron'. See *The Complete Works of W. H. Auden: Prose*, ed. Edward Mendelson, 6 vols. (Princeton: Princeton University Press, 1996–2015), I, 489; Seamus Perry, 'What Auden Made of Byron', in *Byron Among the English Poets: Literary Tradition and Poetic Legacy*, ed. Clare Bucknell and Matthew Ward (Cambridge: Cambridge University Press, 2021), 303–16, p. 305.
71. As Peter Manning puts it, 'Byron can assert identity only through a perpetual re-establishment of his difference'. See Peter J. Manning, *Byron and His Fictions* (Detroit: Wayne State University Press, 1978), 243.
72. Bernard Beatty, *Byron's Don Juan*, 2nd ed. (London: Routledge, 2016), 231.

Bibliography

Addison, Catherine, 'Heritage and Innovation in Byron's Narrative Stanzas', *Byron Journal*, 32 (2004), 9–20.

Amis, Kingsley, ed., *The New Oxford Book of Light Verse* (Oxford: Oxford University Press, 1978).

Anon., *'Don John', or Don Juan Unmasked* (London: William Hone, 1819).

Auden, W. H., ed., *The Oxford Book of Light Verse* (Oxford: Oxford University Press, 1938).

Bainbridge, Clare, ed., Thomas Henry Lister, *Granby*, vol. 1 of *Silver Fork Novels, 1826–1841*, gen. ed. Harriet Devine Jump (London: Pickering and Chatto, 2005).

Barton, Anne, '*Don Juan* Reconsidered: The Haidée Episode', *Byron Journal*, 15 (1987), 11–20.

Beaton, Roderick, *Byron's War: Romantic Rebellion, Greek Revolution* (Cambridge: Cambridge University Press, 2013).

Beatty, Bernard, *Byron's Don Juan*, 2nd ed. (London: Routledge, 2016).

Beatty, Bernard, Tony Howe and Charles E. Robinson, eds., *Liberty and Poetic Licence: New Essays on Byron* (Liverpool: Liverpool University Press, 2008).

Beatty, Bernard, and Vincent Newey, eds., *Byron and the Limits of Fiction* (Liverpool: Liverpool University Press, 1988).

Beaty, Frederick L., 'Harlequin Don Juan', *Journal of English and Germanic Philology*, 67.3 (1968), 395–405.

Byron the Satirist (DeKalb: Illinois University Press, 1985).

Bevis, Matthew, 'Byron's Feet', in *Meter Matters: Verse Cultures of the Long Nineteenth Century*, ed. Jason David Hall (Athens: Ohio University Press, 2011), 78–104.

Blair, Hugh, *A Critical Dissertation on the Poems of Ossian*, 2nd ed. (London: T. Becket and P. A. De Hondt, 1765).

Bone, Drummond, *Byron* (Tavistock: Northcote House, 2000).

Borusko, Matthew C., 'History, Historicism, and Agency at Byron's Ismail', *ELH*, 81.1 (Spring 2014), 269–97.

Boyd, Elizabeth French, *Byron's Don Juan* (London: Routledge and Kegan Paul, 1945).

Boyd, Olivier, ed., *The Diary of Virginia Woolf* (London: Hogarth Press, 1977).

Brett-Smith, H. F. B., and C. E. Jones, eds., *Halliford Edition of the Works of Thomas Love Peacock*, 10 vols. (London: Constable, 1934).

Brownstein, Rachel Mayer, 'Byron's *Don Juan*: Some Reasons for the Rhymes', *Modern Language Quarterly*, 28.2 (1967), 177–91.

Bulwer, Edward Lytton, *England and the English*, 2 vols. (London: R. Bentley, 1833).

Byron, Lord, *Don Juan* (London: Hodgson, 1822).

Camilleri, Anna, 'Byron's Cunning Poetics', *Essays in Criticism*, 66.2 (April 2016), 221–41.

Cantor, Paul, 'The Politics of the Epic: Wordsworth, Byron, and the Romantic Redefinition of Heroism', *The Review of Politics*, 69 (2007), 375–401.

Chandler, James, *England in 1819: The Politics of Literary Culture and the Case of Romantic Historicism* (Chicago: Chicago University Press, 1998).

Cheeke, Stephen, *Byron and Place* (Houndsmills: Palgrave Macmillan, 2003).

Christensen, Jerome, *Lord Byron's Strength: Romantic Writing and Commercial Society* (Baltimore: Johns Hopkins University Press, 1993).

Cochran, Peter, ed., *Byron's Correspondence*, https://petercochran.files.wordpress .com/2009/02/15-genoa-1822-182312.pdf.

    Byron and Bob: Lord Byron's Relationship with Robert Southey (Newcastle: Cambridge Scholars, 2010).

Cocola, Jim, 'Renunciations of Rhyme in Byron's "Don Juan"', *Studies in English Literature, 1500–1900*, 49.4 (Autumn 2009), 841–62.

Coleridge, Samuel Taylor, *The Complete Poems*, ed. William Keach (London: Penguin, 1997).

Cooke, Michael G., *The Blind Man Traces the Circle* (Princeton: Princeton University Press, 1969).

Copeland, Edward, *The Silver Fork Novel: Fashionable Fiction in the Age of Reform* (Cambridge: Cambridge University Press, 2012).

Colton, Charles C., *Remarks Critical and Moral on the Talents of Lord Byron and the Tendencies of Don Juan* (London, 1819).

Craig, David M., 'The Origins of "Liberalism" in Britain: The Case of *The Liberal*', *Historical Research*, 85 (August 2012), 469–87.

Crompton, Louis, *Byron and Greek Love: Homophobia in 19th-Century England* (Berkeley: University of California Press, 1985).

Cronin, Richard, *Romantic Victorians: English Literature, 1824–1840* (Basingstoke: Palgrave, 2002).

    'Words and the Word: The Diction of *Don Juan*', in *Romanticism and Religion from William Cowper to Wallace Stevens*, ed. Gavin Hopps and Jane Stabler (Aldershot: Ashgate, 2006), 137–54.

    'Byron, Clough, and the Grounding of Victorian Poetry', *Romanticism*, 14 (April 2008), 13–24.

    Paper Pellets: British Literary Culture after Waterloo (Oxford: Oxford University Press, 2010).

    'Words of Love: The Erotics of Romantic Writing', *Coleridge Bulletin*, 41 (Summer 2013), 1–12.

'A. C. Swinburne and Byron's Bad Ear', in *Byron Among the English Poets: Literary Tradition and Poetic Legacy*, ed. Clare Bucknell and Matthew Ward (Cambridge: Cambridge University Press, 2021), 287–302.

Curran, Stuart, *Poetic Form and British Romanticism* (Oxford: Oxford University Press, 1986).

Daly, Kirsten, 'Worlds Beyond England: *Don Juan* and the Legacy of Enlightenment Cosmopolitanism', *Romanticism*, 4.2 (1998), 189–201.

Disraeli, Benjamin, *Vivian Grey* (London: Henry Colburn, 1826).

The Young Duke (London: Henry Colburn, 1831).

Dixon, W. MacNeile, *English Epic and Heroic Poetry* (London: J. M. Dent, 1912).

Donelan, Charles, 'Learning to Say Juan', in *Romanticism and Male Fantasy in Byron's Don Juan: A Marketable Vice* (Houndsmills: Macmillan, 2000), 31–67.

Douglas, David, ed., *The Journal of Sir Walter Scott*, 2 vols. (Cambridge: Cambridge University Press, 1980).

Dowden, Wilfred S., ed., *The Journal of Thomas Moore*, 6 vols. (Newark: University of Delaware Press, 1983).

Dyer, Gary, 'Thieves, Boxers, Sodomites, Poets: Being Flash to Byron's Don Juan', *Publications of the Modern Language Association of America*, 116.3 (May 2001), 562–78.

Eckermann, Johann Peter, *Conversations with Goethe, from the German of Eckermann*, trans. Margaret Fuller (Boston: Hilliard, Gray, 1839).

Elledge, Paul, 'Parting Shots: Byron Ending Don Juan I', *Studies in Romanticism*, 27.4 (1988), 563–77.

'Never Say(ing) Goodbye: Mediated Valediction in Byron's "Don Juan" XI', *Byron Journal*, 20 (1992), 17–26.

Erickson, Lee, *The Economy of Literary Form* (Baltimore: Johns Hopkins University Press, 1996).

Esterhammer, Angela, *Print and Performance in the 1820s: Improvisation, Speculation, Identity* (Cambridge: Cambridge University Press, 2020).

Franklin, Caroline, *Byron's Heroines* (Oxford: Clarendon Press, 1992).

Fuess, Claude, *Lord Byron as a Satirist in Verse* (New York: Columbia University Press, 1912).

Gabelman, Daniel, 'Bubbles, Butterflies and Bores: Play and Boredom in Don Juan', *Byron Journal*, 38.2 (2010), 145–56.

Gardiner, Marguerite, Countess of Blessington, *Conversations of Lord Byron with the Countess of Blessington* (London: Henry Colburn, 1834).

Gardner, John, *Poetry and Popular Protest: Peterloo, Cato Street, and the Queen Caroline Controversy* (Basingstoke: Palgrave Macmillan, 2011).

Gleckner, Robert F., *Byron and the Ruins of Paradise* (Baltimore: Johns Hopkins University Press, 1967).

Gore, Catherine, *Women as They Are, or the Manners of the Day* (London: Henry Colburn and Richard Bentley, 1830).

Cecil: Or, the Adventures of a Coxcomb, vol. 6 of *Silver Fork Novels, 1826–1841*, gen. ed. Harriet Devine Jump (London: Pickering and Chatto, 2005).

Graham, Peter W., ed., *Byron's Bulldog: The Letters of John Cam Hobhouse to Lord Byron* (Columbus: Ohio State University Press, 1984).

Don Juan and Regency England (Charlottesville: University Press of Virginia, 1990).

Griggs, Earl Leslie, ed., *Collected Letters of Samuel Taylor Coleridge*, 6 vols. (Oxford: Clarendon Press, 1956–71).

Gross, Jonathan, 'Hazlitt's Worshipping Practice in Liber Amoris', *SEL*, 35 (1995), 707–21.

Byron: The Erotic Liberal (New York: Rowman and Littlefield, 2001).

Groth, Helen, 'Kaleidoscopic Vision and Literary Invention in an "Age of Things": David Brewster, *Don Juan*, and "A Lady's Kaleidoscope"', *ELH*, 74.1 (2007), 217–37.

Halmi, Nicholas, 'The Very Model of a Modern Epic Poem', *European Romantic Review*, 21 (2010), 589–600.

Haslett, Moyra, *Byron's Don Juan and the Don Juan Legend* (Oxford: Clarendon Press, 1997).

Hay, Daisy, 'Liberals, *Liberales* and *The Liberal*: A Reassessment', *European Romantic Review*, 19.4 (2008), 307–20.

Hibbard, Andrea, and Edward Copeland, eds., Catherine Gore, *Cecil: Or, the Adventures of a Coxcomb*, vol. 6 of *Silver Fork Novels, 1826–1841*, gen. ed. Harriet Devine Jump (London: Pickering and Chatto, 2005).

Hill, George Birkbeck Norman, and Lawrence F. Powell, eds., *Boswell's Life of Johnson*, 6 vols. (Oxford: Oxford University Press, 1934).

Hoagwood, Terence Allan, *Byron's Dialectic: Skepticism and the Critique of Culture* (Lewisburg: Bucknell University Press, 1993).

Hone, William, ed., *Poems on His Domestic Circumstances by Lord Byron* (London: William Hone, 1816).

Don Juan, Canto III, 1–35. https://petercochran.files.wordpress.com/2009/03/canto-iii.pdf.

Hopps, Gavin, '"Eden's Door": The Porous Worlds of Don Juan and Childe Harold's Pilgrimage', *Byron Journal*, 37.2 (2009), 109–20.

'Byron and the Post-Secular: Quia Impossibile', *Byron Journal*, 43.2 (2015), 91–108.

Howe, Anthony, 'Uncircumscribing Poetry: Byron, Johnson, and the Bowles Controversy', in *Liberty and Poetic Licence: New Essays on Byron*, ed. Bernard Beatty, Tony Howe, and Charles E. Robinson (Liverpool: Liverpool University Press, 2008), 206–18.

Byron and the Forms of Thought (Liverpool: Liverpool University Press, 2013).

Hunt, Leigh, *Foliage; or Poems Original and Translated* (London: C. and J. Ollier, 1818).

Lord Byron and Some of His Contemporaries, 2 vols. (London: Henry Colburn, 1828).

Jackson, H. J., ed., *Samuel Taylor Coleridge: Selected Letters* (Oxford: Clarendon Press, 1987).

Johnson, Edgar, *Walter Scott: The Great Unknown*, 2 vols. (London: Hamish Hamilton, 1970).

Kahn, Arthur D., 'Byron's Single Difference with Homer and Virgil: The Redefinition of the Epic in "Don Juan"', *Arcadia*, 5.2 (January 1970), 143–62.

Kareem, Sarah Tindal, 'Enlightenment Bubbles, Romantic Worlds', *Eighteenth Century*, 56.1 (2015), 85–104.

Kelsall, Malcolm, *Byron's Politics* (Sussex: Harvester, 1987).

Kendra, April, 'Gendering the Silver Fork: Catherine Gore and the Society Novel', *Women's Writing*, 11.1 (2004), 25–39.

Kennedy, James, *Conversations on Religion with Lord Byron, and Others* (London: John Murray, 1830).

Kovesi, Simon, 'Masculinity, Misogyny and the Marketplace: Clare's "Don Juan A Poem"', in *John Clare: New Approaches*, ed. John Goodridge and Simon Kovesi (Peterborough: The John Clare Society, 2000), 187–201.

Landon, Letitia, *Romance and Reality*, ed. Cynthia Lawford, vol. 2 of *Silver Fork Novels, 1826–1841*, gen. ed. Harriet Devine Jump (London: Pickering and Chatto, 2005).

Lansdown, Richard, 'The Novelized Poem and the Poeticized Novel: Byron's "Don Juan" and Victorian Fiction', *Critical Review*, 39 (1999), 119–41.

Lauber, John, 'Don Juan as Anti-Epic', *Studies in English Literature, 1500–1900*, 8 (1968), 607–19.

Lindop, Grevel, ed., *The Works of Thomas De Quincey*, 21 vols. (London: Chatto and Pickering, 2000–1).

[Lockhart, J. G.], *John Bull's Letter to Lord Byron*, ed. Alan Lang Strout (Norman: University of Oklahoma Press, 1947).

Some Passages in the Life of Mr Adam Blair, Minister of the Gospel at Cross-Meikle (Edinburgh: Edinburgh University Press, 1963).

MacCarthy, Fiona, *Byron: Life and Legend* (New York: Farrar, Straus and Giroux, 2002).

Manning, Peter J., *Byron and His Fictions* (Detroit: Wayne State University Press, 1978).

'Byron's Imperceptiveness to the English Word', in *Longman Critical Readers: Byron*, ed. Jane Stabler (London: Longman, 1998), 180–93.

McDonald, Peter, *Sound Intentions: The Workings of Rhyme in Nineteenth-Century Poetry* (Oxford: Oxford University Press, 2012).

McGann, Jerome J., *Don Juan in Context* (London: John Murray, 1976).

The Beauty of Inflections: Literary Investigations in Historical Method and Theory (Oxford: Clarendon Press, 1985).

'The *Biographia Literaria* and the Contentions of English Romanticism', in *Coleridge's Biographia Literaria: Text and Meaning*, ed. Frederick Burwick (Columbus: Ohio State University Press, 1989), 233–54.

Towards a Literature of Knowledge (Oxford: Clarendon Press, 1989).

Byron and Romanticism, ed. James Soderholm (Cambridge: Cambridge University Press, 2002).

Medwin, Thomas, *Conversations of Lord Byron: Noted During a Residence with His Lordship at Pisa in the Years 1821 and 1822* (London: Henry Colburn, 1825).

Micklewright, F. H. Amphlett, 'On the Bishop of Clogher's Case', *Notes and Queries*, 214 (November 1969), 421–30.

Minta, Stephen, *On a Voiceless Shore: Byron in Greece* (New York: Holt, 1998).

Mozer, Hadley J., '"I Want a Hero": Advertising for an Epic Hero in Don Juan', *Studies in Romanticism*, 44.2 (2005), 239–60.

Nellist, Brian, 'Lyric Presence in Byron: From the *Tales* to *Don Juan*', in *Byron and the Limits of Fiction*, ed. Bernard Beatty and Vincent Newey (Liverpool: Liverpool University Press, 1988), 39–77.

Nicholson, Andrew, ed., *The Letters of John Murray to Lord Byron* (Liverpool: Liverpool University Press, 2007).

Normanby, Lord, *Matilda: A Tale of the Day* (London: Henry Colburn, 1825).

O'Neill, Michael, *Romanticism and the Self-Conscious Poem* (Oxford: Clarendon Press, 1997).

Owen, W. J. B., and Jane Worthington Smyser, eds., *The Prose Works of William Wordsworth*, 3 vols. (Oxford: Clarendon Press, 1974).

Perry, Seamus, 'What Auden Made of Byron', in *Byron Among the English Poets: Literary Tradition and Poetic Legacy*, ed. Clare Bucknell and Matthew Ward (Cambridge: Cambridge University Press, 2021), 303–16.

Peterfreund, Stuart, 'Juan the Memorious: The Feinaiglian Narrative Dynamics of Don Juan', *European Romantic Review*, 17.4 (October 2006), 403–18.

Pomarè, Carl, *Byron and the Discourses of History* (Farnham: Ashgate, 2013).

Procter, Bryan (Barry Cornwall), *An Autobiographical Fragment and Biographical Notes* (London: Bell, 1877).

Reiman, Donald H., and Neil Fraistat, eds., *Shelley's Poetry and Prose* (New York: W. W. Norton, 2002).

Ridenour, George M., *The Style of Don Juan* (New Haven: Yale University Press, 1960).

Rollins, Hyder Edward, ed., *The Letters of John Keats*, 2 vols. (Cambridge: Cambridge University Press, 1958).

Saglia, Diego, '"Freedom's Charter'd Air": The Voices of Liberalism in Felicia Heman's The Vespers of Palermo', *Nineteenth-Century Literature*, 58 (2003), 326–67.

Salomon, Roger B., 'Mock-Heroes and Mock-Heroic Narrative: Byron's Don Juan in the Context of Cervantes', *Studies in the Literary Imagination*, 9.1 (1976), 69–87.

Schoina, Maria, 'Revisiting Byron's Italian Style', *Byron Journal*, 36.1 (2008), 19–27.

Siskin, Clifford, *System: The Shaping of Modern Knowledge* (Cambridge, MA: MIT Press, 2016).

Smiles, Samuel, *A Publisher and His Friends: Memoir and Correspondence of the Late John Murray*, 2 vols. (London: John Murray, 1891).

Southey, Robert, *The Poetical Works of Robert Southey* (London: Longman, Green, 1876).

St Clair, William, *That Greece Might Still Be Free: The Philhellenes in the War of Independence* (London: Oxford University Press, 1972).

The Reading Nation in the Romantic Period (Cambridge: Cambridge University Press, 2004).

Stabler, Jane, ed., *Longman Critical Readers: Byron* (London: Longman, 1998).

Byron, Poetics and History (Cambridge: Cambridge University Press, 2002).

'Byron and "The Excursion"', *Wordsworth Circle*, 45.2 (2014), 137–47.

'Religious Liberty in the "Liberal"', *BRANCH: Britain, Representation and Nineteenth-Century History*, ed. Dino Franco Felluga, extension of Romanticism and Victorianism on the Net (20 August 2020).

Stewart, David, *Romantic Magazines and Metropolitan Literary Culture* (Basingstoke: Palgrave Macmillan, 2011).

'The End of Conversation: Byron's *Don Juan* at the Newcastle Lit & Phil', *Review of English Studies*, n. s. 66 (April 2015), 322–41.

Thackeray, William M., *The Works of William Makepeace Thackeray*, 22 vols. (London: Smith, Elder, 1869).

Thorslev, Peter L., Jr., *The Byronic Hero: Types and Prototypes* (Minneapolis: University of Minnesota Press, 1964).

'Post-Waterloo Liberalism: The Second Generation', *Studies in Romanticism*, 28 (Fall 1989), 437–61.

Trelawny, Edward J., *Recollections of the Last Days of Shelley and Byron* (London: Edward Moxon, 1858).

Tucker, Herbert F., *Epic: Britain's Heroic Muse 1790–1910* (Oxford: Oxford University Press, 2008).

Tuite, Clara, *Lord Byron and Scandalous Celebrity* (Cambridge: Cambridge University Press, 2015).

'Lord Byron's Preposterous Liberalism', *Occasion*, 11 (2018), 1–17.

Ulmer, William A., *Shelleyan Eros: The Rhetoric of Romantic Love* (Princeton: Princeton University Press, 1990).

Vassallo, Peter, *Byron, the Italian Literary Influence* (London: Macmillan, 1984).

Webb, Timothy, 'Free Quills and Poetic Licences: Byron and the Politics of Publication', in *Liberty and Poetic Licence: New Essays on Byron*, ed. Bernard Beatty, Tony Howe and Charles E. Robinson (Liverpool: Liverpool University Press, 2008), 219–32.

West, Paul, *Byron and the Spoiler's Art* (London: Chatto & Windus, 1960).

Wilson, Frances, ed., *Byromania: Portraits of the Artist in Nineteenth- and Twentieth-Century Culture* (London: Macmillan, 1999).

Wilson, Mona, *The Life of William Blake*, ed. Geoffrey Keynes (Oxford: Oxford University Press, 1971).

Wolfson, Susan J., '"Their She Condition": Cross-Dressing and the Politics of Gender in Don Juan', *ELH*, 54 (Autumn 1987), 585–617.

Woodhouse, David, 'The Dedication to Don Juan Re-Examined: Hazlitt – *Wat Tyler* – *Don Giovanni*', *Byron Journal*, 45.2 (December 2017), 141–53.

'Hazlitt and Byron: Hereditary Prejudices and Liberal Sympathies', *The Hazlitt Review*, 12 (2019), 37–60.

Index

CAMBRIDGE STUDIES IN ROMANTICISM

General Editor
JAMES CHANDLER, *University of Chicago*

Ingram Content Group UK Ltd.
Milton Keynes UK
UKHW021939220623
423851UK00006B/29